Abject visions

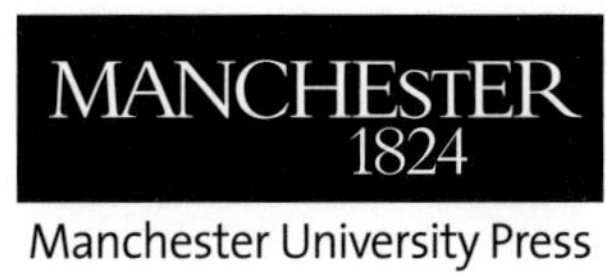

Manchester University Press

Abject visions

Powers of horror in art and visual culture

Edited by
RINA ARYA AND NICHOLAS CHARE

Manchester University Press

Published by Manchester University Press
Altrincham Street, Manchester M1 7JA
www.manchesteruniversitypress.co.uk

British Library Cataloguing-in-Publication Data
A catalogue record for this book is available from the British Library

Library of Congress Cataloging-in-Publication Data applied for

ISBN 978 0 7190 9628 0 hardback

ISBN 978 0 7190 9629 7 paperback

First published 2016

Typeset by
Servis Filmsetting Ltd, Stockport, Cheshire
Printed in Great Britain by
TJ International Ltd, Padstow

Contents

List of figures *page* vi
List of contributors vii
Acknowledgements xi

Introduction: approaching abjection – *Rina Arya and Nicholas Chare* 1
1 Abjection, art and bare life – *John Lechte* 14
2 Queering abjection: a lesbian, feminist and Canadian perspective – *Jayne Wark* 30
3 Manet's abject Surrealism – *Nicholas Chare* 51
4 Juan Davila's abject after-image – *Rex Butler and A. D. S. Donaldson* 71
5 Animals, art, abjection – *Barbara Creed and Jeanette Hoorn* 90
6 The fragmented body as an index of abjection – *Rina Arya* 105
7 Skin, body, self: the question of the abject in the work of Francis Bacon – *Ernst van Alphen* 119
8 Abjection, melancholia and ambiguity in the works of Catherine Bell – *Estelle Barrett* 130
9 Corpus delicti – *Kerstin Mey* 144
10 Art is on the way: from the abject opening of *Underworld* to the shitty ending of *Oblivion* – *Calvin Thomas* 160
11 Base materials: performing the abject object – *Daniel Watt* 189

Index 202

Figures

1 Allyson Mitchell, *Big Trubs*, 2004. Synthetic fur, wood, styrofoam, wire and found acrylic textiles, 320.04 x 228.6 cm. Reproduced courtesy of the artist. Photograph: Thomas Mitchell. *page* 45
2 Juan Davila, *A Man Renounces Love*, 2010. Oil on canvas, 200 × 280 cm. © Juan Davila. Courtesy of Kalli Rolfe Contemporary Art. 80
3 Juan Davila, *After Image. A Man Renounces Love*, 2010. Oil on canvas, 200 × 280 cm. © Juan Davila. Courtesy of Kalli Rolfe Contemporary Art. 80
4 Patricia Piccinini, *The Young Family*, 2002. Silicone, fibreglass, leather, human hair and plywood, 85 × 150 × 120 cm approx. Courtesy of the artist, Tolarno and Roslyn Oxley9 Galleries. Photograph: Graham Baring. 97
5 Louise Bourgeois, *Maman*, 1999. Steel and marble, 9.2 × 8.91 × 10.23 m. Courtesy of the Art Archive / Manuel Cohen. Photograph by Manuel Cohen. 103
6 Catherine Bell, *Heavy Petal* (detail), 2012. Flower petals, conservation medium, wooden board, 25 × 30 cm. Courtesy of the artist and Sutton Gallery, Melbourne. Photograph: Andrew Curtis. 140
7 Catherine Bell, *Nanny Safari*, 2010 (Installation view). Dual audio visual projection, artificial grass. HD DVD 1,54 mins, HD DVD 2,35 mins. Courtesy of the artist and Sutton Gallery, Melbourne. Photograph: Christian Capurro. 142

Contributors

Rina Arya is Reader in Visual Communication at the University of Wolverhampton. Areas of specialism include Francis Bacon, Georges Bataille, abjection, and the relationship between the visual arts and theology. Recent publications include *Francis Bacon: Painting in a Godless World* (2012); *Chila Kumari Burman: Shakti, Sexuality and Bindi Girls* (2012); *Contemplations of the Spiritual in Art* (2013); and *Abjection and Representation: An Exploration of Abjection in the Visual Arts, Film and Literature* (2014). With Nicholas Chare, she was the guest editor for 'On Abjection' for *Performance Research* (2014).

Estelle Barrett is Professor and HDR Coordinator at the Institute of Koorie Education, Deakin University. She has co-edited three books with Barbara Bolt: *Practice as Research: Approaches to Creative Arts Enquiry* (2007; reprinted 2010), *Carnal Knowledge: Towards a 'New Materialism' Through the Arts* (2012) and *Material Inventions: Applying Creative Research* (2014). She has published reviews and articles in *Cultural Studies Review, Zetesis, Real Time, Artlink, Text, Social Semiotics, Double Dialogues, The International Journal of Critical Arts* and the *Journal of Visual Arts Practice*. Her monograph, *Kristeva Reframed: Interpreting Key Thinkers for the Arts* (2011), examines the relevance of the work of Julia Kristeva for the creative arts and creative arts research. She is an international Research Fellow of the International Centre for Fine Arts Research, Birmingham University.

Rex Butler is Associate Professor and Reader in Art History in the School of English, Media Studies and Art History at the University of Queensland. He is author of *Borges' Short Stories: A Reader's Guide* (2010), *Deleuze and Guattari's What is Philosophy? A Reader's Guide* (2014) and editor of *The*

Žižek Dictionary (2013). He is currently working on a book about Colin McCahon with Laurence Simmons, and on a history of UnAustralian art with A. D. S Donaldson.

Nicholas Chare is Associate Professor of Art History in the Department of History of Art and Film Studies at the Université de Montréal. He is the author of *Auschwitz and Afterimages: Abjection, Witnessing and Representation* (2011) and *After Francis Bacon: Synaesthesia and Sex in Paint* (2012). He has also co-authored *Matters of Testimony: Interpreting the Scrolls of Auschwitz* (2016) and co-edited the collection *Representing Auschwitz: At the Margins of Testimony* (2013) with Dominic Williams. He is a former editor of the international journal of critical theory *parallax.*

Barbara Creed is Professor of Film and Screen Studies at the University of Melbourne. Her areas of research are film, feminism and psychoanalytic theory, the impact of Darwinian theory on the cinema, the cinema of human rights and human animal studies. Her publications include *The Monstrous-Feminine: Film, Feminism, Psychoanalysis* (1993), *Phallic Panic: Film, Horror and the Primal Uncanny* (2005), and *Darwin's Screens: Evolutionary Aesthetics, Time and Sexual Display in the Cinema* (2009). She is Director of the Human Rights and Animal Ethics Research Network (HRAE) in the Arts Faculty at the University of Melbourne.

A. D. S. Donaldson is a practising artist and art historian who teaches at the National Art School in Sydney. He completed a PhD on the Australian expatriate artist Mary Webb and recently co-curated with Ann Stephen the exhibition J. W. Power: Abstraction-Creation: Paris 1934. His work is held in the Art Gallery of New South Wales, the Museum of Contemporary Art, Sydney, the National Gallery of Victoria and the Queensland Art Gallery. His work received a retrospective at the University of Queensland Art Museum in 2002. He is currently working on a history of UnAustralian art with Rex Butler.

Jeanette Hoorn is Professor of Visual Cultures at the University of Melbourne. She has worked in the fields of race, gender and colonialism throughout her career. Her most recent research is in the field of the representation of emotions in narratives contained in eighteenth-century British and French academic painting about human beings and domestic animals. She is currently developing an on-line course with the Coursera Platform entitled Sexing the Canvas, in which theories of sexuality and gender are explored through masterpieces held in the collections of the National Gallery of Victoria, Melbourne, the Museum of Modern Art, New York and the Huntington in Pasadena.

John Lechte is Adjunct Professor of Sociology at Macquarie University where he researches in social and European cultural theory. A former student of Julia Kristeva, he has published extensively on her work. His publications include *Julia Kristeva: Live Theory* (with Maria Margaroni, 2004); *Fifty Key Contemporary Thinkers: From Structuralism to Post-Humanism* (2008); *Agamben and the Politics of Human Rights: Statelessness, Images, Violence* (with Saul Newman, 2012); *Genealogy and Ontology of the Image and its Digital Future* (2012).

Kerstin Mey is Professor of Contemporary Art and Theory at the University of Westminster, where she holds responsibility as Dean of the Faculty of Media, Arts and Design. With a background in Art and German language and literature, her own cross-disciplinary research has been concerned with the situatedness of twentieth-century and current cultural practices. She has an interest in digital literacies, art and the production of publics, and knowledge-making at the interface of art and science. Publications include *Sculpsit: Contemporary Artists on Sculpture and Beyond* (2001); *Art in the Making: Aesthetics Historicity and Practice* (2004); with M. Kroenke and Y. Spielmann *Kulturelle Umbrüche: Identitäten, Räume, Repräsentationen* (2007); *Art and Obscenity* (2007); and with Smite and Smites: *Art as Research* (2012)

Calvin Thomas is Professor of English at Georgia State University in Atlanta. His publications include *Male Matters: Masculinity, Anxiety, and the Male Body on the Line* (1996); *Straight with a Twist: Queer Theory and the Subject of Heterosexuality* (2000); *Masculinity, Psychoanalysis, Straight Queer Theory: Essays on Abjection in Literature, Mass Culture, and Film* (2008); and *Ten Lessons in Theory: An Introduction to Theoretical Writing* (2013). He plans to expand his contribution to the present volume into a book called *Adventures in American Abjection.*

Ernst van Alphen is Professor of Literary Studies at Leiden University. His books include *Francis Bacon and The Loss of Self* (1992); *Caught By History: Holocaust Effects in Contemporary Art, Literature, and Theory* (1998); *Armando: Shaping Memories* (2000); *Art in Mind: How Contemporary Images Shape Thought* (2005); and *Staging the Archive: Art and Photography In Times of New Media* (2014).

Jayne Wark is Professor in Art History and Critical Studies at the Nova Scotia College of Art and Design University in Halifax, Canada. Her main areas of research and publication include performance, video and conceptual art from the 1970s to the present, with a particular focus on feminist art, theory and politics. She is the author of *Radical Gestures: Feminism and Performance*

Art in North America (2006). She was also a co-curator and co-author of the exhibition and publication, *Traffic: Conceptual Art in Canada 1965–1980*, which toured across Canada as well as to Karlsruhe, Germany and Paris from 2010 to 2014.

Daniel Watt is Senior Lecturer in English and Drama at Loughborough University. His research interests include fragmentary writing, ethics and literature and philosophical and literary influences on theatre and performance in the twentieth century, particularly in the work of Tadeusz Kantor. Other research is focused on the literary/theatrical fantastic and 'Weird Fiction', death in performance and culture, and the nature of the puppet, or abject object, in performance. Recent publications have appeared in *Performance Research Journal*, *Polish Theatre Perspectives* and *Puppet Notebook*. He was co-investigator in the Object Theatre Network and is a founding core-convenor of the Performance Philosophy Network.

Acknowledgements

The editors would like to thank the contributors for their scholarship and commitment, without which the volume would not have been possible. We would like to express our appreciation to the two anonymous reviewers for their invaluable comments and encouragement regarding the book. We are also grateful to Rachel Evans, Manchester University Press staff, and especially Emma Brennan for their enthusiasm and support throughout this project.

Introduction: approaching abjection

Rina Arya and Nicholas Chare

'Abjection' is a word with a long history in the English language. In *The Oxford Dictionary of English Etymology* its use is traced back to the fifteenth century. At that time, someone who had been brought low, rendered despondent or dejected for whatever reason, was referred to as abject. The term assumed its more familiar meaning of being degraded or despicable in the sixteenth century. Its etymological roots are to be found in the Latin word *abicere* meaning to cast away or rebuff. In contemporary cultural theory, however, the term 'abjection' is commonly associated with the psychoanalytic theories of Julia Kristeva.[1] In 1980, Kristeva published *Pouvoirs de l'horreur: Essai sur l'abjection* (Kristeva, 1980). The book was swiftly translated into English, appearing in 1982 as *Powers of Horror: An Essay on Abjection* (Kristeva, 1982). It notably preceded the English-language translation of Kristeva's ground-breaking *Revolution in Poetic Language* which was published in French in 1974 (Kristeva, 1974) but only translated into English in 1984. *Powers of Horror* provided the English-language reader with the first monograph (rather than collection of essays) by Kristeva and subsequently profoundly shaped the Anglophone reception of her work.

Sylvère Lotringer has suggested that Kristeva's work, coupled with the Whitney Museum exhibition *Abject Art: Repulsion and Desire in American Art* of late June to late August 1993, contributed to abjection gaining wide currency (Lotringer, 1994: 2). These two impetuses will now be analysed for the insights they provide into what comprises abjection and also the possible restrictions they place on our understanding. In the context of the constraints that accompany operating with a purely Kristevan notion of the abject, Lotringer suggests that the significant attention given to *Powers of Horror* has obscured Georges Bataille's earlier theorisation of abjection. Bataille's treatment of abjection is different from Kristeva's. He does not use the term very much nor does he develop it into an elaborate theory in the way that Kristeva does. He explicitly addressed abjection in a short essay he drafted in 1934, 'Abjection and Miserable Forms'. This was published posthumously as part of *Essais de sociologie* in 1970,[2] where it is clear that his focus is rooted in the socio-political (rather than the psychoanalytic, which is where Kristeva's predominant focus lies) and accounts for the dynamic of rejection and exclusion in relation to the socially disenfranchised. But if we consider abjection as a concept within a larger theory of the sacred, particularly in relation to Bataille's work on desire and eroticism (see Wirth, 1999) then we can make the case that it was integral because it contributed to his aesthetic and philosophical view of desublimation (Arya, 2014: chapter 3).

Kristeva's *Powers of Horror* is a book of three distinct parts. It begins with a psychoanalytic exegesis of the concept of abjection. This is followed by a Western cultural anthropology of the abject. The book concludes with a literary analysis of the role of the abject in the writing of Louis-Ferdinand Céline. Working within a predominantly Lacanian paradigm, abjection is identified by Kristeva as a process that initially pre-figures the mirror-stage in the psychic development of an infant. It comprises the period when the child begins to separate from the figure of the Mother. Prior to the child's misrecognition of itself in the mirror, it must first become estranged from this Mother. Kristeva writes: 'Even before being *like*, "I" am not but do *separate*, *reject*, *ab-ject*' (Kristeva, 1982: 13).[3] Abjection therefore occurs before the subject's positioning in language, anterior to the emergence of the 'I'. It is a provisional, transitory sense of differentiation from the maternal: a fragile, unbecoming and unknowing sense of self.

Abject materials, such as bodily excretions like menses, urine, faeces, mucus or spit, are capable of triggering memories of this archaic stage of psychic life, of abjection, in later psychic life. Excretions, for example, travel from inside to outside the body, thereby troubling any sense of it having secure borders. The acquaintance such materials provide us with regarding the lack of assurance of our physical borders is supplemented by recognition of the precariousness of our psychic borders, our sense of self. This renders abject materials psychically threatening. Cultures therefore frequently develop rituals for policing encounters with such substances. Kristeva explores how in a Judeo-Christian context religion has assumed the role of guarding against the abject. For her, the rise of secularism in modernity has led art to take over this function. Avant-garde literature of the kind practised by Céline provides the means by which Western culture manages the abject.

In the Anglophone world, however, abjection is predominantly associated with art rather than literature. This situation can be attributed to the cultural impact of the Whitney exhibition, which was formed from a selection of works from the gallery's permanent collection of American Art.[4] The exhibition was curated by Craig Houser, Leslie Jones and Simon Taylor. As is evident from their individual contributions to the catalogue that accompanied the exhibition, each conceived of abject art in markedly distinct ways. The exhibition featured a selection of works, mainly produced post-1945, which the curators felt spoke to their varied ideas of the abject. Several video works by Jennifer Montgomery, Azian Nurudin and Suzie Silver were from the early 1990s. Many of the other artworks were from the 1960s.

The Introduction to the catalogue for the exhibition endeavours to synthesise the diverse approaches to abjection adopted by the curators. In the essay, the curators state that they are operating with a theory of abjection drawn from two key constituents: a psychoanalytic component related to the blurring of boundaries between self and other and a philosophical dimension originating in Georges Bataille's notion of 'base materialism' which challenges mind-body dualism and established taboos (Ben-Levi et al., 1993: 7).[5] Abject art displays boundary breakdown and/or base materialism. The curators conceive of such art not as a specific movement within art's history but as a particular physical quality which potentially manifests across diverse periods.

The term 'abject art' is used by the Whitney curators to group together a varied body of works that engage with materials culturally coded as abject in order 'to confront taboo issues of gender and sexuality' (Ben-Levi et al., 1993: 7). Abject art comprises a group of works, a corpus, which 'incorporates or suggests abject materials such as dirt, hair, excrement, dead animals, menstrual blood and rotting food' (7). The abject quality ascribed to some artworks therefore inheres in particular kinds of substances. Some of these are referenced in subsequent essays in the catalogue. Leslie Jones, for example, refers to the incorporation of 'untraditional substances' in artworks of the 1970s and provides the example of Judy Chicago's *Menstruation Bathroom* of 1972, which comprised 'a trash can overflowing with bloodied tampons and pads' (Jones, 1993: 36–37). Hannah Wilke's use of chewing gum is also foregrounded (50–51). Taylor draws attention to the use of wax in Kiki Smith's *Untitled* (1990) (Taylor, 1993: 65).

For the curators, the abject is therefore signalled first and foremost at the level of form. Works composed from, or connoting, abject materials also frequently feature abject subject matter (Ben-Levi et al., 1993: 7). Such subject matter is of a kind that has been 'deemed inappropriate by a conservative dominant culture' (7). For the curators, the subject matter invariably relates to issues of gender and sexuality. In his catalogue essay 'I, Abject', Houser (who had advance access to the manuscript of *Bodies that Matter: On the Discursive Limits of 'Sex'*) draws on Judith Butler's identification of abjection as a 'strategy used to remove the different threats gays and lesbians present to the heterosexual' (Houser, 1993: 86). The heterosexual subject, Butler explains, comes into being through 'the simultaneous production of a domain of abject beings, those who are not yet "subjects," but who form the constitutive outside to the domain of the subject' (Butler, 1993: 3). This outside exists inside the heterosexual subject as 'its own founding repudiation' (3).

The gay and lesbian as figures of this outside are meant to live as abject beings, to perform the role of bodies that do not matter. This 'exclusionary matrix', as Butler calls it, has a long history in Western culture. Marcel Jouhandeau's 1939 work *De l'abjection*, for example, describes the hate speech gay subjects are subjected to, speech that demarcates them as abject. In a passage that prefigures Butler's affirmation that performing sexuality is not equivalent to 'taking on a mask', Jouhandeau describes the impact of verbal abuse directed at him because of his sexuality (Butler, 1993: 7). He writes of the insults: 'At first you try to pretend that it's not real, that it's only a mask, a theatre costume mockingly thrown on you that you want to tear, but no; they cling so much that they are already your face and your flesh and it is yourself that you rend by wanting to strip off' (Jouhandeau, 2006 [1939]: 191).[6] Here Jouhandeau harrowingly captures the materialisation of an abject subjectivity and the role of others, those who embody regulatory norms, in producing it.

For Butler, the process of abjection that produces bodies which do and do not matter, which generates the wholesome and the abject sexual being, provides a critical resource. When they work collectively, those who dis-identify with dominant identity categories such as the heterosexual 'can facilitate a reconceptualization of which bodies matter, and which bodies are yet to emerge as critical matters of concern' (Butler, 1993: 4). In this sense, embracing an abject subject position can become a means by which to renegotiate that position. The curators of the Whitney exhibition also recognised the political potential of the abject. For them aesthetic practices which unfold across the terrain of the abject can exploit base materials to promote a radical sexual politics. Abject art then becomes a means by which to challenge the status quo. In his catalogue essay, Taylor describes abject art as manifesting an 'insurgent materialism' that acts 'against societal repression' (1993: 59). This insurrectionary capacity, Taylor goes on to explain, is triggered through the production of artworks that transgress social taboos (66). Abject art can potentially reshape the social conditions from out of which it emerges.

The essays in this volume communicate the enduring power and relevance of the abject by explaining how it conveys ideas about aesthetic, social and moral conventions with regards to representation and viewing. In their chosen themes and artists, the contributors draw on the ideas of Bataille and Kristeva, and others such as Judith Butler, Hal Foster and Rosalind Krauss, as part of their approach to extending current ways of conceiving abjection. The majority of the essays focus on the visual arts although there are also considerations of how attending to the abject can inform readings of film, theatre and literature, a fact which attests to its enduring relevance in culture, and how abjection is starting to be discussed by disciplines which hitherto have not broached the topic.[7]

John Lechte's essay for this volume, 'Abjection, art and bare life', develops the idea of the abject as being beyond objectification. Grounding his argument in Kant's conception of the beautiful as that which has no concept, Lechte asks if there can really be an art of the abject given the concept's elusive status. He answers this question through an analysis of the film *Sombre* (Dir. Philippe Grandrieux, France, 1998). For Lechte, the abject 'represents' a radical immanence. Abject art is therefore art that takes the non-object as its object. Grandrieux's films, through their chiaroscuro cinematography, comprise works in which the medium of film appears to be foregrounded. The sombre lighting makes objects difficult to discern. This has led some commentators to contend that Grandrieux brings the materiality of film to the screen. Lechte, however, argues that materiality is always already screened, barred from us, by the very process of signification that seeks to capture it. In this light, if there is an abject element to *Sombre* it can only ever be evoked rather than clearly represented for to represent it would be to abolish it.

The radical power of abjection is examined in a number of essays in this volume. Jayne Wark, for example, draws on the ideas of Judith Butler and Kristeva as a means to examine the political potency of a number of works by the Canadian artists Allyson Mitchell, Shawna Dempsey and Lorri Millan, and Rosalie Favell whose practices are informed by feminist and lesbian politics. The artists strive to problematise fixed identity categories. Wark seeks to move beyond what she perceives to be the limiting outlook of the Whitney conceptualisation of abject art because it lacked nuance and was too wedded to the political climate of the United States of the early 1990s. The Whitney curators had a national agenda and were responding to efforts to censor art and censure certain artists, such as Robert Mapplethorpe, Andres Serrano, Annie Sprinkle and Karen Finlay, in the United States in the 1980s and early 1990s (Ben-Levi et al., 1993: 8). Their political motivations do not seamlessly transfer to a consideration of contemporary Canadian art.

For Wark, each of the artists she considers strives, in different ways, to resignify the abject. They therefore employ it as a critical resource in the way Butler envisages. As the Whitney exhibition and the essay by Wark demonstrate, thinking about modernist and contemporary works through the prism of abjection allows us to recognise their political radicalism and to understand how they confront the repressive tendencies of dominant culture at specific historical moments. The Whitney curators identified many now 'canonical' artists as having produced abject art, naming Carl Andre, Marcel Duchamp, Jasper Johns, Claes Oldenburg, Robert Rauschenberg, Cy Twombly and Andy Warhol among others as exemplary. In their different ways, each of these artists drew attention to the human body, a body capable of oozing, festering, mouldering and dirtying. Warhol's *Oxidation Painting* (1978), for example, was produced by the Pop artist urinating on a ground of copper-based paint. For the curators, this action 'suggested an ironic relation between [Jackson] Pollock's painting procedure and his exhibitionist habit of pissing in public, pointing to how the issue of the body had been elided in discussions of the artist's work' (Ben-Levi et al., 1993: 9).[8]

The example of Warhol highlights the limits of the Whitney's historical overview. The interpretation, Warhol's perceived piss-take, is premised on Pollock not himself recognising the parallels between dripping paint from a stick and the act of a man urinating. If Pollock did perceive continuity between the two forms of expression then, for him, the canvas already formed a figurative urinal. The connection between penis and paintbrush (a glorified stick) is longstanding. Pollock's technique has also sometimes been viewed as ejaculatory and as being closely bound up with his masculinity.[9] Equating paint with sperm, another abject material not discussed by the curators, is commonplace.[10] If paint possesses a spermatic symbolic potential then many artworks in traditional media such as egg tempera, gouache, oil and watercolour, and also those made from baser material such as house-paint, possess an abject capacity. Nicholas Chare's essay 'Manet's abject Surrealism' examines this possibility.

Chare suggests that the Surrealist project possessed an underlying sadistic impulse that was prefigured in the art of Édouard Manet. Manet exploited paint's potentially aberrant qualities through an aggressive approach to composition and handling. Artworks that exhibit a deviant painterliness often function within Surrealism to question dominant ideas about identity, particularly sexual identity. Manet's works prompt such a questioning. Chare contrasts Manet's technique with Jackson Pollock's to tease out the nature of the former's brutal formalism, his Surrealism, and elaborate on its capacity to recast identity without losing sight of the self entirely.

The curators at the Whitney included works by women artists in their exhibition but the history of art they promoted was still overwhelmingly a white history. In this context, Wark's analysis of artworks by a Métis, a group of Canadian people of First Nations and European heritage, forms a valuable counterpoint to what can still be seen as the prevailing narrative of abject art. The essay by Rex Butler and A. S. Donaldson in this collection also challenges the conventional focus on artists operating within a European or American context. Building on the theories of Kristeva and Slavoj Žižek, Butler and Donaldson explore how debates about modernism and postmodernism are played out in the work of Chilean-Australian artist Juan Davila. Davila's Antipodean and South American background render him an outsider in the Whitney's terms. The abject assumes a central role in these debates as it cannot be equated either with the medium or the message of art. It falls outside polarising arguments over the privileging of surface or subject matter. The abject is not present in Davila's paintings as it cannot become their subject given its quality as a non-object. The abject is rather that which resists becoming subject. It refuses to be made to matter as a subject because it refuses objectification. It is, however, not a simple matter. It is a kind of arrested or abeyant signification: it occupies the gap between matter and meaning. Butler and Donaldson show how Davila works within this gap exploiting the abject's slipperiness in his recent pictures as a means to intervene in contemporary aesthetic disputes about the role of the medium in art.

Taylor's Whitney catalogue essay identifies abject art as comprising works that raise various challenges to Clement Greenberg's aesthetics of purity and to the White Cube format of exhibiting art. He draws on Barbara Creed's Kristevan-inspired idea of the 'monstrous feminine', which describes men's perception of women due to their dread of the female genitals, to explain the impact of works such as Cindy Sherman's *Untitled* (1987) and Kiki Smith's *Untitled* (1990) on gallery goers. Creed initially formulated the 'monstrous feminine' as a means to explain the attraction and repugnance generated by horror films such as *Aliens* (Dir. James Cameron, USA, 1986).[11] In this volume, however, in collaboration with the art historian Jeanette Hoorn, Creed explores art in relation to abjection. Creed and Hoorn's essay, 'Animals, art, abjection', teases out the implications of Kristeva's contention in *Powers of Horror* that the abject engenders a fragile state within which the human strays on the territory of the animal (Kristeva, 1982: 12). For Kristeva, some cultures have branded animals as abject and as 'representatives of sex and murder' (13). In such cultures, the animal is figured in negative terms, and notions of animalism, of the human as an animal species, are suppressed.

Animals therefore figure as impure and are made to form the constitutive outside to the human. Creed and Hoorn, however, argue that contemporary art practices that explore animals and animality do so as a means to challenge the notion that animals form humankind's abject other. In this context, the artworks do not function to purify the abject but rather embrace what has hitherto been labelled as abject as a means to renegotiate its status from within an anthropocentric society. The emancipatory logic outlined by Judith Butler in relation to gender is here transferred to the matter of the animal. Jouhandeau's *De l'abjection* displays anthropocentrism of the kind Creed and Hoorn seek to combat. He describes the descent into abjection as becoming animal and then plant: 'become foul animal and then muddy plant, acclimatised to withdrawal into a shameful crevice of hell, suddenly you become less than that, protoplasm, and next, something so eminently close to "nothing" that in the blink of an eye you have witnessed that vertigo that is the other aspect of us all: negation, absolute nothingness' (2006: 182).

Rina Arya's essay continues in the vein of investigating the amorphous body that is in between different states, such as the human-animal, by examining abjection in relation to the fragmented body. She starts by exploring the significance of the boundary in relation to the body proper before moving on to look at what happens when we look at distorted or fragmented bodies that do not adhere to the normal conventions of how we read a body. In the ordered body, abjection occurs at its margins, which corresponds to the points of the greatest vulnerability and the body is regulated accordingly. Abjection is harder to establish in the case where the body is fragmented and does not conform to being an organically ordered and functioning body. How are we to think about the boundary when it is not clear where the body starts or ends? Arya considers the cases of two twentieth-century artists, Hans Bellmer and Francis Bacon, who both employ fragmentation in order to release the somatic and expressive potential of the body but also to critique longstanding traditions of the art historical representative tradition.

Ernst van Alphen's essay is a consolidated study of abjection in the context of Francis Bacon's art, and investigates the various ways and senses in which Bacon's art can be described as abject. On an unstudied level Bacon's paintings are understood as abject but this needs to be probed further to examine the significance of the boundary between matter and representation, for instance, and of his figures themselves which are fragmented and which demonstrate various positions of subjecthood at risk. Calling on the work of other theorists, including Mikhail Bakhtin and Roland Barthes, van Alphen explores the identity of the Baconian figure and argues for a revived way of thinking about the abject condition of Bacon's figures. A further area of study in van Alphen's essay draws on Hal Foster's work and concerns how the viewer is provoked to complete the operation of the abject, which results in a reshattering of the viewer's sense of self. Van Alphen's study shows how abjection can be used to elicit a host of other Baconian themes about representation, viewing and identity.

The next two contributions by Estelle Barrett and Kerstin Mey continue with the theme of the applicability of abjection in twentieth-century art and examine more contemporary artworks. Barrett is concerned with the multidisciplinary practice of the Australian artist Catherine Bell and aims to show how artistic practice can extend, develop and reconfigure established conceptions of abjection, in particular Kristeva's and Bataille's. She argues that extant commentaries about abjection remain within the parameters of exposition and referentiality but do not adequately articulate the implications of abjection for understanding the aesthetic experience in both the making and viewing of art. This is often characterised by ambivalence (namely attraction and repulsion) and Barrett explores the transgressive (in the Bataillean sense) in the photographic and video work of Bell. By shifting the focus from the reading of an artwork to an experiential encounter, Barrett conveys the power of Bell's practice to evoke a complex of sensory and cognitive feelings that often involves ambivalence. Abjection then is reconceived as an operational function and as a process that is engendered by aesthetic experience in the making and viewing of art, thus reinvigorating its potential.

Kerstin Mey's essay takes us to the heart of abjection by examining the vilest 'object' of abjection, that is, the corpse. Mey considers how although death and its concomitant connotations – disease and demise – has been removed from the public gaze in the West, this has not reduced our fascination with these subjects. Nor has it removed its exploration through various forms of mediatised culture, including graphic video games, films and the visual arts. She examines the mass appeal of the anatomist Gunther von Hagens' *Body Worlds*, which was a worldwide touring exhibition shown in North America, Asia and Europe between 1995 and 2011, and focused on the display of preserved corpses and body fragments. The scientific process of Plastination was employed to preserve the body tissue and reveal inner anatomical structures which gave the specimens a hyperreal coloration, somewhat departing from the visceral ghastliness expected of bodily parts but in other ways imparting the starkness of our grim destinies, especially given the lifelike poses of the corpses. Von Hagens pushed the boundaries of acceptability in other ways by performing the first public autopsy in 2002, and in 2009 unveiling a plastinate of a couple having sex. Mey's essay details the different aspects of von Hagens' controversial but influential work and also examines the work of other artists who are engaged in similar subject matter, such as Joel-Peter Witkin, the art group AES + F and Andres Serrano's morgue series.

In the first essay of this volume Lechte attends to Kristeva's belief that the abject can form the subject of art and literature. Kristeva has claimed that the abject features as a theme in much avant-garde art. She also asserts that the experience of abjection accompanies this art's production and reception. Her theory of abjection is therefore one that encompasses the abject and abjection, substance and process. For her it is necessary to generate artworks that trigger abjection as a means to purge individual and social anxieties surrounding the abject. The Whitney exhibition did not conceive of art in this way. It was in the exhibition catalogue for a later exhibition, *Rites of Passage: Art for the End of the Century* which was held at the Tate Gallery in 1995, as part of an interview with Charles Penwarden, that Kristeva conceded there is a relationship between abjection and rites of passage in that the latter, as rituals, are bound up with purification (Penwarden and Kristeva, 1995: 23). In this context abject art can be read as a ritual practice that performs a purifying function. Artworks that attend to the abject, coming close to it while refusing to collapse into it, provide a cathartic value. (23).

For Kristeva the danger of not discharging social anxieties related to abjection is that they will be exploited to advance extreme politics. Abjection threatens identity and there is a danger that to counteract it individuals or groups will project their fears on to an Other. In Céline's case this Other was the Jew and the homosexual. In Jouhandeau's case it was the Jew. His anti-Semitism might be read as an effort to counteract the abject status he felt his homosexuality brought him.[12] Jacqueline Rose reads Céline's writings as symptoms that reveal how horror can become a matter for power (Rose, 1993). Céline wrote out his hatred rather than physically enacting it. The Nazis, however, contemporaneously exploited this hatred which was foundational to their politics and acted upon it through their anti-Semitic policies and the genocide they perpetrated. For Kristeva and Rose culture can therefore potentially play a vital role in combatting extremism. Art and literature have a critical purgative role to play in contemporary society.

Kristeva's literary examples are exclusively modernist. In this volume, however, Calvin Thomas explores the differing roles of the abject as a theme in the writings of the contemporary authors Don DeLillo and David Foster Wallace. For Thomas, Wallace's novella 'The Suffering Channel', which features an artist who claims to excrete fully modelled figurative sculptures, demonstrates how literature provides a crucial means to convey abject suffering. The scatological art produced by the fictional artist in the novella, Brint Molke, would not have been out of place in the history of modern art. Molke's excremental oeuvre would have added to a long history of artists talking shit to each other through their work. This ongoing conversation includes Piero Manzoni's 1961 work *Artist's Shit*, Carl Andre's 1962 *Dog Turd Sculptures*, Sam Goodman's and Boris Lurie's 1964 *Shit Sculptures*, Lynda Benglis's seeming riposte to Andre, *Quartered Meteor*, of 1969, and Mary Kelly's faecal stains in the 1974 *Post-Partum Document*, a prototype for which formed part of *Abject Art*. More recently, Chris Ofili has incorporated elephant dung in works such as *No Woman, No Cry* of 1998 which forms a tribute to the murdered black teenager Stephen Lawrence. For Thomas, Wallace's faecal theme provides the means by which the author explores abjected masculinity in contemporary America and also art's claim to use stories to reveal truths.

The final essay in this volume, Daniel Watt's 'Base materials: performing the abject object', configures abjection within the performing arts, and in particular within theatre, thereby underscoring the significance of catharsis in abjection as grounded by Antonin Artaud's work. Watt examines the radical theatre practices of Tadeusz Kantor, who co-founded the Cricot2 theatre in 1955, and Jerzy Grotowski's theatre company, which began in 1959. What these share is the view of the practice of immersion in abjection. The actor in Kantor's theatre, the bio-object (which is neither human nor object) is transformed throughout the performances from persons to things. In Grotowskian performance the body is sacrificed in total theatre. Both cases articulate how the sacrificial abjection of the performing object reveals a vision of reality, in a Bataillean sense, that conveys the potentiality of theatre as one that unveils the human, through a different type of communal event that entails the dissolution of selfhood (*jouissance*) and the power of horror. The task of performance becomes one of immersion in abjection.

The rich variety of essays in *Abject visions* demonstrates that abjection as a concept continues to hold great value as an aid to cultural understanding and a prompt to critical reflection. The profound interest abjection as an idea continues to inspire in the present signals its enduring newness. Theories of the abject are key to understanding the contemporary. This is because abject art and literature are not bound to a particular period or geographical location. They adapt to reflect changing times and contexts. The essays in this volume cumulatively demonstrate that abjection is not singular but plural and multiform. Something of the concept's lasting value and significance may inhere in its elusiveness. Kristeva's magisterial *Powers of Horror*, for instance, is marked by shifting notions of what comprises abjection. It refuses to be bounded. The power of abjection is its refusal to be too easily and rapidly explained.

Abjection's resistance to thought, a resistance that is also simultaneously a challenge and an invitation, has not prevented Kristeva's psychoanalytic exegesis in particular from being subject to cursory and uninformed readings that focus solely on the visceral aspect of her argument. Adrian Rifkin has rightly drawn attention to the tendency to 'pillage' *Powers of Horror* for 'conveniently sized "bleeding chunks"' (1998: 136). The phrase 'bleeding chunks' derives from Donald Tovey's essay on Anton Bruckner's Symphony No. 4, first published in 1935, in which he chastises concert audiences who delight in 'the bleeding chunks of butcher's meat chopped from Wagner's operas and served up on Wagner nights' (2015: 254–255). Tovey is criticising the practice of plundering operas for what are perceived to be the best bits. He regards it as akin to butchery. Operas understood only through excerpts, the perceived highlights, lose their integrity. This volume is also important because through the fine, nuanced readings it provides of Kristeva it additionally serves as a valuable corrective to the kind of practice Rifkin identifies.

Tovey's image of butcher's meat dripping with blood is purposely gruesome. He has chosen a horrible analogy to drive home his point. In a sense, Tovey recognises the power of horror. The image repels yet fascinates. It is striking. Classical music is not often discussed in relation to earthy matters such as butcher's meat. Music, however, like all culture is founded on horror. In *Powers of Horror*, Kristeva seeks to lay bare what lies beneath 'the cunning, orderly surface of civilizations' (1982: 210). She strives to reveal the 'nurturing horror' that civilisations seek to push aside through 'purifying, systematizing and thinking' (210). The essays in this volume can all be said, in their different ways, to join her in this effort.

Notes

1 For a brief summary of the various criticisms that have been levelled at Kristeva's conception of abjection see Rina Arya and Nicholas Chare's introduction to the special issue of *Performance Research*, 'On Abjection', devoted to the theme of abjection in relation to a number of performance practices (Arya and Chare, 2014). See also Arya, 2014 for a comprehensive elucidation of the concept of abjection in culture.
2 This essay is included in volume H of the author's *Œuvres complètes* (Bataille, 1970).
3 These are Kristeva's emphases. Unless otherwise stated all emphases are our own.
4 For an interesting analysis of the American artist as abject figure in relation to nationalism see Julie Codell's reading of cinematic depictions of artists in 'Nationalizing Abject American Artists' (Codell, 2011). For Codell, minoritarian abject artists reveal the underside of national identity but their filmic representations re-inscribe hegemonic values in relation to their personalities and works.
5 Kristeva's indebtedness to Bataille in *Powers of Horror* is evident in her book's third chapter which begins with an epigraph related to abjection taken from his *Essais de sociologie*.
6 Our translation. All translations are our own unless otherwise stated.
7 See Rina Arya and Nicholas Chare's guest edited volume 'On Abjection' for *Performance Research*, which is a comprehensive exploration of abjection in performance studies and related areas.
8 The idea that the bodily component to Pollock's practice was not hitherto recognised is, of course, belied by Harold Rosenberg's 'The American Action Painters' (Rosenberg, 1962).
9 See Chare, *After Francis Bacon* (2012: 77–100).
10 For a discussion of the history of this equivalence see Chare, 'Sexing the Canvas' (Chare, 2009).
11 See Barbara Creed, *The Monstrous Feminine* (1993).
12 For a discussion of Jouhandeau in this context see Rifkin's 'Does Gay Sex Need Queer Theory?' (2012).

References

Arya, R. 2014. *Abjection and Representation: An Exploration of Abjection in the Visual Arts, Film and Literature*. Basingstoke: Palgrave Macmillan.

Arya, R. and Chare, N. 2014. On Abjection. *Performance Research* 19(1), pp. 1–134.

Bataille, G. 1970. *Œuvres complètes*. Paris: Gallimard.

Ben-Levi et al. 1993. Introduction. In Ben-Levi, J., Jones, L., Taylor, S. and Houser, C. eds. *Abject Art: Repulsion and Desire in American Art*. New York: Whitney Museum of American Art, pp. 6–15.

Butler, J. 1993. *Bodies that Matter: On the Discursive Limits of 'Sex'*. New York: Routledge.

Chanter, T. 2007. *The Picture of Abjection: Film, Fetish and the Nature of Difference.* Bloomington: Indiana University Press.

Chare, N. 2009. Sexing the Canvas: Calling on the Medium. *Art History* 32(4), pp. 664–689.

Chare, N. 2012. *After Francis Bacon: Synaesthesia and Sex in Paint.* Farnham: Ashgate.

Codell, J. 2011. Nationalizing Abject American Artists: Jackson Pollock, Lee Krasner, and Jean-Michel Basquiat. *Auto/Biography Studies* 26(1), pp. 118–137.

Creed, B. 1993. *The Monstrous Feminine: Film, Feminism, Psychoanalysis.* London: Routledge.

Houser, C. 1993. I, Abject. In Ben-Levi, J., Jones, L., Taylor, S. and Houser, C. eds. *Abject Art: Repulsion and Desire in American Art.* New York: Whitney Museum of American Art, pp. 84–100.

Jones, L. C. 1993. Transgressive Femininity: Art and Gender in the Sixties and Seventies. In Ben-Levi, J., Jones, L., Taylor, S. and Houser, C. eds. *Abject Art: Repulsion and Desire in American Art.* New York: Whitney Museum of American Art, pp. 32–57.

Jouhandeau, M. 2006 [1939]. *De l'abjection.* Paris: Gallimard.

Krauss, R. 1996. 'Informe' without Conclusion. *October* 78, pp. 89–105.

Kristeva, J. 1974. *La révolution du langage poétique.* Paris: Éditions de Seuil.

Kristeva, J. 1980. *Pouvoirs de l'horreur: essai sur l'abjection.* Paris: Éditions de Seuil.

Kristeva, J. 1982 [1980]. *Powers of Horror: An Essay on Abjection.* New York: Columbia University Press.

Lotringer, S. 1994. Les Miserables. In Lotringer, S. ed. *More & Less.* New York: Semiotext(e), pp. 2–7.

Penwarden, C. and Kristeva, J. 1995. Of Word and Flesh. In Morgan, S. and Morris, F. eds. *Rites of Passage: Art for the End of the Century.* London: Tate Gallery Publications, pp. 21–7.

Rifkin, A. 1998. Julia Kristeva and Her Histories. *parallax* 4(3), pp. 135–141.

Rifkin, A. 2012. Does Gay Sex Need Queer Theory? *Paragraph* 35(2), pp. 197–214.

Rose, J. 1993. Julia Kristeva-Take Two. In Oliver, K. ed. *Ethics, Politics, and Difference in Julia Kristeva's Writings.* London: Routledge, pp. 41–61.

Rosenberg, H. 1962. The American Action Painters. In Rosenberg, H. *The Tradition of the New.* London: Thames & Hudson, pp. 23–39.

Ross, C. 1997. Redefinitions of Abjection in Contemporary Performances of the Female Body. *RES* 31, pp. 149–156.

Taylor, S. 1993. The Phobic Object: Abjection in Contemporary Art. In Ben-Levi, J., Jones, L., Taylor, S. and Houser, C. eds. *Abject Art: Repulsion and Desire in American Art.* New York: Whitney Museum of American Art, pp. 58–83.

Tovey, D. F. 2015. *Symphonies and Other Orchestral Works: Selections from Musical Analysis.* New York: Dover.

Wirth, J. M. 1999. Wretched Desire: Bataille and Kristeva on Abjection. *Philosophy Today* 33, pp. 169–176.

1

Abjection, art and bare life

John Lechte

> When I saw the 'Abject Art' show at the Whitney, I thought, What is abject about it? Everything was very neat; the objects were clearly art works. They were on the side of the victor. (Denis Hollier)

The domain of abjection and the excluded part

Since the publication in 1980 of Julia Kristeva's innovative work (Kristeva, 1980), we know that, psychoanalytically, the subject is put in question by abjection – or, better: that there is no fully formed subject in abjection because there is no object before which subjectivity (including an ego) could emerge. While it may be true that subjectivity is in part constituted by an effort of expulsion of the abject 'thing' and that this can have echoes throughout the life of the individual, it is not a matter of an object with a negative sign (abject) opposed to one with a positive sign (object of desire). As Kristeva makes clear in a passage which has not received the attention which it deserves – perhaps not even from Kristeva herself[1] – we note that: 'The abject is not an ob-ject facing me, which I name or imagine. Nor is it an ob-jest [*ob-jeu*], an *objet petit "a"* ceaselessly fleeing in the systematic quest of desire' (Kristeva, 1982: 1, trans. modified). Least of all, then, can the abject be contained in a representation in as far as every representation is based on an object-ification. The abject is thus not to be confused with the object in the mirror stage which, as Jacques Lacan said, is based in identification and is formative of the 'I' (subject). Indeed, if the object is the mediating thing through which the subject can gauge itself in the world, abjection evokes an immediate force that fragments the embryonic ego/subject. There is no room to manoeuvre in an immersion in meaninglessness, repugnance and incoherence – everything, in effect, that subjectivity will strive to keep at bay in its ego life within the borders of sociality.

Anthropologically, abjection has been seen to do with the ambiguity of borders, in particular, those of the body and its markers (hair of the head, nails, body fluids, human excreta, erotic sexuality) and those of transitional states (menstruation, childhood/adulthood, marriage, the cadaver) and things that do not fit in and are excluded from social life (rubbish or filth, individuals who are different – 'unclean' (the leper), food that is out of place (not blessed). The abject must be dealt with, lest purity be undermined; but it is, at the same time, what one would prefer not to know about and which, in a sense, one cannot 'know', to the extent that knowledge privileges the object.

Ambivalence in relation to abjection emerges with regard to an identity which becomes fragile and ambiguous, especially if we recall Bataille's idea of 'continuity' or communication as the blurring of borders between beings, most notably in eroticism. Both anthropology (Mary Douglas), and psychoanalysis (Kristeva) see ambivalent states of the sacred and the concomitant fragility of identity as key components of culture, eliciting as they do religious rituals and prohibitions along with innovative symbolic incarnations, which, Kristeva suggests, keep abjection at bay. The correlate is that when symbolic forms break down, there is a risk of abjection taking hold.

As I have shown, crime is also part of the abject, especially as corruption (cf. Lechte, 2011). For then, what appears as upright behaviour becomes a cover for hypocritical self-interest. Crime is thus double-edged, as far as abjection is concerned: on the one hand, the criminal who openly flouts the law is not abject and may well deserve the status of a hero. On the other hand, the judge and similar persons of status and authority who publicly, but hypocritically, uphold the law while secretly on the take are abject. Such behaviour is the subject of revulsion before it can be represented or objectified. It is not immoral – which can be proclaimed – but is amoral, with which it is impossible to identify – an impossibility that also pertains to the one engaged in amoral behaviour.

Crime, then, is abject when it cannot be made to come under the auspices of the law (including the moral law) or even under the sway of language, to the extent that a key element of language is codification and abjection defies codification. At the level of sociality, one assumption is that the law's *raison d'être* is to purify – or at minimum deal with – criminality. Another is that the law creates the criminal (Michel Foucault) and that it is first a form of violence (Walter Benjamin) before it is peaceful codification. Whatever the case, the basis of the law remains the subject of profound ambiguity and uncertainty. Freud's founding myth of the primal horde only confounds the ambiguity; for, as Freud himself acknowledges, the 'murder' of the father is only possible *after* the father's death at the hands of the sons, that is to say, retrospectively, something that goes against the whole meaning of law. The law, in a sense, can have no origin (it would be an-archical) – or rather, a profound law-lessness is at the origin of the law. But this does not make sense; we do not want (in a profoundly visceral sense) to accept it; it is abject!

Be all this as it may, the question that must now be put to art and science is: can abjection truly be incorporated in an object of appreciation and knowledge? Would it not rather be that abjection undermines art and knowledge? For, to repeat, the abject is not an object, which it needs to be to enter the realms of art or epistemology. It is not for nothing that art is referred to as the sphere of the 'art object'. Let us look at the notion of 'heterology' in this light.

Heterology

In Bataille's to date unpublished piece on heterology,[2] we can see the coincidence, at certain points, of heterology and abjection. Heterology – or, as Bataille's manuscript puts it: 'the science of the heterogeneous. That is to say, the science of the excluded part (or at the very least of the mode of exclusion that creates this part)' – would seek to bring the excluded part into the fold of science in order that it might be objectified. But, as we have said, the abject is beyond, or prior to objectification. It is not therefore amenable to 'heterology'; for it is not amenable to the logos (discourse, science) of hetero-logy (science of difference).

As Kristeva notes, Bataille wrote an early essay on abjection, albeit from the perspective of those subject to abject poverty (*misère*). Of importance here is the idea that the abject poor, who have become things, must be excluded from society proper and this gesture of exclusion is yet constitutive of social life. Indeed, according to Bataille, it makes possible the sovereignty of a heterogeneous nobility: 'The act of exclusion has the same meaning as social or divine sovereignty, but it is not located on the same level; it is precisely located in the domain of things and not, like sovereignty, in the domain of persons' (Bataille, 1970: 220). This 'act of exclusion' coincides with Bataille's concept of community as the union of 'those who have no community' – that is, of those who, as a kind of non-group, are thoroughly heterogeneous to all forms of society and even to the human as a whole (recall Agamben's *homo sacer*).

Heterology, then, as the 'science of the excluded part', points to a domain that is entirely other and foreign to identity and the order of the Same. And it is this which requires scrutiny and interpretation. Accordingly, the following is the key passage: 'Heterology receives therefore from the start a minimum definition – as the knowledge of what appears as completely other'.

When abjection is under scrutiny, though, it is a matter of deciding whether what is 'completely other' – a definition which, for all intents and purposes, also applies to the abject – leads to the destruction of art and knowledge rather than being part of their fulfilment. Can there really be an art of the abject?

'Return of the real' and cinema

> Duchamp, I think single-handedly, demonstrated that it is entirely possible for something to be art without having anything to do with taste at all, good or bad. Thus he put an end to that period of aesthetic thought and practice which was concerned, to use a title of David Hume's, with the standard of taste. This does not mean that the era of taste (*goût*) has been succeeded by the era of disgust (*dégoût*). It means, rather, that the era of taste has been succeeded by the era of meaning. The question is not whether something is in good or bad taste, but what does it mean [*sic*]. (Danto, 2000: 9)

This is a fundamental point, especially in light of what was said above about abjection. For, in highlighting meaning, Danto might seem to have changed the terms of the debate. However, if the debate is about whether or not the abject as such can appear, meaning thus becomes embroiled with the appearance or non-appearance of the abject. It is worth presenting other aspects of Danto's take on abject art. We find that even though the abject is what cannot appear – it keeps on appearing![3]

As Danto explains, 'What was initially so revolting to viewers of Modern Art, whenever it began, was that it itself gave offense, not that it represented offensive things' (2000: 3). However, even though the material content of what was frequently called disgusting and implicitly placed in the category of abject art (in particular, Duchamp's urinal) was rarely as objectionable as some critics (e.g., Jean Claire, director of the Musée Picasso in Paris) made out, there is no doubt that Danto, like most critics, accepts that in the last two decades of the twentieth century a transformation occurred where, instead of aiming to present, in the Kantian manner, what was pleasing, artists evoked Duchamp's gesture of 1917 when the now legendary urinal, signed 'R. Mutt' was submitted to, and rejected by, the Society of Independent Artists for its annual exhibition. According to Danto, this gesture prompted art practice to reorient itself and to confront the viewer with what was and often is disturbing, or repulsive, if not abject. Indeed, 'a case *can* be made' says our critic, 'that Duchamp made it possible for artists today to use "abject" materials to produce experiences in viewers' (2000: 9). Once artists are no longer constrained by the notion of 'good taste', they are then at liberty to broaden the materials repertoire of art and for this they are, argues Danto, to be applauded.

In engaging with this theme, the art historian and theorist, Hal Foster, adopts a Lacanian stance in arguing that what is called the abject in art is in fact a return of the real as a missed encounter – of the real experienced as a trauma that can only ever be repeated, as is exemplified, says Foster, by the work of Andy Warhol, work that becomes an instance of the compulsion to repeat characteristic of the trauma of the missed encounter (Foster, 1996: 127–168). In his analysis of the 'cult' of the abject in art asks Foster: 'Why this fascination with trauma, this envy of abjection today?' (1996: 166). This is an important question to which we shall later return.

In cinema, too, Martine Beugnet, after referring to Foster's notion of a 'return of the real' in art is moved to say that:

> A comparable shift is noticeable in the work of a film-maker like Grandrieux, whose achievement, as Nicole Brenez emphasizes, rests specifically on the willingness to use cinema to approach these borderline experiences of the human condition that both Lacan and Bataille evoked in their writing. (Beugnet, 2005: 178)

According to Brenez, as cited by Beugnet:

> 'The image is no longer given as a reflection, discourse, or the currency of whatever absolute value; it works to invest immanence, using every type of sensation, drive and affect. To make a film means [...] confronting the sheer terror of the death drive (*Sombre*), or the still more immense and bottomless terror of the unconscious, of total opacity (*La Vie nouvelle*).' (Brenez, 2003 in Beugnet, 2005: 178)

More specifically, for Beugnet,

> The fluid, elliptical structure of the two films thus eschews conventional dramatic progression. There are no precise, explicit motivations to the actions of *Sombre*'s main characters, and their journey does not seem to lead anywhere in particular. Similarly, *La Vie nouvelle* offers a nondescript geographical and fictional space of devastation, where the characters appear in erratic, elliptical fashion, to enact an obscure tale of desire and revenge. (180)

In *La Vie nouvelle*

> The bodies thus metamorphose into monstrous creatures, eyeless, translucent silhouettes, part-human, part-animal, howling and hovering blindly in the dark, and tearing up each others' flesh – a scene of utter chaos, filled by the mixed sounds of a rumbling noise and distorted yells. (182)

Often, Beugnet notes, background and figures in both films become so indistinct that one is reminded of Georges Bataille's notion of the *informe* (the formless), a term used by a number of commentators as a synonym for the abject. And, indeed, it evokes the struggle for identity that takes place to avoid the merging of self and other deemed to be at the heart of the Kristevan, psychoanalytic view of the abject.[4]

Thus, as with the other arts, so too with cinema: the effort to please is replaced by a desire to shock, or to let appear what was previously thought should not appear – or so it would seem. In any event, something has happened in art and cinema. But is it to do with the representation or presentation of the real or the abject *as such*? Clearly, to the extent that the abject is defined as that which cannot be represented or presented – as that which cannot be objectified – it cannot appear in the objectifications in art or cinema. On the other hand, it might be that the mode of appearing of the abject is entirely unique and that it is this which needs to be addressed. For instance, we could propose that the abject appears in the same way that style does in art. And that just as there is no singular entity that can encapsulate the style of a work, so there is no abject object. Or again, it may be that the kind of presence that the abject has in art and cinema is analogous to the semiotic in Kristeva's sense. The semiotic is in language and signs – it is the level of *signifiance* – yet cannot appear in its own right independently of the symbolic. It is nevertheless distinct from the symbolic.

That it is difficult to avoid objectifying the abject can be intuited from Levinas's now famous philosophy of the ethical where he points out that Western philosophy is an 'egology', by which is meant that every effort to do justice to the other results in the other being objectified within the order of the Same. The other thus becomes, in the tradition, the ego's other, not the other as such (see Levinas, 1969). Instead, Levinas directs us to the other as infinity and transcendence that is *immediately* experienced. The other is prior to the self, prior to the same – prior to essence – and has its impact beyond any subjectivity understood as forged through a relation to an object, as it is beyond all forms of totality. The other, in short, cannot be represented.

By way of analogy, then, the abject is an immediacy beyond the present structure of objectification and representation. While Levinas is concerned with transcendence, the abject would be radically immanent. As such, it is not at the disposition of any subjectivity to control or manipulate. This is its difference from an object that inevitably exists for a subject in the order of the Same. Epistemology does nothing other than reinforce this latter relation. What about art?

As a first step to a response to this question, I cite a passage from my essay on crime culture that concerns the abject in art:

> I do not deny that the abject can appear in artistic presentations; and certainly Kristeva's work claims as much. But how it does so is a key element in making contact with it, much as the ugly poses a conundrum for art of the beautiful when presented artistically. If the abject *is* in art content this can also be a way of muting it, in the sense that a symbolic form (an interpretation) would enable it to see the light of day, as it were, the manifestation of that which otherwise remains hidden, secret, indistinct, just as the unconscious is rendered relatively benign by language. (Lechte, 2011: 60)[5]

Just how the abject appears in art is thus one issue along with that of whether symbolic form mutes the abject so that it becomes an object to be observed, if it is not something with which one can identify. A clichéd abject – much like a clichéd, shadowy figure in movies – might then be substituted for what is genuinely revolting.[6]

But more importantly, perhaps, than issues of representation, because linked to a political take on the abject, we should ask: can its cultural version (as described by ethnology), where general prohibitions come into play, be more than – as Foster has recognised – 'the condition *to be abject*' (Foster, 1996: 156)? The 'condition to be abject' is the negative, passive position, contrasting with the drive 'to abject' – to keep abjection at bay in the formation of subjectivity. It is the cultural version of abjection which thus becomes worrying when persons are implicated. The abject being (the one of the lower cast, clan, or class, or the being of the lower gender, or simply: the other as the necessarily excluded part) risks being the victim of forms of persecution and hatred which bypass intellectual scrutiny. It is thus clear that prejudice is based in abjection in this sense. Keeping abjection at bay thus remains perfectly fine when confined to things, but becomes noxious when humans become the target. To repeat: this is an impulse (or feeling) that bypasses the intellect and, as such, appears to be (relatively) automatic. Power can thus sense that expelling the other or keeping the other at bay (turning back the asylum seeker and refugee boats, in the Australian case) will not be resisted; for the other is abject, the excluded part that forms the basis of every phobia. To fight for human rights under these circumstances, would thus seem to entail a fight against 'the condition to be abject'.

Art, for its part, would seem to be unavoidably implicated in the abject in the sense that it is founded in feeling (cf. Immanuel Kant's definition of the beautiful, which has no concept).

But, then, perhaps the point that the abject is not an object and cannot be represented needs further elaboration when it comes to politico-cultural matters. Just as Kant said that there is no beautiful object as such, only a subjective feeling of beauty, so there is no abject object/person as such, even if the play of power opens up a certain vulnerability in this domain. For power wants to unite abject and object. It wants an immediacy of response in relation to an object (hatred of a person, or group of persons), whereas the abject arises precisely when there is no object that can be the vehicle of identification, albeit negative. Power can exploit the abject impulse; for just as the void calls for something to stand for it, just as a shadow is an index of something else that the subject calls to appear, just as what is murky and ambiguous calls to be clarified and thus turned into something, so, in similar fashion, an experience of the abject calls for an object to stand for it, however misleading this might be when it comes to the true nature of the abject. Calling on an object (calling an object abject) is a way of assuaging the discomfort of the abject. Such discomfort may be pushed to the point of quasi-institutionalisation.[7]

We are now at the point where uncertainty arises regarding the status of art as embodied in an object – and this would include film as the cinema object.

Surely, even for conceptual art, there must be an art object at work in order that the ideas at play can see the light of day?

Were we to take an approach similar to that of Danto, there would hardly be a problem; for, as we saw, he says that 'abject' materials have come to assume an important place in art practice since Duchamp, and that the representation of the disgusting (abject) thing has the same impact as the real thing. To what extent is Danto correct here? And to what extent, by contrast, is Hollier, as cited in the epigraph, correct when he implies that art and the abject are at opposite poles to each other? – that the abject is so subterranean that anything that appears in its name (comes into the light, so to speak) is a falsification of it. Philippe Grandieux's film *Sombre* might, in this regard, provide us with an insight into the relationship between the abject and art.

Sombre

As Martine Beugnet notes, Grandrieux, along with a select number of other directors, has become known for what has been called a 'cinema of the senses'. Instead of being based in intrigue and narrative, the film highlights the way images are constructed and engage the senses and accompanying emotions – including the abject and the Freudian death drive. *Sombre* plays on this by having images only partially lit and often so murky that forms are impossible to distinguish clearly, sounds often being all that remains to guide the viewer in determining the nature of events that carry the loosely developed plot of a serial killer's journey through a 'sombre' countryside. Dark themes (figuratively speaking) could thus be said to be treated in darkness, or sombreness (artistically speaking). Where would the abject lie, if it appears at all? Would it be in the actions of the killer, or is it elsewhere? Like Brenez, cited above, Grandrieux himself has said in interviews that he set out to explore the themes of the human that were close to the truth of the human, but which were rarely exposed. To do this, a narrative, albeit minimal, is necessary otherwise what is produced verges on the purely experimental, a genre Grandrieux is interested in as a spectator but not as a film maker.

It is clear from interviews that, in terms of the understanding he has of a film like *Sombre*, Grandrieux has a Freudian take on violence and murder. When prompted to explain how a certain '*éblouissement*' (bedazzlement) derives from murder, Grandrieux claims that it is not a matter of social reality, but of the real, of the unconscious and of dream, which blurs what is possible and impossible, permitted and forbidden, a world that is more obscure and opaque than the social world: 'The material of *Sombre* comes very much from that, not as a representation of a dream in cinema, but indeed as something from the unconscious' (Grandrieux, 1999). Despite acknowledging that it is not about the representation of dream, there is still a question of the mode of appearing of dream-like material and material from the unconscious. There are actors, there are images and scenes, there is dialogue – albeit minimal – there is music. If it is not a matter of social reality, but one of an encounter with the real, are we to assume that, indeed, Grandrieux, has produced a poetic film that, in certain respects, highlights the semiotic in Kristeva's sense: rhythmical images and sounds, expressionist images, images that highlight the fact of the image as such and where meaning breaks down – opaque images – images with a poetic status, images that lay claim to being purely aesthetic, either beautiful or ugly or at one moment beautiful at another ugly. But what of the film not being experimental? Grandrieux here wants, as we have said, to hold on to narrative such that there is a definable structure to the film: all is not fluidity, murkiness and strange contrasts of light and dark. Jean, the puppeteer and murderer, embarks on his killing spree and travels down the mountain with Claire, following the *Tour de France* bicycle race. Various characters are met with along the way, and with each meeting Jean exhibits his inability to communicate with others or with himself. Driving the narrative is the sense that Jean may kill again. Will it be another prostitute? Is Claire in danger? Killing, therefore, is what holds the film together. It is the basis of the narrative. The poetics of the image intervene to blur and to dissolve the trajectory of the narrative. But the fact remains that killing wins through. The film is about killing: about the act of killing and the prospect of killing – killing framed by an experimentalism, or a poetics/semiotics of the image. That is what is scandalous and what maybe even abject. Poetics is nihilistic and indifferent to murder. It is this (about killing and poetics) more than it is about Jean, the killer, about whom the spectator knows hardly anything. This is where, to repeat, the abject is located – in the killing (even the thought of which, under the circumstances is abject) and in its banality, to the extent that it is the basis of the film *as* film. It is barely possible to name this abject banality; for it is not quite in the killing as such or in the actions of the killer nor exactly in the film as film but in all these simultaneously. This abject is an experience that we can only gesture towards, but not name.

The difference from the horror movie is quite striking; for, there, an object (ghost, monster, evil doer, ugly object) arises which provokes fear or repulsion, but which does not put identity into question. To desire entails to hate; to embrace something or someone entails the potential to reject, to exclude. Clearly, we are in the realm of negative identification, whereas the abject is neither positive nor negative (cf. nihilism with regard to murder) and constitutes a threat to identity. Or, as Kristeva shows (1982: 31–55), if an object provokes fear, it is not always the object itself of which the subject is fearful, but something else (as with a phobic fear) – something more inaccessible to language and signification.

Certainly, Grandrieux's and the critics' references to the 'materiality' of the film and of film in general should be taken into account here. For, it is not just a matter of the cinema screen, the technology (analogue or digital), the context of projection (private or public), the style of editing or the duration of takes, the play of sound, but a matter of how the poetics/semiotics of the image relates to the structure of the film provided by the narrative. To thematise materiality, however, really means to thematise the medium irrespective of the content or what film, in this case, brings in terms of a message or meaning. To the extent that meaningful content is uppermost, the film is transparent, whereas it becomes opaque and intransigent when the material medium is to the fore. But can a medium be opaque and still appear as a medium? In my study of the image (Lechte, 2012), I have suggested that it cannot and that to hold that it can is to fall into the error that Jean-Paul Sartre called the 'illusion of immanence', by which he meant treating the image as an object separately from its content, the point being that the image is the 'presence of the thing in its absence' (see Sartre, 2004). In effect, a medium cannot appear as such; it cannot become an object and still remain a 'medium', the essential quality of the medium being its transparency.

Media studies takes a very different view. For this discipline, media can be objectified and still remain media. Little wonder that, today, the abject is frequently described as an 'abject object', there being no recognition that this is an oxymoron.[8] If a medium is an object, so is the abject – both media and abject being the outcomes of a theorising that, to be what it is, must objectify.

Although the profundity of his philosophising is difficult to match, we need to move in the direction of Levinas's thinking when he speaks of the face of the other as beyond what might be circumscribed by a phenomenology or be the object of theory. The Other (*autrui*) cannot be objectified, which means that it cannot be contained within the order of the Same (see Levinas, 1969: 33–81). Any claim by Western philosophy to have captured the other only reiterates the fact that it is philosophy's other that has been captured, not the other as such.

So where does this leave us with regard to the so-called materiality of film? It leaves us with the paradoxes arising from any attempt to objectify media. As has been said, to objectify media is to be left with objects – not media! It is to have failed to have come abreast of the distinction made in 1941 by Sartre between perception and image. To perceive is to objectify and to lay claim to objectivity; with regard to the image it is a matter of being in touch with the thing itself, without mediation. Thus with a painting of Pierre, Pierre is not contained in a perception of the brushstrokes on the canvas. Pierre is not equivalent to the paint, as a naive materialism might claim.[9] Rather, Pierre is transported directly into my presence as spectator. Through the image, I commune with Pierre. Pierre's presence transcends any perception of brushstrokes. The analogous question vis-à-vis film might be: how does the play of light (the equivalent of brushstrokes) as such become the imaged entity? If a picture proposed itself as nothing other than brush strokes and colour (shades of Abstract Expressionism?) would this mean that the materiality of the medium had finally been captured – just as the play of light and movement might be presented in cinema as nothing other than light and movement? Would we – do we – in works of this genre confront the true bases of art and film? In writing, the equivalent would be the mark as the foundation of the materiality of writing. Do we confront the mark as such – a mark bereft of all signification? The answer to the preceding questions is that: brushstrokes *as such*, cannot appear; light and movement *as such* in film cannot appear; the mark *as such* in writing and art cannot appear. For what has no symbolic form cannot appear. And they are the media – the condition of possibility – for the appearing of meaning, but, qua media, cannot themselves appear.[10] Guy Debord's experimental cinema proves that even a dark screen appears as something significant – that darkness (sombreness!) cannot appear as such (maybe against Debord's intention).

So, the claim that Grandrieux's film, *Sombre*, allows the materiality of the film to appear[11] needs to be reconsidered. To the extent that the materiality (sound, rhythm and movement, light, type of technology) of film is objectified – is rendered present through perception – it ceases to figure in film qua film. That is, to the extent that a spectator is aware – whether through the senses and/or the mind (but how can these be separated?) – of the materiality in a pure form (light qua light, etc.) of a film, it ceases to work as film – as a cinematic event.

From his interviews, it is clear, as we have already indicated, that Grandrieux includes as part of the narrative aspect of his cinema the play of the drives, of dream and of the unconscious, all of which, he implies exist in a more or less explicit state in childhood – hence the significance of the children's reactions, mirrored on their faces, to Jean's Punch and Judy show at the beginning of *Sombre*. However, assuming that what Grandrieux thinks he is doing *is* what he is doing, this idea (and it is an idea) of childhood is highly problematic if it proposes that, for a child, everything tends to be blurred in conjunction with the absence of the lineaments of a moral universe. This we could almost say is the idea of childhood as 'bare life' (existence as pure biological survival), where a *way of life* would be yet to emerge and the little individual is more or less the plaything of instinct and the indifferent perpetrator of violence. This is quite a *narrative*![12]

A quite different narrative (for those who believe this is significant) is proposed by Julia Kristeva who refers to Freud's vision of the 'father of individual pre-history', where a loving father, corresponding to the loving mother, supports the child in an environment of *agape* love (Kristeva, 1987: 26). Here, while the surrounding world might take on an air of fluidity, the first impulse is not self-preservation – the presupposition of those who view the human as essentially 'bare life' – but the rudiments of a way of life in which the other is at least as present as the self. Socially speaking, therefore, the child is not, as Grandrieux seems to argue, an archetypal psychopath – even if keeping the abject at bay entails keeping the (archaic) mother at bay. At the level of the abject, as Kristeva proposes it, I can be drowned in love. Thus to say that *Sombre* is governed by a child's view of the world is quite problematic, the result of a retrospective illusion.

Conclusion

The main concern of this essay has been about the presentation of the abject. Kristeva herself, we have noted, exhibits a certain ambivalence in her theory. For, on the one hand, the abject is connected to 'the instability of the symbolic function' (Kristeva, 1982: 14), which implies that the possibility of using language is inhibited, and on the other hand, the abject is deemed to appear in literature – the realisation and confirmation of the symbolic function. It is as though we were left with the fundamental ambiguity of abjection itself:[13] can it appear in symbolic form, however elementary, or should we conclude that it cannot appear, according to the principle that the impossibility of its appearing as an object or even entity is its essential quality?

Could there be a third position – namely, that although it cannot appear as such, the abject can be evoked and in this way be more effectively dealt with? Such might be the significance of the horror film genre and of the features of literary works referred to by Kristeva. Just as the ineffable, the inexpressible and the unpresentable can be evoked through symbolic means (including words), so the abject would appear without fully appearing. This may well be satisfactory as far as it goes and would imply that, as a work fitting into the horror film genre, *Sombre* evokes abjection. In the film, we see that the character, Jean the killer, in his very ambiguity as a human being, evokes abjection. The darkness surrounding this character and the darkness of the film generally, a darkness which heightens ambiguity, evokes abjection.

What such an approach does not address, however, is the possibility that a work as such (not just its content) is abject. In this regard, certain critics (e.g., Adrian Martin) do not seem to have had trouble identifying with the film as such, even if they have found the content challenging. Here, let us recall Hal Foster's point that the 'crucial ambiguity in Kristeva is her slippage between the operation *to abject* and the condition *to be abject*' (Foster, 1996: 156). Would this imply that while the operation 'to abject' is prior to any object, 'to be abject' is tinged with objectivity and thus allows things to be classified or categorised as abject, with all the negative consequences that this might entail.[14] 'Attract' or 'repel' are part of the everyday universe of words. They are terms pointing to the possibility of an identification – whether positive or negative – in relation to which the ego is in control. The abject – if this term is to have real significance – is radically other by comparison. It is the unimaginable, the unsayable – that which grabs me by the throat and bowls me over and in relation to which I can do nothing! In fact, I cease to know who I am other than this wave of nausea that will not recede. The abject thing thus becomes indistinguishable from *abjecting*. It is a matter of getting the context right – not the context to do with the everyday mantras of 'I like this' and 'I hate that', 'I desire this' or 'I'm repelled by that', but the context in which being as such is undermined.[15] The stakes are thus much higher than is generally appreciated. Overall, far from being the plaything of art – or its Duchampesque component (Danto) – the abject is what problematises the very possibility of an art object. However, for a modernist disposition there is nothing that cannot be captured within the realm of knowledge, nothing that in principle escapes the confines of science or philosophy. Were this to be the case – were a radical immanence to be challenged by a transcendence that cannot appear, the whole fabric of modernist order would be under threat. To evoke Levinas, we could say that the order of the Same would be under threat. In itself, the abject appears to be anything but transcendent – at least when it is associated with filth and defilement. However, it is the inside/outside ambiguity which is of relevance here more than any dirt as such. It is perhaps not for nothing that the sacred has come into play in precisely this context. Oddly, then, the lowest of the low, seems to evoke the 'most high' – a dimension that is no longer at the disposition of any knowledge and which can barely be thought. It is no doubt because it almost escapes thought that it continually calls to be thought. And part of this thinking that results from this call will concern the question of whether things (e.g. the sacred) can appear in thought without being objectified.

The abject, then, is that entity which, above all raises the question of the possibility or impossibility of its appearing. If cinema is a privileged form of art in its encounter with abjection, it may be because films, such as *Sombre*, are able to evoke the fact that the abject is that which, for artistic thought, borders on what is most unpresentable.

Notes

1 The reason being that Kristeva not only proceeds to describe the abject as supposedly presented in art and literature (e.g., Dostoyevsky, Proust, Joyce, Borges, etc.), but she also evokes objects (food items) that become vehicles of the abject, as if the latter could be represented in a certain sense. I will suggest, by contrast, that the implications of the abject for philosophy and theory are much more radical than we find in *Powers of Horror* (1982).

2 Georges Bataille, 'Definition of heterology' Introduction, by Marina Galetti (University of Rome III). Translated by Roy Boyne; Professor Emeritus, Durham University. This translation is likely to be published in the near future. Maria Galetti says, in part, that: 'Remaining unpublished until now, this text is preserved among Bataille's papers deposited with the Manuscripts Department at the Nouvelle Bibliothèque in Paris [Boite 13 C, 85–101]'.

3 That the issue is often about the appearance or non-appearance of the abject is often linked to the appearance or non-appearance of things that are repressed and located in the unconscious and that this repression, as implied by Grandrieux (see below), is not a good thing. More colloquially, it is said that Western society is too 'hung up' about excreta and the body – a view which entirely forgets the connection of the repressed things to the sacred. To the extent that the argument is that *everything* can appear, we have a further proof of Levinas's philosophy as 'egology' (Levinas, 1969: 44).

4 In her book-length study of recent French cinema, Beugnet refers to the emergence of a cinema of 'sensation' (= the body) (Beugnet, 2007: 2–10).

5 In a similar vein, Hal Foster raises crucial questions with regard to the abject: 'Can the abject be represented at all? If it is opposed to culture, can it be exposed *in* culture? If it is unconscious, can it be made conscious and remain abject? In other words, can there be a *conscientious abjection*, or is this all there can be? Can abject art ever escape an instrumental, indeed moralistic, use of the abject?' (Foster, 1996: 156. Foster's emphasis.)

6 The extent to which Philippe Grandrieux's film, *Sombre* (2006) also plays on this cliché of horror evoked by shadows needs to be considered. I have more to say below on this film.

7 Twenty years ago, in a discussion of the abject and the *informe*, Denis Hollier could remark: 'Today I think there is a strange institutionalization of the beyond of the pleasure principle. And I think the fascination with the abject is involved' (Hollier in Foster, et al., 1994: 21)

8 For instance, Rosalind Krauss, in discussion, says, 'But Kristeva's project is all about recuperating certain objects as abject' (in Foster et al., 1994: 3). Another participant in the discussion, Helen Molesworth, asks: 'Why do artists want to make objects that are abject?' (in Foster et al., 1994: 21).

9 This can serve as a reminder that a semiotic approach as exemplified by the work of Umberto Eco in the 1970s and 1980s (cf. Eco, 1979), made a big issue of the fact that realism in the theory of the icon was thwarted because the materiality of the representation was in no way equivalent to the materiality of the real thing – a classic instance of the 'illusion of immanence'.

10 Greg Hainge argues that this, 'leads to the presentation not of a transcendent story for which the medium is merely a transparent vehicle but, rather, of a series of objects formed of the very materiality of the medium' (Hainge, 2007: 160).

11 As is claimed, for example, by Greg Hainge: 'For Grandrieux, then, it is the materiality of the medium in which he works that precedes the structure' (Hainge, 2007: 160). And our critic, along with others, sums up what Grandrieux stands for as a contemporary *auteur* director: 'This truly is the cinema made flesh' (Hainge, 2007:

164). Finally, because of this materiality, when talking of Grandrieux's films: 'it serves no purpose to attempt to give an account of the film's narrative structure' (2007: 167) Hainge says this despite the fact that Grandrieux (whom Hainge cites as an authority on numerous occasions), as we have seen, applies the notion of narrative to his own work to distinguish is from purely experimental cinema.

12 To confirm his idea, Grandrieux also refers to the Freudian myth in *Totem and Taboo* of the primal horde and the killing of the father by the sons – thus establishing the rule of law and civilisation.

13 Cf.: 'abjection is above all ambiguity' (Kristeva, 1982: 9).

14 Pierre Bourdieu recalls that, 'to categorise' originally meant: 'to accuse publicly' – from the Greek, *kategoresthai* (Bourdieu 1985: 729).

15 Emmanual Levinas's philosophy, which evokes an 'otherwise than being', makes this statement all the more plausible (see Levinas 1998).

References

Bataille, G. 1970. *Œuvres complètes II: Écrits posthumes, 1922–1940*. Paris: Gallimard.

Beugnet, M. 2005. Evil and the Senses: Philippe Grandrieux's *Sombre* and *La Vie Nouvelle. Studies in French Cinema* 5(3), pp. 175–184.

Beugnet, M. 2007. *Cinema and Sensation: French Film and the Art of Transgression*. Edinburgh: Edinburgh University Press.

Bourdieu, P. 1985. The Social Space and Genesis of Groups. *Theory and Society* 14(6), pp. 723–744.

Brenez, N. 2003. The Body's Night: An Interview with Philippe Grandrieux. Trans. A. Martin, *Rouge*. 1 [Accessed 5 August 2013]. Available at: www.rouge.com.au/1/grandrieux.

Danto, A. 2000. Marcel Duchamp and the End of Taste: A Defense of Contemporary Art. [Accessed 12 August 2013]. Available at: www.kim-cohen.com/artmusictheoryassets/artmusictheorytexts/Danto_Duchamp.pdf.

Eco, U. 1979. *A Theory of Semiotics*, Bloomington: Indiana University Press.

Foster, H. 1996. *The Return of the Real: The Avant-Garde at the End of the Century*. Cambridge, MA, and London: The MIT Press.

Foster, H. et al. 1994. The Politics of the Signifier II: A Conversation on the 'Informe' and the Abject. *October* 67 (Winter), pp. 3–21.

Grandrieux, P. 1999. Entretien avec Philippe Grandrieux. [Accessed 5 August 2013]. Available at: www.horschamp.qc.ca/Emulsions/grandrieux.html.

Hainge, G. 2007. *Le corps concret*: Of Bodily and Filmic Material Excess in Philippe Grandrieux's Cinema. *Australian Journal of French Studies* 44(2), pp. 153–171.

Kristeva, J. 1980. *Pouvoirs de l'horreur: essai sur l'abjection*. Paris: Seuil.

Kristeva, J. 1982 [1980]. *Powers of Horror: An Essay on Abjection*. Trans. L. S. Roudiez. New York: Columbia University.

Kristeva, J. 1987. *Tales of Love*. Trans. Leon S. Roudiez. New York: Columbia University Press.

Koerner, J. L. 1997. The Abject of Art History. *Res* 31 (Spring), pp. 5–8.

Lacan, J. 1977. The Mirror Stage as Formative of the Function of the I as Revealed

in Psychoanalytic Experience. In *Écrits: A Selection*. Trans. A. Sheridan. London: Tavistock, pp. 1–7.
Lechte, J. 2011. Crime, Abjection, Transgression and the Image. In Nicol, B., McNulty, E. and Pulham, P. eds. *Crime Cultures: Figuring Criminality in Fiction and Film*. London and New York: Continuum, pp. 51–67.
Lechte, J. 2012. *Genealogy and Ontology of the Western Image and its Digital Future*. New York and London: Routledge.
Levinas, E. 1969. *Totality and Infinity: An Essay on Exteriority*. Trans. A. Lingis. Pittsburgh, PA: Duquesne University Press.
Levinas, E. 1998. *Otherwise than Being, Or Beyond Essence*. Trans. A. Lingis. Pittsburgh, PA: Duquesne University Press.
Sartre, J-P. 2004. *The Imaginary: A Phenomenological Psychology of the Imagination*. Trans. J. Webber. London and New York: Routledge.

2

Queering abjection: a lesbian, feminist and Canadian perspective

Jayne Wark

The intersection of abjection and queerness

Envision a gargantuan hairy goddess slapped together with fun fur and hot glue, a pair of lesbians masquerading as rangers at a world-famous national park, a video diary documenting a day in the life of a bull dyke, and blown-up Polaroids of a former lover's face with eyes obliterated by black strips recalling squalid 1960s detective novels. All these are artworks made respectively by four Canadian artists to be discussed in this essay: Allyson Mitchell, Shawna Dempsey and Lorri Millan, and Rosalie Favell.

Such things confound our expectations to be rewarded by art's aesthetic pleasures of craft, beauty and uplifting idealism. Although such pleasures have been frequently contested throughout the history of modern art, the term 'abject art' entered the art world lexicon in the early 1990s to denote a specific type of work preoccupied with taboo, and transgressive and disturbing subject matter and forms. The crystallisation of this term came about in 1993 when the Whitney Museum in New York held an exhibition called *Abject Art: Repulsion and Desire in American Art*. As a result of this designation of previously inchoate tendencies in contemporary American art, the type of art included in that show has come to dominate our conception of abjection in art and thus preclude other ways of understanding its role and significance.

This essay will consider some of these other possible understandings by examining the work of Favell, Dempsey, Millan and Mitchell from the perspective of its queer – or more precisely, lesbian – connotations. Although the relationship between queerness and abjection has been explored in philosophy, feminism and queer theory, I contend that so far it has only been incorporated into art discourse in a very circumscribed way, one that has been overdetermined by the Abject Art show. My goal is to bring attention to how these artists' approaches to the configuration of abjection and queerness can deepen our understanding of this connection in three principal ways: they complicate the generality of the term 'queer' by inflecting it with the particularity of lesbianism and its attendant politics, they counter the prevailing view of abject art presented in the 1993 Whitney show, and they challenge our received thinking about the theoretical framework that informs the discourse on abjection. I will begin by reviewing the theoretical writings on abjection by Julia Kristeva and Georges Bataille that helped shape the Abject Art exhibition. I will then reconsider aspects of Kristeva's theories, along with Judith Butler's discussion of abjection from a queer perspective, so as to integrate these into an analysis that sheds light on the role of abjection in the work of Favell, Mitchell, Dempsey and Millan from a lesbian, feminist, queer and Canadian perspective.

From theory to art: the American culture wars

The theoretical touchstone for any discussion of abjection is Julia Kristeva's book, *Powers of Horror: An Essay on Abjection*. In it she identified abjection both as a state of degradation and as a social position or domain that 'disturbs identity, system [and] order' because it refuses to 'respect borders, positions [and] rules' (Kristeva, 1982: 4). Overall, Kristeva regards abjection as our human responses of repulsion and horror to the breakdown of meaning caused by the disintegration of distinctions between subject and object, self and other. The kind of examples she provided include food, filth, waste or dung that induces spasms and vomiting, most famously the skin that forms on the surface of milk (2).

Kristeva's conception of abjection was manifestly evident in the Whitney's 1993 Abject Art show, which included artists such as Robert Gober, Andres Serrano, Kiki Smith and Cindy Sherman, whose work incorporates disturbing bodily aberrations, grotesque materials, messy forms and taboo social acts and relations. In her excellent undergraduate honours paper, 'Abjection: The Theory and the Moment', Amy Zurek posited this exhibition as the historical moment when an interest in abjection coalesced within the art world for two main reasons (Zurek, 2011: 3). First, it was a crucial retaliatory salvo in the so-called culture wars that had been raging in the United States since the late 1980s between right-wing forces and the artists and art institutions they deemed immoral. The attacks were so ferocious that they resulted in National Endowment for the Arts grants being withdrawn or denied, institutional censorship and charges of obscenity (Dubin, 1992). Second, it coincided with and articulated a growing body of scholarly and critical thinking about the idea of abjection in relation to art. I concur with Zurek's appraisal of this situation, but I wish to explore more fully how aspects of this body of thought converged to influence the formation of the Abject Art exhibition. As I will argue, this convergence furnished the theoretical foundations for the retaliatory and hostile incentives that shaped the Abject Art show within its particular historical moment. By identifying the connection between these theoretical and historical factors more precisely, we can then establish the grounds for differentiating between the Whitney show's approach to abjection and art and the one I wish to develop here in relation to the work of Favell, Dempsey, Millan and Mitchell.

The connection between these theoretical and historical factors that underpinned the Abject Art show must take into account the renewed interest at that time in the writings of the French intellectual Georges Bataille. Bataille was a dissident Surrealist who countered André Breton's idealist conception of Surrealism as rising and 'phallic' with his materialist preference for art that was base, 'anal' and *informe* (literally unformed or formless), and thus aesthetically abject (Spector, 1997: 84). In her 1985 book, *The Originality of the Avant-Garde and Other Modernist Myths*, historian Rosalind Krauss revived Bataille from obscurity in her analysis of Alberto Giacometti's sculpture (Krauss, 1985: 52–55). That same year, Krauss collaborated with Jane Livingston on the exhibition and publication *L'Amour fou: Photography and Surrealism*, which manoeuvred photography from the margins to the centre of Surrealism and positioned Bataille as the lynchpin of this alternate view (57, 64–65, 165–175). Krauss's interest in Bataille and the *informe* was subsequently passed on to her doctoral student, Hal Foster, who completed his dissertation on Surrealism in 1990 at the City University of New York.

A direct link can be traced from Foster to the Abject Art show. Foster was director of the Whitney's Curatorial and Critical Studies programme from 1987 till 1991, the same programme in which the three curators of the show – Craig Houser, Leslie C. Jones and Simon Taylor – were enrolled in 1992–93. Given this link, as well as the prominence of Krauss and Foster as editors of *October* magazine, it is implausible that these student curators were unaware of this rehabilitation of Bataille. It is understandable, therefore, that their curatorial premise would augment Kristeva's theory of abjection with Bataille's less well-known version as articulated in his 1934 essay, 'L'Abjection et les forms misérables' (Bataille, 1970: 217–222).

As Zurek has noted, Bataille's essay on abjection differed significantly from Kristeva's by taking a sociological rather than psychoanalytic approach (6–8). Written a year after the Nazis came to power in neighbouring Germany and built Dachau to imprison their political enemies (communists and labour leaders), Bataille's essay was a critique of how the oppressors subordinate the oppressed through mechanisms of exclusion and degradation that consign them to the realm of abjection. For Bataille, therefore, abjection could only have the negative connotations of exclusion: '*Les choses abjectes peuvent être définies ... négativement – comme objets de l'acte impératif d'exclusion'* (220).

Bataille's negative conception of abjection as social exclusion suited the curators' agenda for the Abject Art exhibition, which was to hit back against the repressive politics of their conservative opponents in the culture wars. As the curators stated in the introduction to the show's accompanying catalogue, they aimed to stick it to these right-wing forces: 'our goal is to talk dirty in the institution and degrade its atmosphere of purity and prudery by foregrounding issues of gender and sexuality in the art exhibited' (Ben-Levi et al., 1993: 7). Their strategy was to adopt Bataille's negative conception of abjection as their conceptual framework and then illustrate this with artworks that manifest the improper and unclean phenomena associated with Kristeva's theory of abjection as that which causes psychic repulsion and horror.

This conjoining of Bataille's negative sociological view of abjection with artworks evoking the disgusting and repulsive elements that Kristeva spoke about was strategically useful at that moment in the American culture wars. By encompassing burgeoning tendencies in art under the newly invented nomenclature 'abject art', the show succeeded in defining and legitimising it both as a category and an aesthetic, one that would become so pervasive in the 1990s that it even led Hal Foster to describe it as 'the shit movement' (1996: 118; cited in Zurek, 2011: 14). As I see it, however, although the version of abjection promulgated by the Whitney show was specific to its American culture-war context, it has come to dominate and skew our understanding of abjection in art. In order to open up other possible readings of abjection that can be brought to bear on the artworks I discuss in this essay, it is necessary to take a closer look at Kristeva's theory of abjection.

Revisiting Kristeva

Kristeva's *Powers of Horror* is a critical reworking of Jacques Lacan's psychoanalytic theory of the process of individuation. Kristeva concurs with Lacan that subjectivity is formed in conjunction with the acquisition and use of language, but she challenges his view that the onset of self-consciousness only comes about through the mirror stage and castration threats (see Lacan, 1977: 1–7). As Kelly Oliver has noted, Kristeva attempts to bring the 'speaking body' back into discourse by arguing that the logic of language is already operating at prior material levels of bodily processes, that bodily drives make their way into language, and that the recognition of these drives contests the traditional dualism between the body and the mind, the biological and the social (Oliver, 1997: xvi–xvii).

Kristeva locates these bodily drives in the pre-Oedipal realm she calls the 'semiotic', a realm that is experienced within the intimacy of the mother–child dyad (Oliver, 71–2). Her theory of abjection aims to account for the significance of this experience in the formation of identity. Unlike Sigmund Freud and Lacan, who regard the maternal body as the infant's first object, Kristeva argues that it is neither object nor non-object for the infant, but something else: it is an abject. Since the maternal body is not an object, or even a partial object, for the infant, this means that subjectivity is a process already underway long before Lacan's mirror stage (Oliver, 1997: 226). As this process develops through the infant's separation from the mother during the course of weaning, the infant undergoes a stage of abjection in which it 'abjects', or finds abject, its mother's body. The infant's first experience of abjection is produced, therefore, as a result of the uncertainty of finding the maternal body fascinating and horrifying all at once. As Sara Beardsworth argues, the value of Kristeva's theory is that it identifies and explicates 'a primitive moment of separateness in the earliest – not only presymbolic but pre-*imaginary* – structure of subjectivity, where the life of the drives is most emphatic' (Beardsworth, 2004: 81; emphasis in original). And because the infant must attempt to deal with its spatial and material ambivalence vis-à-vis its simultaneous attraction to and repulsion of the mother's body, it is no wonder, Beardsworth writes, 'that Kristeva claims that abjection is above all ambiguity' (82).

This ambiguity persists through the process of individuation because in order for the child to complete its separation from the mother and enter into the Symbolic Order or 'law of the father', it must 'revolt against that which gave us our own existence', which is the maternal body and everything associated with it (Pentony, 1996). This revolt is never complete, however, which is why Kristeva regards the abject not, as we might ordinarily think, as the grotesque, degraded or unclean, but rather as something that more profoundly 'calls borders into question and threatens identity' (Oliver, 1997: 225). Yet it is precisely encounters with such repellant things as bodily fluids, waste or matter out of place that cause us to relive the trauma of this revolt (Kristeva, 1982; 13). These encounters fill us with revulsion and we regard them as abject because they threaten us with the disintegration of the orderly borders we presume to exist between self and other, identity and non-identity, human and non-human. The abject is what we disavow or try to cast out. As Kristeva writes, 'the abject has only one quality of the object – that of being opposed to I' (1).

Although we are repelled by the otherness of the abject, we are simultaneously drawn to it through *jouissance*: 'One does not know it, one does not desire it, one joys in it [*on enjouit*]' (9). This duality is fascinating to Kristeva and indeed becomes central to her theory of how abjection pertains to art and culture. On the one hand, she says, abjection is 'perverse' because it refuses to accept prohibitions, rules or laws and instead 'turns them aside, misleads, corrupts; uses them, takes advantage of them, the better to deny them' (15). On the other hand, abjection can be purified through catharsis, beginning with 'the history of religions, and end[ing] up with that catharsis par excellence called art' (17). Abjection is thus valuable to art for two reasons: it signifies the critical disruption of rules and prohibitions, whilst art can in turn purify abjection, thereby enacting a positive force for cultural intervention and social change.

Because Kristeva's central preoccupation is with the relationship between language and subjectivity, she explores the cultural aspects of abjection exclusively in relation to literature (this may account for why art-based discussions of her theory of abjection have largely ignored these in favour of making more simplistic formal and material analogies to her descriptions of its grotesque, taboo and unclean manifestations). While the subject's acquisition of social language in its passage into the Symbolic realm results in the repression of the pre-Oedipal or semiotic realm, which Kristeva also refers to as the maternal *chora* (13–14), she sees literature as a form of cultural creativity that can resist that repression by reaching back into the semiotic dimension of language. The 'aesthetic task', she says, is to retrace 'the fragile limits of the speaking being, closest to its dawn', to a place where "subject" and "object" push each other away, confront each other, collapse, and start again – inseparable, contaminated, condemned, at the boundary of what is assimilable, thinkable: abject. Great modern literature unfolds over that terrain: Dostoyevsky, Lautréamont, Proust, Artaud, Kafka, Céline' (18). Kristeva regards such literature as redemptive because it propounds 'a sublimation of abjection' (26). This sublimation is the counterpart to abjection's value as the place where prohibitions are refused and boundaries are broken. As a result of this duality, 'abjection is eminently productive of culture. Its symptom is the rejection and reconstruction of languages' (45).

If we transpose Kristeva's views on abjection from literature to art, they offer a way of thinking about abjection that differs from the Abject Art exhibition, which, I have argued, was preoccupied with Bataille's negative conception of abjection as a socially exclusionary force, and limited in its incorporation of Kristeva's theory to her handful of concrete examples of abjection's visceral and embodied repulsiveness. By reconsidering her ideas about the ambiguity at the core of abjection, its simultaneously critical and productive aspects, we can move beyond the American-centric version of abject art that has come to dominate the discourse and consider other possible approaches, as I propose to do in the next sections of this essay.

Canadian and queer: a distinct nexus

I stress the need to move beyond the conception of abjection promoted by the Whitney's Abject Art show because it cannot account for the role of abjection in the work of the artists I wish to discuss here – Rosalie Favell, Shawna Dempsey, Lorri Millan and Allyson Mitchell. While their work has some similarities with that included in the Abject Art exhibition, there are also crucial differences that pertain both to its distinctively feminist-lesbian-queer orientation and its Canadian historical and political context.

First and foremost, these artists produced their work in a socio-political context quite unlike that of the American culture war milieu that raged around the Whitney's Abject Art show. In that culture war, as Catherine Lord has noted, the right-wing forces took especial aim at the increasingly visible presence of gays and lesbians in art and culture. They deployed a 'family values' agenda that exploited the AIDS crisis to target homosexuals as immoral deviants and thus justify cutting off publicly funded arts grants to them and their supporting institutions (2013: 32, 37–38). Although Canada certainly has its share of conservatives, the 'family values' agenda has never taken hold, nor has its principal public arts funding agency, the Canada Council for the Arts, ever been forced to submit to such political interference. Canada has not been entirely immune to right-wing attacks against cultural displays deemed to be immoral or deviant, as indicated, for example, by the censoring of Toronto's gay magazine, *The Body Politic*, in 1982, but these never had the fury of those in the US. In short, the cultural conflict that provoked the Abject Art show simply had no parallel in Canada.

Second, as a corollary to the former, although the work of the artists I will be considering here addresses lesbian and/or queer experiences of the sort that would be denounced by the American 'family values' perspective, it bears no resemblance to the crisis-driven model of abjection that shaped the Abject Art show. Rather than aiming to 'talk dirty in the institution and degrade its atmosphere of purity and prudery', these artists' work instead seeks something of the *redemptive* potential of abjection proposed by Kristeva. This body of work explores that potential across a spectrum ranging from the probing of private and intimate experiences to the advocating of the normalness of queerness within the public sphere.

Third, although Favell, Dempsey, Millan and Mitchell make work about their experiences as lesbians, neither they nor I treat lesbianism as a fixed identity category, but rather as a problematising of such categories. For this reason, I also use the word queer to talk about their work. This term surfaced on the streets in the 1980s to indicate resistance to norms and it passed into academic usage in the 1990s as a critique of identity-based programmes (Lord, 2013: 30). This critique developed largely out of the 1980s intersection between feminism and postmodernism, whereby postmodern feminists criticised the essentialism of early feminism as naïve and exclusionary. These ideas were forcefully articulated in Judith Butler's landmark book, *Gender Trouble*, which argued that biological sex does not presuppose or dictate the outcome of gender identity, which is instead 'constructed' through the unconscious and repeated iteration of 'performative acts' that appear to produce gender as a natural effect of biological sex (Butler, 1990: 9–10, 25, 173–180).

Gender Trouble was a body blow to prevailing notions of gender identity politics, causing much confusion and backlash. Butler responded with *Bodies That Matter*, which aimed both to clarify her ideas about gender performativity and how its normative heterosexual imperatives could be resisted by performing gender differently. These imperatives, which enable certain sexed identifications and foreclose or disavow others, consign people who do not conform to the norms – that is, queers – to the realm of abjection: 'This exclusionary matrix by which subjects are formed thus requires the simultaneous production of a domain of abject beings, those who are not yet "subjects," but who form the constitutive outside to the domain of the subject' (Butler, 1993: 3). These abject beings are relegated to those zones of social life that are excluded as 'unlivable' or 'uninhabitable'. And yet they are necessary because they 'circumscribe the domain of the subject' by producing that subject's 'abjected outside, which is, after all, "inside" the subject as its own founding repudiation' (3).

Despite this bleak prognosis for abject beings, Butler also proposed that abjection might be a form of political agency able to resist and challenge the heterosexual matrix:

> I suggest that the contentious practices of 'queerness' might be understood not only as an example of citational politics, but as a specific reworking of abjection into political agency ... The public assertion of 'queerness' enacts performativity as citationality for the purposes of resignifying the abjection of homosexuality into defiance and legitimacy ... [T]his is the politicization of abjection in the effort to rewrite the history of the term, and to force it into a demanding resignification (21).

Butler's call for a reworking of abjection as a force for political agency and resignification resonates with Kristeva's opinion that 'abjection is eminently productive of culture. Its symptom is the rejection and reconstruction of languages' (Kristeva, 1982: 45). It must be noted, however, that although Butler never discusses Kristeva's essay on abjection, she harshly criticises the theory on which it rests, namely that the maternal semiotic realm can serve 'as a perpetual source of subversion within the Symbolic' through poetic language and art (Butler, 1990: 101–102). Her core argument is that Kristeva is an essentialist because she accepts the maternal body and our relationship to it as prior to culture and discourse. These disagreements notwithstanding, there is concurrence between Kristeva and Butler on three points that are central to the analysis I will develop here of the works of Favell, Dempsey, Millan and Mitchell: First, culture is ruled by the paternal laws of the Symbolic and 'is predicated upon a repudiation of women's bodies' (Butler, 1990: 118). Second, subversion of the paternal laws is possible and necessary in order to attain 'an open future of cultural possibilities' (119). Third, since 'abjection is eminently productive of culture', it can be reworked 'into political agency' (Kristeva, 1982: 45; Butler, 1993: 21). Let us turn now to a consideration of how these artists negotiate abjection's psychic and social complexities in order to resist abjection and attain its possible resignification.

Rosalie Favell: queer and Aboriginal

Such complexities abound in the work of Rosalie Favell. Favell is a Métis artist from Winnipeg, Manitoba, a mid-size city on the eastern edge of the vast western Canadian Prairie, and home to many Métis among its large population of urban Aboriginals. Métis is a specifically Canadian term, derived from the Old French word meaning mixed race and referring to the offspring of unions between indigenous people and European settlers. It has thus always denoted the contamination of miscegenation and exclusion that designate abject social status. The Métis only became legally recognised in 2003 as one of Canada's First Nations. Until then they existed in social and political limbo, lacking even the meagre rights extended to other Aboriginals under the Indian Act.

Favell emerged as a professional artist in 1985, long before this legal recognition of the Métis's First Nations' status. Her early work thus probed the uncertainty and invisibility of her Métis identity by culling and repurposing photographs of her maternal ancestors found in family albums. While the work is shaped by a desire to know more about a cultural heritage that has been systematically repressed and destroyed by policies of apartheid and assimilation, the images of her family members must also be seen as an intervention into the vast photographic archive of unnamed Aboriginal women produced as documents of colonising practices in Canada (Taunton, 2013). Favell's work, therefore, is no mere nostalgic or essentialist longing for a lost past, but rather is an assertion of political resistance to Canada's deplorable colonial history.

Favell put an even sharper point on the political edge of her work with *Living Evidence* (1994). This work consists of a series of thirty Polaroid photographs taken by Favell either of her lesbian partner, also an indigenous woman, or 'selfies' of the two of them together. In shifting the focus from historical representations of Aboriginal women to Favell's own experiences as a contemporary woman, *Living Evidence* was groundbreaking because it was one of the first acts of *self-representation* by an Aboriginal Canadian artist.

Living Evidence's audaciousness was further heightened by Favell's outing of herself as lesbian. This isn't explicit in the snapshots themselves, but is made clear by the superimposed handwritten texts from Favell's diary declaring her love for her partner, and her despair and pain over the ending of this relationship. The trauma of her loss is also manifest visually by masking out the lover's eyes with black tape, thus producing a violent erasure of her identity and a jarring contrast to the photographic documents of happier times.

When *Living Evidence* was first exhibited in 1994 at the Dunlop Art Gallery in Regina, Saskatchewan, curator Ingrid Jenkner remarked on the difference between the private context in which the photographs were made and their display in the gallery. She noted, for instance, that despite having been greatly enlarged (61 x 51 cm each), they are mounted with black photo corners of the sort used in family albums. But instead of the usual smiling family souvenirs one finds in such albums, Favell's photographs and diary excerpts reveal the unorthodox (and troubled) relationship between the women as a lesbian couple. Yet as much as Favell exposes, she also holds back by concealing the lover's identity with the black tape. As Jenkner wrote, 'with the shift from private memento to public exhibition, homophobia enters the picture, and Favell makes it visible, like a disfiguring scar. She must anticipate that her decisions will affect the social well-being of both subjects in her pictures' (Jenkner, 1994, n.p.).

By thus making homophobia visible in *Living Evidence*, Favell drew attention to the strictures that consign her lesbian relationship to what Butler called the 'abjected outside' of normative heterosexual subjectivity and sociality (1993: 3). Yet by simultaneously making her homosexuality visible in the gallery, Favell's work is also an instance of Butler's 'citational politics', whereby the abjection of queerness can be reworked into political agency (21). Furthermore, by bringing herself and her lover into view as queer *and* Aboriginal, Favell reveals how experiences of abjection can collide, intersect and overlap in multiple ways.

Since Favell's work was the outcome of an intentional creative act, it raises a crucial question about the applicability of Butler's theories of performativity to art practice that entails the performance of gender. As we recall, Butler defined performativity in *Gender Trouble* as the unconscious and repeated iteration of 'performative acts' that appear to produce gender as a natural effect of biological sex (1990: 173–180). Because she insists that there is no conscious subject behind these acts, no 'doer behind the deed', Butler distinguishes performativity from performance because the latter presupposes a preexisting subject (25). As she put it in *Bodies That Matter*, 'performance as bounded "act" is distinguished from performativity insofar as the latter … cannot be taken as the fabrication of the performer's "will" or "choice"' (1993: 234). This statement has caused consternation among some feminist scholars, especially in theatre and performance studies, who interpret it to exclude the possibility of cultural forms of performance as sites where gender norms can be performatively subverted and/or reimagined (Diamond, 1997: 46–47; Harris, 1999: 174–175). Although this is a misinterpretation of her theory, Butler must take some responsibility for it since she has, as Sara Salih has noted, created confusion by sometimes eliding and waffling on performance and performativity (Salih, 2002: 56).

Butler elaborated on the subject's relation to will, agency and performativity in her 1997 book, *Excitable Speech*. Written and focused exclusively on the American context at the height of its 1990s culture wars, *Excitable Speech* examines both how hate speech is an injurious *act* that threatens or solicits violence against minority groups, and how the judiciary's attempt to regulate it imposes its own form of censure and violence, which is often paradoxically directed against minority groups. Butler's central claim is that hate speech and its adjudication operate within a discursive field of power that exceeds individual subjects. We are mistaken in thinking that the one who utters hate speech is a 'sovereign subject' in control of its meaning and effect upon the one to whom it is addressed (Butler, 1997: 15). The subject who utters hate speech is certainly responsible for its utterance, but the hate speech does not originate with that subject. As Butler writes, 'the agency of the subject is not a property of the subject, an inherent will or freedom, but an effect of power' (139). The hate speech utterance is thus an instance of a performative citation of the conventions of hate already established within the social discourse, which are in turn re-cited in its adjudication by the courts (33–34).

On these grounds, Butler rejects the notion of the 'sovereign subject' because what the subject is, says and does always derives 'from elsewhere'. She maintains that this critique of sovereignty is not the demolition of agency, but rather that 'agency begins where sovereignty wanes' (15–16). Since all subjects are formed within discursive operations that they neither wholly determine nor are determined by, Butler reconceives of agency in terms of the 'post-sovereign subject'. The agency of this subject does not simply invoke the freedom to 'speak "against"' the discourses of power, but rather speaks 'performatively' within them so as to confound, disrupt and redirect their original signification (139–140).

Butler's call in *Excitable Speech* for resistance to the power effects of hate speech by performing signification differently echoes the views about gender performativity she previously advanced in *Gender Trouble* and *Bodies That Matter*. As the post-sovereign subject may speak back to hate speech, so too might this subject perform gender differently by means of such cultural forms as drag and gender parody (1990: 137). Although Salih is right that Butler sometimes elided the distinctions between performativity and performance, the notion of the post-sovereign subject articulated in *Excitable Speech* enables us to understand better how she accords agency not only to performative acts that 'resignify' or 'queer' heterosexist gender norms, but also to the 'theatricality' of performance as a way to contest 'the terms of sexual legitimacy' (Butler, 1993: 232). Indeed Butler advocates the 'politicization *of* theatricality', examples of which include cross-dressing, drag balls, AIDS benefits, 'the convergence of theatrical work with theatrical activism' and 'performing excessive lesbian sexuality and iconography that effectively counters the desexualization of the lesbian' (233). Butler regrettably never addresses the relationship between performativity and performance in art, but the parallels seem clear between her theory of queer performativity as a 'reworking of abjection into political agency' and artworks like Favell's *Living Evidence* (21). The connection is even more evident with explicitly performative artwork, such as that by Shawna Dempsey and Lorri Millan.

Shawna Dempsey and Lorri Millan: lesbians go public!

Shawna Dempsey and Lorri Millan have collaborated since 1989. Like Favell, they live in Winnipeg, which they call 'The Lesbian Capital of the Universe' (Bell and Williamson, 1998–99: 57). In contrast to Favell's painful revelations of her lesbian identity, however, Dempsey and Millan flaunt theirs with unruly gusto. Their performances, videos, films and public art projects combine preposterous skits, costumes and monologues with a wry humour that simultaneously disarms hostility to homosexuality and affirms lesbian identification. As Paulina Palmer has argued, the lesbian has been consigned to the abject domain not only because she embodies Kristeva's definition of that which disturbs identity, system and order, but also because she threatens the regulation of heterosexual femininity within the Symbolic Order by usurping the male prerogative to take a woman as a lover (Palmer, 2007: 49–50). Dempsey and Millan upend this abject relegation and turn it into cause for celebration.

The humorous charge of their performative work is hard to convey in words, akin to explaining why a joke is funny (Goldie and Schellekens, 2010: 101). It often consists of pseudo-vaudevillian skits such as *We're Talking Vulva* (1990), featuring Dempsey in an anatomically explicit full-body costume doing a song-and-dance tribute to this female nether region:

> The vulva's something that men have feared. It looks innocent enough, a bit like a beard. On the outside it's fuzzy, it's fluffy, it's hairy – open it up, it gets pretty scary. Yippers! It gives us pleasure, it makes us feel good, we can touch ourselves better than lots of men could. Many don't want to, we remind them of mother, that we all come from here, this hole and none other. (Dempsey and Millan, 1990)

As I have written elsewhere, nothing is sacrosanct in Dempsey and Millan's comedic inversions of what is officially designated as 'normal' or 'deviant'

(Wark, 2006: 202). In *Growing Up* (1996), for instance, Dempsey dons her mother's 1960s-era 'industrial strength' foundation garments while recounting how the women who modelled such lingerie in mail order catalogues triggered her adolescent lesbian desire for those 'unimaginable body parts so powerful they needed architecture to keep them in place' (Dempsey and Millan, 1999). This performative and parodic outing of 'illicit' lesbian desire both elicits and gratifies lesbian identification and creates what Cheryl Kader has called a 'community of spectators' (1990: 46; cited in Auslander, 1997: 112). As Dempsey and Millan put it, their use of time-based media to connect with this community is no coincidence: 'It is our hope that by existing simultaneously in space with our audience, there is the potential for dialogue, for movement, for the creation of individual and hence political change' (Dempsey and Millan, 1996: 69).

But while it is paramount for Dempsey and Millan to speak *to* the lesbian community within its traditionally intimate and underground enclaves, they also speak *for* this community at wider public levels, thus countering its social invisibility (Lord, 2013: 31). Some works, like *What Does a Lesbian Look Like?* (1994), a short video that exposes every myth about lesbians (and reveals they're all true!), have the semblance of public service announcements. Others, however, such as *A Day in the Life of a Bull Dyke* (1995), which follows the ups and downs of a bulldagger in a mockumentary style pillorying the crude sensationalism of journalism, are full-on confrontations with the social opprobrium leveled at butch dykes who are perceived as monstrous aberrations of femininity (Bell and Williamson, 1998–99: 66–67).

Such performances would have been excoriated and/or denied public funding in the context of the American culture wars, but not so in Canada. *What Does a Lesbian Look Like?* was co-produced with Much Music (Canada's version of MTV) and aired on rotation in 1994–95, *We're Talking Vulva* was created for the National Film Board of Canada's Feminist Minutes series and *A Day in the Life* was the recipient of multiple awards. This situation stands in sharp contrast to the contemporaneous American one where, as Catherine Lord has argued, the attacks on homosexuals had the effect of making '"the public" a club with a limited membership' (Lord, 2013: 38). But because queer or otherwise controversial artists were not cut off from public interaction or funding in Canada, this explains why the crisis-driven and deadly serious model of the Whitney's Abject Art exhibition didn't resonate in the same way. It also explains why Canadian artists were able to use humour as a strategy for resisting and sublimating abjection.

This strategy is brilliantly revealed in Dempsey and Millan's best-known work, *Lesbian National Parks & Services*. This began in 1997 as an artist-in-residency project funded from multi-level public grants at Banff National Park and is ongoing in various permutations. Located in the Rocky Mountains of

Western Canada, Banff is surrounded by spectacular landscape and is a tourism mecca. Dempsey and Millan's gambit was 'to insert a lesbian presence into the landscape' (Dempsey and Millan, 'Lesbian National Parks and Services', artists' website). Wearing classic ranger uniforms, they blended seamlessly into the milieu except for the crests on their caps denoting them as Lesbian Park Rangers. Some of their activities documented in the accompanying video include patrolling the parklands, researching the flora and fauna, giving directions to lost tourists and holding a recruitment drive. At this event, the friendly Rangers are seated at an outdoor table with a big banner reading 'Lesbian National Parks & Services Wants You!' At one point, several groups of children come bounding up for free lemonade, oblivious to the hilarity of their lesbian 'recruitment'.

This absurd scene perfectly captures Dempsey and Millan's strategies for resisting abjection. Their playful humour enables them to bring a visible homosexual presence into spaces that are ostensibly public, but are in practice designated as heterosexual family spaces. These public interactions aim 'to help people learn about the fascinating and fragile lesbian ecosystem' so as to help make 'the world a happier, safer place for lesbians' (Dempsey and Millan, 2001: 4). Ultimately, they renounce abjection by demonstrating that lesbians are not social deviants.

Allyson Mitchell: Deep Lez

Allyson Mitchell is a Toronto-based artist who shares these goals and use of humour to resignify 'the abjection of homosexuality' (Butler, 1993: 21). Her approach is to meld feminism and popular culture to investigate both from a lesbian perspective. Mitchell is part of the 1990s generation of women who split into third-wave and postfeminist camps, with the former critiquing but extending feminist politics into a new era and the latter abandoning feminism as passé and irrelevant (McRobbie, 2007; Pinterics, 2001). Holding a PhD in Women and Gender Studies from York University and now teaching in that programme, Mitchell renounces postfeminist depoliticisation and seeks instead to build bridges over feminism's generational waves.

Mitchell's practice is diverse, encompassing sculpture, performance, installation, film and handcrafted multiples. Representations or reflections on the body and sexuality feature prominently throughout her repertoire, and are treated with a joyous, irreverent and downright bawdy humour. Works like *The Fluff Stands Alone* (2003), for example, lampoon *Playboy* magazine's 1970s heyday by recasting its 'dirty joke' cartoons in wall hangings made of old bedspreads and garish fun fur. Revelling in their campy splendour, these racially diverse and corpulently sexy mammas thwart the crudely chauvinistic one-liners of the original cartoons. Mitchell further lacerated *Playboy's* ideal notion of femininity with *Big Trubs* (2004; Figure 1), a hybrid of the Playboy Bunny, the Venus of Willendorf and Roman war victory statues. Standing ten feet high and measuring over seven feet in girth, *Big Trubs* is a fun-fur goddess come to earth to celebrate 'excess and pleasure' and 'fight fat phobia' (Mitchell, 'Big Trubs,' artist's website).

While fat activism is important in Mitchell's work, her broader concern is to redress the ongoing degradation of women, especially lesbian women, who can't or won't meet the persistently oppressive ideals of commodified femininity. Mitchell's use of materials and techniques associated with femininity is a key strategy in this respect, as seen with *The Fluff Stands Alone* (bedspreads and thrift shop fabrics) and *Big Trubs* (fun fur and a glue gun). Such materials and techniques are wildly popular with amateur crafters (who are overwhelmingly women), and thus disdained within the world of professional craft. Or so it was until the term 'sloppy craft' began to gain traction among professional craftspeople after it surfaced in 2007 at the international NeoCraft conference, held at the Nova Scotia College of Art and Design in Halifax, Canada, and in Glenn Adamson's subsequent *Crafts* magazine article, 'When Craft Gets Sloppy'. Adamson described it as the 'calculated sloppiness' embraced by 'post-disciplinary' craft education, and aligned it with early feminist reclamations of domestic craft, the fascination with low or 'abject' art forms in the 1990s and the growing popularity of the DIY movement today (Adamson, 2008: 36, 41).

Mitchell's use of materials and techniques appears to share some of the sloppy craft characteristics Adamson outlined, but these resemblances are superficial. While sloppy crafters abandon the hallmarks of expertise that have traditionally distinguished professional from amateur craft by embracing lowly and unaesthetic (and thus abject) forms and techniques, they do so within a discourse that is purely aesthetic because the goal is merely to assert such work as an ironically knowing variation of professional craft. Mitchell's work, by contrast, counters such aesthetic conceits by foregrounding its critical and political goals. It not only encompasses her fat activism, but also revitalises feminist politics for a new generation by bridging the gap that opened up between feminists and lesbians in the early 1980s over charges of heterosexism by the latter against straight feminists (Lord, 2013: 34–35).

Mitchell's Deep Lez project is central to these critical and political goals. Deep Lez is a broad enterprise bringing together artists, academics and activists seeking to make 'a strategic return to the herstories of radical and lesbian feminisms' (Mitchell, 'Deep Lez', artist's website). In her book, *Time Binds: Queer Temporalities, Queer Histories,* Elizabeth Freeman refers to this kind of return as 'temporal drag', a term implying 'retrogression, delay, and the pull of the past on the present'. Freeman is critical of how the popularisation

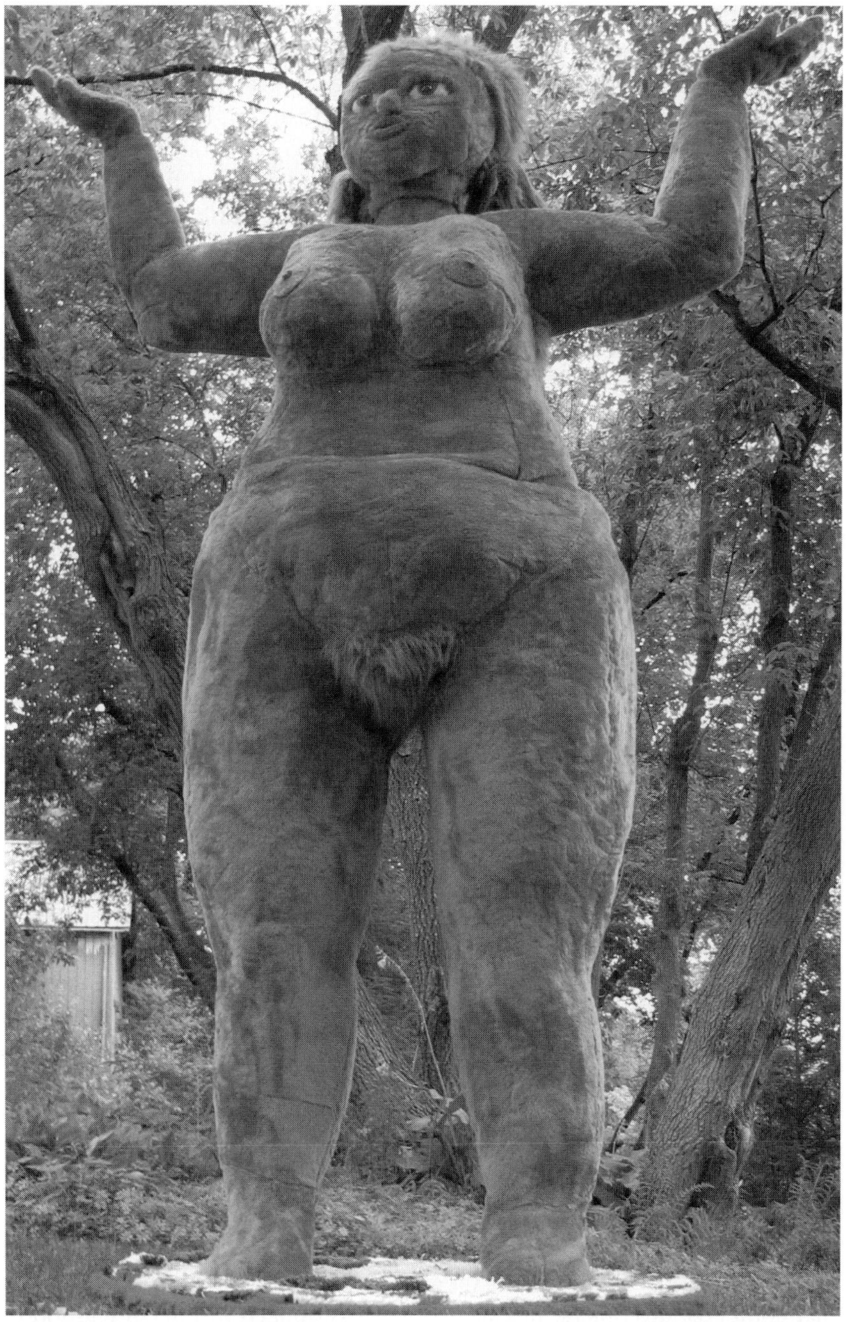

1 Allyson Mitchell, *Big Trubs*, 2004. Synthetic fur, wood, styrofoam, wire and found acrylic textiles, 320.04 × 228.6 cm. Courtesy of the artist. Photograph: Thomas Mitchell.

of *queer* theory and politics emanating from Butler's texts has resulted in casting the lesbian who remains committed to feminism as 'the big drag', an anachronistic relic from the days of essentialised bodies and single-issue identity politics. Her concern is that Butler's prioritising of the future-oriented transformative potential of her theory might also have had the deleterious effect of devaluing anything that generates continuity with the past, including feminism and 'political history itself' (Freeman, 2010: 62–63). Freeman thus proposes the notion of 'temporal drag' as a way to return to the history of feminism and its hoped-for collective politics. She regards Mitchell's Deep Lez project, with its 'temporal binding of past and present lesbian cultures', as constitutive of this political goal (65, 85).

As Freeman recounts from a 2004 interview with Mitchell, Deep Lez originated with a trip to a thrift shop during which Mitchell and a gay male friend found an old macramé wall-hanging in the shape of an owl and decorated with wooden beads and dried nuts. 'Oh my god', said Mitchell's friend, 'that's so deep lez' (cited in Freeman, 85). This discarded handicraft from a bygone era struck Mitchell as a metaphor or omen of the past lurking in the present. It unleashed the creation not only of *Big Trubs*, but also the giant *Lady Sasquatches* (2006–10), lesbian versions of an ancient Aboriginal mythological figure who valorises 'cellulite, dirty fingernails, tattoos, big butts, fangs, collectivity and collaboration' (Mitchell, 'Ladies Sasquatch', artist's website). As Freeman observes, the *Lady Sasquatches* 'reanimate all kinds of cultural dinosaurs: the legend of Sasquatch, the sexually excessive racial primitive, the hairy radical feminist, the Wiccan icon, the home arts' (89).

The home arts aspect of Deep Lez, as embodied in the macramé talisman, is directly invoked in Mitchell's *Fat Craft* project, an ongoing series of needlepoint, crochet and pompom samplers embroidered with slogans such as 'Fat Forever', 'Sedentary Lifestyle', 'No Cookie for Fattie', etc. Despite any superficial resemblances to sloppy craft, Mitchell's *Fat Craft* is not an ironic parody of amateur craft, but rather stems from a genuine admiration for and emulation of 'wimmin's' craft history. It thus invokes early feminist projects like Judy Chicago's famous *Dinner Party*, but without needing to elevate craft from amateur to professional status, as Chicago did. *Fat Craft* echoes those early feminist politics – daringly so, considering *The Dinner Party's* contentious reception among both feminists and mainstream art critics (Jones, 1996) – and recycles them through 'temporal drag' into a contemporary lesbian assertion of interracial and non-heteronormative body politics. Mitchell's fat activism reminds us, says Freeman, 'that the stigmatic histories of *female* fatness and lesbianism interlock on a single body': the 'fat dyke'. As she further contends, this linkage has been largely overlooked within contemporary queer theory, which 'has generally treated lesbian stigma as if it were coded primarily by transgender embodiment', thus ignoring the actual social coding of lesbian bodies, unlike those of gay men, 'as a problem of sizable bodily proportions' (Freeman, 2010: 91).

I concur with Freeman's assessment of how Mitchell's work reanimates supposedly obsolete and unfashionable feminisms in order both to redress 'white feminism's failed concatenation with antiracist organizing' and to bring the lesbian back into the feminist history of 'the shared culture making we call "movements"' (91, 93). Yet I also want to consider this assessment in relation to how Mitchell's art and activism both instantiates and sublimates the psychic and social reverberations of abjection. It does so by invoking the disdained and degraded in multiple ways, ranging from the insertion of fat female and explicitly eroticised lesbian bodies into the spheres of art and public spaces; the alliance with discarded feminist histories and collectivist politics; the refusal of postfemininism's commercialised and depoliticised individualism; to the retrieval of the dowdy, dusty, outmoded (or never in mode) and abandoned forms of women's domestic craft.

These bodies, identities, political movements and crafts have been deemed undesirable, deviant, passé and crudely amateurish. As such, they inhabit the border zones of abjection, the murky spaces between what is or is not culturally recognisable and socially sanctioned. Yet Mitchell renounces their designation as abject and instead calls upon us to avow their value as agencies of creative and enfranchised political change. Hers is a reclamation project, analogous to the recuperation of the word 'queer' from its pejorative meaning to one of positive identification and defiance against social conformity and prohibitions. It is, therefore, the 'reworking of abjection into political agency' that Butler calls for, a 'resignifying [of] the abjection of homosexuality into defiance and legitimacy' (1993: 21).

Conclusion

My analysis of this work by Flavell, Dempsey, Millan, and Mitchell has argued that it presents a way of thinking about abjection in art differently from the connotations advanced in the Whitney's Abject Art exhibition. The acrimonious and earnest rhetoric of that show served its political purpose at that historical moment in the American culture wars. But as the first articulation of the notion of abjection in relation to contemporary art, the Whitney show's designation of it as the taboo, the transgressive and the grotesque has inordinately come to dominate our understanding of its role and meaning in contemporary art.

By my sights, the value of the different approach to abjection in the work of Flavell, Dempsey, Millan and Mitchell lies in its strategies for creating progressive social change, not merely confrontational antagonism. They certainly acknowledge the consignment of homosexuals – most specifically lesbians

– to the realm of abjection, but they also supersede its negative connotations by invoking Kristeva's and Butler's conceptions of its potential for psychic and social transformation. This is manifested in Flavell's courageousness in coming out as a lesbian and also being one of the first Canadian Aboriginal artists to assert the right to self-representation. Dempsey and Millan, meanwhile, have used humour to bring lesbian discourse and practice out from its 'hidden' community of bars and clubs into the public realm in an effort to dislodge homophobia. For her part, Mitchell has salvaged discarded feminist histories, denigrated female bodies and amateur crafts in a campaign for constructive community activism and political movement-making. While this ability to engage constructively rather than combatively with queer abjection in the cultural sphere may be facilitated by the relatively tolerant and liberal Canadian milieu, the struggle against homophobia, sexism, the legacy of colonial oppression and other forms of social abjection is far from over. This is no time for complacency, either in Canada or elsewhere.

References

Adamson, G. 2008. When Craft Gets Sloppy. *Crafts* 211 (March/April), pp. 36–41.

Auslander, P. 1997. *From Acting to Performance: Essays in Modernism and Postmodernism*. New York and London: Routledge.

Bataille, G. 1970. L'Abjection et les forms misérables. In *Écrits posthumes, 1922–1940*. Vol. 2 of *Œuvres complètes*. Paris: Gallimard, pp. 217–222.

Beardsworth, S. 2004. *Julia Kristeva: Psychoanalysis and Modernity*. Albany, NY: State University of New York.

Bell, L. and Williamson, J. 1998–99. Public Warning! Sexing the Public Spheres: A Conversation with Shawna Dempsey and Lorri Millan. *Tessera* 25 (Winter–Spring), pp. 57–77.

Ben-Levi, J., Houser, C., Jones, L. C. and Taylor, S. 1993. Introduction. In *Abject Art: Repulsion and Desire in American Art*. New York: Whitney Museum of American Art, pp. 7–15.

Butler, J. 1993. *Bodies That Matter: On the Discursive Limits of Sex*. New York and London: Routledge.

Butler, J. 1997. *Excitable Speech: A Politics of the Performative*. New York and London: Routledge.

Butler, J. 1990. *Gender Trouble: Feminism and the Subversion of Identity*. London and New York: Routledge.

Dempsey, S. and Millan, L. Finger in the Dyke Productions. [Artists' website]. [Accessed 15 October 2014]. Available at: http://fingerinthedyke.ca.

Dempsey, S. and Millan, L. 1990. We're Talking Vulva. [Online Video Resource]. [Accessed 15 October 2014] Available at: http://fingerinthedyke.ca/were_talking_vulva_mov.html.

Dempsey, S. and Millan, L. 1996. Shawna Dempsey and Lorri Millan. In May, L. W.

ed. *The Feminist Reconstruction of Space*. St. Norbert, Man.: St. Norbert Arts and Cultural Centre, pp. 66–83.

Dempsey, S. and Millan, L. 1999. *A Live Decade: 1989–1999*. [Video compilation]. Winnipeg: Finger-in-the-Dyke Productions.

Dempsey, S. and Millan, L. 2001. *Handbook of the Junior Lesbian Ranger*. Winnipeg: Lesbian National Parks and Services.

Diamond, E. 1997. *Unmaking Mimesis: Essays on Feminism and Theatre*. New York and London: Routledge.

Dubin, S. C. 1992. *Arresting Images: Impolitic Art and Uncivil Actions*. New York and London: Routledge.

Foster, H. 1996. Obscene, Abject, Traumatic. *October* 78 (Autumn), pp. 106–24.

Freeman, E. 2010. *Time Binds: Queer Temporalities, Queer Histories*. Durham, NC: Duke University Press.

Goldie, P. and Schellekens, E. 2010. *Who's Afraid of Conceptual Art?* New York and London: Routledge.

Harris, G. 1999. *Staging Femininities: Performance and Performativity*. Manchester: Manchester University Press.

Houser, C., Jones, L.C., and Taylor, S. eds. 1993. *Abject Art: Repulsion and Desire in American Art*. New York: Whitney Museum of American Art.

Jenkner, I. 1994. *Rosalie Favell: Living Evidence*. Regina, Sask.: Dunlop Art Gallery.

Jones, A. ed. 1996. *Sexual Politics: Judy Chicago's* Dinner Party *in Feminist History*. Los Angeles: Armand Hammer Museum of Art and Cultural Center in association with University of California Press, Berkeley.

Kader, C. 1990. Kate Clinton: The Production and Reception of Feminist Humor. In Raymond, D. ed. *Sexual Politics and Popular Culture*. Bowling Green, OH: Popular Press, pp. 42–55.

Krauss, R. 1985. *The Originality of the Avant-Garde and Other Modernist Myths*. Cambridge, MA: MIT Press.

Krauss, R. and Livingston, J. eds. 1985. *L'Amour fou: Photography and Surrealism*. Washington: Corcoran Gallery and New York: Abbeville Press.

Kristeva, J. 1982 [1980]. *Powers of Horror: An Essay on Abjection*. Trans. L. S. Roudiez. New York: Columbia University Press.

Lord, C. 2013. Inside the Body Politic: 1980 – Present. In Lord, C. and Meyer, R. eds. *Queer Art and Culture*. London: Phaidon, pp. 29–45.

McRobbie, A. 2007. Postfeminism and Popular Culture. In Tasker, Y. and Negra, D. eds. *Interrogating Postfeminism: Gender and the Politics of Popular Culture*. Durham, NC: Duke University Press, pp. 1–39.

Mitchell, A. Allyson Mitchell. [Artists' website]. [Accessed 15 October 2014]. Available at: www.allysonmitchell.com.

Oliver, K. ed. 1997. Introduction: Kristeva's Revolutions; Individual and National Identity. In *The Portable Kristeva*. New York: Columbia University Press, pp. xi–xxix; pp. 225–227.

Palmer, P. 2007. Queer Transformations: Renegotiating the Abject in Contemporary Anglo-American Lesbian Fiction. In Mueller, M. and Kutzbach, K. eds. *The Abject of Desire: The Aestheticization of the Unaesthetic in Contemporary Literature and Culture*. Amsterdam and New York: Rodopi, pp. 49–67.

Pentony, S. 1996. How Kristeva's Theory of Abjection Works in Relation to the Fairy Tale and Post Colonial Novel: Angela Carter's *The Bloody Chamber*, and Keri Hulme's *The Bone People*. *Deep South*. [Accessed 15 October 2014] 2(3) [no pagination]. Available at: www.otago.ac.nz/deepsouth/vol2no3/pentony.html.

Pinterics, N. 2001. Riding the Feminist Waves: In with the Third? *Canadian Woman Studies* 21(4) [pp. 15–21]. Available at: http://cws.journals.yorku.ca/index.php/cws/article/view/6899/6083.

Salih, S. 2002. *Judith Butler*. New York and London: Routledge.

Spector, J. 1997. *Surrealist Art and Writing, 1919–39: The Gold of Time*. Cambridge: Cambridge University Press.

Taunton, C. 2013. Personal Conversation with the Author about Self-Representation in the Work of Rosalie Favell, Halifax, 25 September 2013.

Wark, J. 2006. *Radical Gestures: Feminism and Performance Art in North America*. Montréal: McGill-Queen's University Press.

Zurek, A. 2011. Abjection: The Theory and the Moment. BA, University of Pennsylvania. [Accessed 15 October 2014] Available at: www.arthistory.upenn.edu/vlst/2011thesis/zurek/AZthesis.pdf.

3

Manet's abject Surrealism

Nicholas Chare

The rest is silence

Surrealism as it is formulated by André Breton in his manifestoes is frequently used by Georges Bataille as a stalking horse. He challenges the movement, rails against its tenets, the better to formulate and further his own beliefs. Surrealism provides a means through which to articulate his philosophy. This includes a desire to strip away 'some of the veils or screens, some of the hypocrisies, with which we try to conceal and make palatable bald existence' (Ades, 1985: 13). He finds Surrealism lacking because in practice the movement manifests 'an evasive and poetic idealism' which is at odds with its theoretical commitment to dialectical materialism (12). It does not intervene sufficiently in concrete reality, the reality that matters to Bataille.

For Bataille, an artist who does confront existence with a frankness he approves of is Édouard Manet. Manet engages in disquieting representational practices as a means by which to forcefully catch what matters to him in paint, the world's baser aspects. He does not aspire to moralise in his paintings, rather his strident picturing focuses upon attacking the figure, the figurative. Manet's work, as will become clearer, is pitiless. It embodies a brutishness engendered primarily by way of a particular kind of handling, a cruel toying with the figure.[1] Manet's brushwork leaves clear traces, marks, of his aggression. Smears, stains of oily pigment are easy to see in his work. The oil is allowed to assert its haecceity. Paint, however, never entirely overawes subject matter. Manet's paintings, as I will demonstrate through comparisons with Jackson Pollock, another artist linked to Surrealism, play with borders and boundaries but draw the line at abandoning them. The playfulness in Manet is bound up with an unsettling of taken for granted assumptions about sexuality. There is a sadistic edge to Manet's play that disquiets in ways that are not unambiguously negative.

Bataille published his book on Manet in 1955, the same year as his volume on Lascaux (1955a; 1955b). Both forms of art, modernist and prehistoric, are united in exhibiting a playfulness lacking in the art produced in the ages that separate them. Theirs is a solemn playfulness, enabling rediscovery of the sensible, the world of the senses, the felt (rather than cognised) world. As Youssef Ishaghpour explains in his exegesis of Bataille's texts on Lascaux and Manet: language is instrumental to becoming human but its invention causes a rupture with the sensible. To be human, however, requires finding the sensible again through the form of play that is art, art not 'as a base return, nor as a reconciliation, but as the radiant presence of an omnipotent, impenetrable world' (Ishaghpour, 1989: 21).[2] For Bataille, prehistoric humans initially discovered their playfulness through hunting, an activity in which they faced death. This encounter gave birth to sacrifice, feasting and art. Art becomes a kind of sacrifice in itself (Bataille, 1955b: 39). The art of Lascaux and Manet, which are both linked to sacrifice in different ways, are united in their intimacy with death (Ishaghpour, 1989: 22). In Manet, death shows itself through a disfiguring, a silencing of illusion.

Such a silencing can be perceived in *Un bar aux Folies-Bergère* (1882, Courtauld Institute of Art, London).[3] The painting of the barmaid at work in the café-concert cum brothel includes a depiction of a mirror in the background which holds the potential to function as a metaphor for painting. It is a mirror that provides an ambiguous reflection of the world that fronts it. The ambiguity is registered through spatial discontinuities between the bar and its mirror-image and also through the roughness of Manet's facture.[4] The backwall and the light fittings are made up of choppy strokes of paint.

The reflection of the face of the customer entreating the barmaid is blotched and smeared rather than sharp. His bulbous nose, comprised of red and white slurs of pigment, explodes. The man's puce hand, perhaps gloved, cannot be called modelled. It is composed of botched, irregular contours which suggest a decrepit, diseased appendage. The spectator who confronts the painting fails to fill the shoes of this customer not simply because, as both Timothy Clark and Michel Foucault have argued, they cannot find a foothold in front of the off kilter reflection but also due to the ghastliness of this reflected bourgeois gentilhomme (Clark, 1984: 251; Foucault, 2004: 45–47). The man in the mirror is deformed, made monstrous. The vagueness of his features goes beyond that of an inviting everyman instead tipping over into abject dissemblance. The borders of this body are too insecure and unstable to encourage any act of identification. Manet, instead, has painted only the repulsive, ghoulish pretence of a human being.[5]

The disturbing figure is rendered such through the loose brushwork the painter has chosen to employ. The features, as the barmaid's face demonstrates, could easily have been honed, secured. There is instead studied indistinctness. The nose and moustache of the fogged face register forcefully as marks of paint (Clark, 1984: 249). They exhibit a substantial, oily obviousness. It is this assertion of pigment as pigment, rather than as pigment as stand-in for things outside the canvas, which lends an underlying aggression to the painting. The opacity of parts of *Un bar*, the stubborn refusal of some strokes of paint to serve illusion and, by extension, the escapist fantasies it facilitates, constitutes Manet's bellicosity. He produces a spectacle that lays into the bourgeois spectator. The matter of paint offends in such a way that it repels contemplation, is found repulsive.[6]

In his 1971 Tunis lecture on Manet, Foucault appears particularly attuned to the painter's formalist brutality. For Foucault, this rough treatment manifests through Manet's approach to depth, lighting and the anticipated positioning of the spectator. He identifies a striking absence of recession in many of Manet's works. In *The Execution of Emperor Maximillian* (1868–69, Mannheim, Städtische Kunsthalle), for example, there is a 'violent emphatic and insistent closure of space' produced by the inclusion of the high wall immediately behind the emperor, his two generals and the firing squad (Foucault, 2004: 27). In *The Balcony* (1868, Paris, Musée d'Orsay), Foucault finds Manet adopting a particularly mean and violent approach to depth (41). Manet's approach to light is also vicious. In *Olympia* (1863, Paris, Musée d'Orsay), for instance, the light: 'is not at all a soft or discreet lateral light, it is a very violent light which strikes [Olympia] head on' (40). A similar frontal assault is detected in *Un bar* (44). As already discussed, *Un bar* also displays a concerted effort to make the spectator uneasy by way of the incongruous reflection in the mirror. Confronted by the reflection, a spectator feels neither here nor there. They are left undecided about where to position themselves (45–47).

In *Un bar*, the compositional aggression leaves the spectator unable to surveil the café-concert with confidence. This painting, like many by the painter, also includes open brushwork. The looseness leads the oil to assert itself, as is evident, for example, in the scalloped paintwork of the central chandelier, the splotched countenance of the customer, the powder blue smutting to the left of the barmaid. The evidentiary roughness of the paint surface suppresses the possibility to engage in an in-depth exploration of any fictional beyond to the picture plane. To Manet's contemporaries it formed a cruel betrayal of bourgeois expectation: works of art were usually designed to encourage escapist reveries with paint put into service to produce otherworldly illusions.

This abrasiveness in Manet extends to the subject matter. The bits of rough in his paintings, such as the working-class women in *Un bar* and *Olympia*, can be read as a studied sullying of academic convention at the level of subject matter. Pierre Bourdieu, for instance, meticulously outlines the calculated transgression of *Le Déjeuner sur l'herbe* (1862–63, Paris, Musée d'Orsay), in which the rural purity of a pastoral scene is muddied by the presence of the corrupt figure of the *grisette*, the metropolitan working girl (Bourdieu, 2013: 58–59). This *fille de joie* stains the country scene with urban matters. She is painted rudely. Her ear, pulled flat against the picture plane, appears swollen, misshapen. The thumb beneath her chin is stodgy, thick and indelicate. Manet's touch here is assiduously coarse, carefully crude. He indelicately fashions a studio scene in a public place (126). *Le Déjeuner*, and works like it, can therefore be seen to carry a taint in terms of both their subject matter and handling. The interrelation of tainted forms and contents redoubles the abject qualities of Manet's art. In some ways, the painter's studied combining of impurities renders him similar to Julia Kristeva's preferred exemplar of an abject author, Louis-Ferdinand Céline, whose foulness manifests through both style and subject.[7] Manet offers a painterly equivalent to Céline's forceful stylistic ingenuity.

Bataille's Manet

Bataille's vision of Surrealism provides a means by which to make sense of the partiality for brutality in Manet's pictures. Bataille saw Manet as a painter who gestured towards base materialism through the way he gave things in his work an unmediated presence (Bataille, 1955a). For Bataille, Manet's canvases were not effusive, voluble or magniloquent which was to their credit. Loquence entered picture-making only as a defect, placing what mattered at a remove. The effective expression of ideas and ideals was therefore to be understood as a fault. Bataille identified such a flaw, such a florid belief in something, in Gustave Courbet. He suggested that: 'the density and fine vital energy of Courbet's art are undeniable, but his realism has not yet been stripped of eloquence, his art pleads nobly, eloquently, for the truth of things and this nobility is the one relic of a dead past to which Courbet clung' (1955a, 72). A work such as *The Stone Breakers* exemplified this identification of Courbet's work with the reliquary. There is a clear moral story to the painting, an obvious narrative content related to ending up: youth is transformed by backbreaking labour into shrivelled agedness. The gravitas of this message, the weight of the moral story, the work's principled patina, gets in the way of the gravity of the paint. It is this conflict of interests between paint and precept that causes the work to disappoint.

What Bataille found in Manet that was lacking in his Realist contemporary was an eschewal of pictorial rhetoric. Manet refused to place his paint in the service of persuasion such that there is no outmoded trace of imploration, no special pleading in his works. Bataille contrasts Manet with Courbet, suggesting that the former provides the spectator with what he describes as a 'laconic elegance' and 'economy of statement' that is not present in the latter (1955a:

73). Manet is a maestro of brevity and concision. He is not one for brashly telling stories. His is a quiet art. His paintings approach a silence that echoes the kind described by Maurice Blanchot in relation to poetry. In poetry, the world 'falls silent' and 'language speaks as the essential', with words 'not obliged to serve to designate anything or give voice to anyone' (Blanchot, 1982: 41). The difference between Blanchot's quietude and Bataille's dwells in the aggressive dimension inherent in the latter's conception of the process of silencing. Bataille sees silence as achieved through violence. The negation of eloquence, Manet's tight-lipped quality, his 'doing-away' with the subject is accomplished via rough means.

Manet's desire not to let a moral message muffle the paint is well illustrated in his still lifes such as *Lemon* (1880, Musée d'Orsay, Paris). The singular lemon does not opine on ephemerality. It is not corrupted by reflections on transience. It is, rather, about the substantial. The rapid smears of yellow oil, the citrus accents upon a diaphanous platter (through which the weave of the canvas shows through) comprise pared painting that pushes materiality to the fore. The object is indifferent to the world, refusing to comment upon it. As with Manet's other still lifes, however, there is 'an element of vague raillery, perhaps stemming from the momentary aggressiveness of his style' (Bataille, 1955: 98).

This focus on Manet's playfulness, his badinage, his cruel jokes, in its praise for surface-effects seemingly resonates with Clement Greenberg's understanding of the artist. Greenberg declares in 'Modernist Painting' that Manet's were the first modernist pictures by virtue of the frankness with which they declared the flat surfaces on which they were painted (Greenberg, 1993: 86). Both Bataille and Greenberg recognised the violence in Manet's treatment of his subject matter. In 'Towards a Newer Laocoon', Greenberg described the painter as 'attacking subject matter on its own terrain by including it in his pictures and exterminating it then and there' (Greenberg, 1986: 29). Rosalind Krauss reads Bataille's *Manet* in a one-dimensional way as simply a paean to surface (Krauss, 1986). She remarks on the book's lightness, its appeals to recognise technical mastery and its disappointing lack of an appetite for destruction (147). There is, however, greater attention to modern art's destructive aspect in Bataille's figuring than Krauss gives credit for. Griselda Pollock has examined how both Bataille and Greenberg take up the theme of 'the idea of artistic advance through destruction' (Pollock, 1996: 229). Bataille's attention to surface in *Manet* should not be confused with the formalist understanding of the term. For Bataille, Pollock explains, the 'surface of the painting can be imagined as a kind of lid, which conceals its deadly freight, like a tombstone in a graveyard covers up a corpse' (230).

In *Manet*, Bataille analogises still life painting with sacrifice. Manet's still lifes are read by Bataille, alongside his other works, as meaningless luminous immolations (1955a: 95–96). Although his works connote the sacrificial, Bataille is at pains to point out that Manet does not kill the subject (96). The subject is not destroyed or disregarded. It is retained but exceeded [*dépassé*] (96). As the discussion of the still lifes demonstrates, Manet does, however, aggress, distress it. He joys in the injurious potential of the paintbrush, the way a particularly free and fast twist of the wrist can transform what was cautious modelling into maiming. Greenberg is therefore mistaken in perceiving Manet as a slayer of the subject. He torments but does not do away with. The horror of Manet is embodied in his willingness to hold fast to the figure at the same time as delighting in damaging it. He models to dissect. Figures are fashioned, to a point, and then attacked. The painter engages in sly or sustained assaults. This places him in opposition to the purely abstract painter who is absorbed in annihilation. There is no cruel toying with the subject, for example, in Pollock's 1948–50 drip paintings. There is no teasing. Pollock destroys.

The tendency towards mutilation that Krauss links to Bataille within Surrealism and that she identifies in the photography associated with *Documents* and *Minotaure* is already visibly at work in Manet's paintings (1986: 154). It is a strand of modernism founded in sadistic impulses.[8] Greenberg recognised this, writing in an overview of twentieth-century American art that works in the United States that were influenced by Surrealism produce 'a fantastic [*baroque*], over-elaborate effect that is reminiscent of Poe and exudes a scatological and sadistic sensibility' (Greenberg, 1946: 350). American painters such as Pollock (who Greenberg mentions alongside William Baziotes and Arshile Gorky in the essay) exhibit this Surrealist taint yet only rarely and in ways moderated by formal concerns related to the treatment of depth in their work. This sensibility is one Manet shares. In his work an unnerving, callous tendency to disfigure can be detected. It is a tendency Greenberg cannot countenance as it would require him to acknowledge Manet's macabre, gothic qualities. The painter forms part of a cruel strand of modernist art-making that Krauss only identifies later in Bataille and Surrealism.

Revolution in pictorial language

Manet's relation with Surrealism is bound up with sadism and abjection and can best be understood through turning to the movement's interest in the Comte de Lautréamont (Isidore Ducasse). David Lomas has explored the abject and sadistic elements present in the poet's writings, tracking their influence upon Surrealism and, particularly, the interest they held for Salvador Dalí (Lomas, 2000: 167–171).[9] It was, notably, to Lautréamont that Breton turned in the Second Manifesto where he wrote: 'I can see nothing which would invalidate a single word of Lautréamont's with respect to events of interest only to the mind' (Breton, 1972: 156). Lautréamont's work combines an innovative approach to writing with debased themes. He is one of the authors chosen by Kristeva as her primary examples (the other being Stéphane Mallarmé) of revolutionaries in poetic language (Kristeva, 1984). For Kristeva, these two writers made explicit, through their use of language, the 'dialectical condition of the subject' (81).

Kristeva's linkage of subjectivity to the exercise or practice of language, building on the ideas of Émile Benveniste, implies that identity is not born of a singular act and then retained but rather emerges and is maintained through repeated designation. The subject exists as a continual process, I *is* in process. Kristeva supplements Benveniste's recognition of the linguistic status of the subject by expanding his conception of language to one formed of two distinct, if inseparable, aspects: the semiotic and the symbolic (it is because there are two aspects that Kristeva writes of the subject's dialectical condition). The semiotic, drive-invested aspect of language emerges in early infancy. It is manifested as rhythms, tones and gestures. In the visual field it also registers as the throb of the chromatic (Kristeva, 1981). The symbolic is the place within the Symbolic order (as conceived of by Jacques Lacan) where the subject can assume a position and is made up of facets of language such as grammar and syntax which serve to ensure communicative clarity.

Kristeva perceives the symbolic aspect of language, the syntactic structures that act as guarantor for specific significations, to be in the ascendant under normal circumstances. The semiotic, however, is ever present. It is what provides language with its brio. The rhythms, modulations that characterise the drive-endowed underside to communication that is the semiotic, are what hooks and guides the listener or reader. The semiotic enlivens. A language devoid of this aspect would be inert, flat, like a monotone voice or a monochrome painting. In the visual field, the smooth Classicism of Jean-Léon Gérôme, described by Linda Nochlin as exhibiting 'a chilly and remote pseudo-scientific naturalism', can be understood as comparably semiotically deprived if not bereft (Nochlin, 1988: 12).

Language pared of the semiotic is language purged, as far as possible, of that aspect which possesses the potential to instigate change. In this context, the semiotic is potentially a force of revolutionary transformation. It is possible to produce forms of language that exploit the semiotic to contest the signifying structures, challenge the preferred meanings set in place by the symbolic. Kristeva believes some avant-garde writers have produced such language. For her, Lautréamont and Mallarmé instituted a poetic revolution. Their writings, which altered and extended the language available to the subject, held the promise of expanding subjective possibilities. The subject, for Kristeva, is, as mentioned earlier, always in process/on trial (Kristeva, 1984: 22). This lack of finish means that it is viable to envisage change in identity. After disrupting the symbolic, it is possible to then return to it on improved terms.

Kristeva does not believe the symbolic should be abandoned altogether. This would lead to psychosis. The semiotic and the symbolic are both indispensable, the two 'irreconcilable elements' are 'separate but inseparable from the *process* in which they assume asymmetrical functions' (82).[10] Only the ascendancy of one or the other can be contested. This means Kristeva has no time for practices which seek to void one or other aspect from language. She specifically rejects 'surrealist automatism' which she perceives as fantasying the negation of the thetic, the gap between word and thing (82).[11] Surrealist practices of the kind advocated by Breton are therefore aligned, by Kristeva, with psychosis.

It is easy to read some of Breton's descriptions of the Surrealist project in this vein, as expressions of the dream of a return to the before of language and subjectivity. He writes, for example, that the idea of the movement is to recover the individual's psychic force

> by a means which is nothing other than the dizzying descent into ourselves, the systematic illumination of hidden places and the progressive darkening of other places, the perpetual excursion into the midst of forbidden territory, and that there is no real danger of its activities coming to an end so long as man still manages to distinguish an animal from a flame or a stone. (Breton, 1972: 137)

In this formulation, Surrealism will only achieve its aim once linguistic difference is abolished. It is only when humanity collapses back into its surroundings, reunites with the animal, the flame, the stone, or, at least, recognises an underlying unity between them, that the project will be accomplished. That the linguistic is key to achieving this state of affairs is made clear later when Breton affirms that Surrealism is 'almost exclusively concerned with the question of language at first' (151).

The author from the past that Breton identifies as most embodying the tenets of Surrealism is the same writer Kristeva singles out as both revealing and preserving the subject's dialectical condition. Lautréamont should not appeal to Breton as despite his stylistic innovativeness he retains a conscious grip on language. His subject matter is depraved, but knowingly so, which means that he practises what Breton calls 'reflected writing' (158). Lautréamont's callousness may therefore be what permits him entry into Breton's Surrealist pantheon. Kristeva writes of the poetic practice that produced *Les Chants de Maldoror* that it was violent and dangerous (Kristeva, 1984: 84). The recognition of aggression as key to social change was obvious to Breton who wrote of Surrealism as striving to provoke '*an attack of conscience*' (Breton, 1972: 123).[12] He argued the movement expected 'nothing save from violence' (125). Xavière Gauthier suggests that 'the strength of

Surrealism is to have proposed that 'art, like revolution, is violent, a kidnapping and a harrowing metamorphosis of the body' (Gauthier, 1971: 67). In this context, Lautréamont's formal brutishness is alluring.

Through de-privileging the symbolic and permitting the semiotic to come to the fore, Lautréamont opens the subject to their heterogeneity, a revelation which is unbearable to them (Kristeva, 1984: 213). Lautréamont inflicts psychic pain on his readers when he shows them that the language they occupy and depend upon for their identity is multiple and malleable, excessive and ungraspable. Manet can be seen to practise something comparable in relation to painting. Through their perfecting of aggression the practices of Lautréamont and Manet intersect. Lautréamont attacks traditional literary forms and Manet confronts time-honoured pictorial language. Manet's aggression towards the figure and figuration, towards a particular mode of Salon-satisfying art-making, is present in many of his works but intensifies towards the end of his career. This can be seen, for instance, in the pastel *Woman Fastening her Garter* (1878, Ordrupgaardsamlingen, Copenhagen) and in the oil painting *The Reader* (1878–79, Art Institute of Chicago, Chicago).

In the balance

In *Woman Fastening her Garter*, with its conventional theme of a woman dressing, Manet's treatment of the figure is noteworthy. The artist carefully shapes fulsome breasts, yet much of the rest of the composition is sketchy. The two focal points in the pastel picture are the breasts (these spill forwards, outwards from the picture plane) and the hands securing the garter. The hands are not meticulously modelled, and contrast markedly with the bosom. The left hand, which 'queases' outwards, becomes an abject exercise in looseness, formlessness. The right hand's stub fingers, potentially the focal point of the woman's gaze, index bodily impairment. A cruel and disturbing vision is cultivated.

In *The Reader*, a woman is shown reading in the outdoors. Anthea Callen celebrates the work for its economy of gesture, particularly in the woman's face, in which 'not a single brushstroke is superfluous' (Callen, 2000: 74). For her visage, pale yellow combines with several rapid strokes of black, ochre, pink and scarlet such that the various colours coalesce into a skilfully composed portrayal of the face when seen from optimum viewing distance. Callen is, however, careful to call the face brilliantly, rather than beautifully, rendered because the skims of brownish-red pigment that delineate the base of the nose, in their colouring, bring a tinge of the excremental to the woman's features. Despite its disturbing faecal trace, the face involves paint applied in such a way that its presence evaporates in the service of illusion when seen from distance. From afar, it is composed of a reassuringly reticent facture.

In other areas of the work, by contrast, paint is made obvious. The woman holds her reading matter up with two gloved hands. The left is well-defined but the right looks less like a hand and more like a gloved stump – signalled by thick smears of tan pigment – upon which her literature appears to be propped. This stub seems to emerge from the woman's lower torso, an amorphous black mass. The illustrated journal or menu it supports is like an abstract canvas, an exercise in the affirmation of flatness achieved through thick blocks and squiggles of oil.

Manet's cruelty traverses both form and content. It is form, however, which is of most interest. He fosters deformation through a handling that is wilful yet, at times, conscientiously laissez-faire. Manet gives freedom, a certain looseness, to the bristles. This leads to the production of thick patches of pigment, obvious coils of paint, and to an assault on the edges that form is tied to, a loss of contour, a troubling of boundaries. Manet's Surrealist sensibility manifests itself most markedly in patches of impasto. These broad touches, touches that stand out in his works as paint, serve like a syntactic disruption. They disturb the pictorial language of naturalism, revolt against it, offending bourgeois expectations of academic painting because they bring the spectator back to the fact of the paint rather than indulging their desire for fantasy. The rough patches form injuries to traditional picture making methods, gaping wounds.

The pain in looking at Manet is achieved through the way he, like Lautréamont, can be seen to reveal the dialectical condition of the subject. This is accomplished by way of bringing the fact of paint or pastel to bear upon the form of the figure, upon figuration, scoring it, excoriating it. The artist exposes the semiotic underside to pictorial language through his contrast of rough and smooth patches of paintwork and through shifts between precise and slack modelling. The painting appear to have two planes, one of illusionism and one that signals a marked refusal of it, one that is syntactic, forged from self-effacing brushstrokes, and one that is rhythmic, a celebration of oily textures.

Manet engages in a balancing act, exposing the dialectic of language, of subjectivity, without abolishing either of the two terms that form it. This necessitates doing violence to language but in a controlled way. His technique is one that dirties traditional Salon painting, introducing impurities, rough oily stuff, within figuration. In this he is, perhaps, the flipside to late Jackson Pollock. In Pollock's final canvases, the purity of his abstraction, his virtuous, virtuoso surface effects, gives way to defiling form. *Search* (1955, New York, Collection Samuel and Ronnie Heyman) appears to be in pursuit of form, an effort to reform the figurative, to retreat from overall abstraction. It is as if the wheel has come full circle. *Search* is haunted by *Untitled [Overall Composition]* (c.1934–38, Houston, Museum of Fine Arts), returning to blocky tubers of red, black, yellow and white paint. His last paintings appear on the cusp of figuring. They are Manet turned inside out.

Pollock's major drip paintings, by contrast, oppose Manet's studied compositions which never writhe in the psychotic semiotic excess that accompanies forms of pure abstraction. Franz Kline's black-and-whites provide another example of such an excess. Kline's and Pollock's sadism assumes such an intensity that the symbolic is obliterated. Kristeva writes of Pollock's drip paintings of 1948–50 that they embody a space that is not symbolic, that does not possess the pictorial syntax of geometry and the forms that derive from it, but is instead semiotic, a space of noise and dancing, of rhythms and cadences (Kristeva, 2013: 61). Manet holds back from total liquidation of the symbolic. He appears to engage, by contrast, in an elaborate role play in which limits are established, agreed upon. The symbolic is aggressed but within boundaries.

Kline's and Pollock's appropriation of violence would meet with Breton's approval. It leads to the production of psychotic episodes such as Pollock's *No.1* (1948, Museum of Modern Art, New York). This work is not, however, Surrealist. It lacks the necessary imagery. Even automatic writing, with the unexpected, unpremeditated word-associations it produces, retains a kind of imagism. There are slivers of sense, meanings or stories, to be extracted from it. The reader of automatic writing may lose their bearings. If they labour, however, they can find a way back into significance. Kristeva's characterisation of automatism as irreconcilable with the aims of poetic revolution therefore appears to do the Surrealist project a disservice. Surrealism seeks to harness the power of the unconscious yet in a balanced way that avoids the trap of psychosis. It is for this reason that Breton is able to write, as quoted earlier, that the movement will initiate a 'systematic illumination' of the hidden places of the mind. There is always structure to the endeavour, exercised restraint.

This system is one that incorporates abject elements. The abject, as Kristeva outlines, is neither an object or, drawing on the work of Pierre Fédida, an *objeu*, a plaything through which to figure (out) separation (Kristeva, 1982: 1). It is more archaic, forming a kind of hinge between the semiotic and the symbolic in Kristevan terms. As a disruptive force abjection, as Kristeva conceives of it, shares characteristics with Bataille's base materialism. Bataille appreciated psychoanalysis for its engagement with base matter, with heterogeneity, with 'resistant phenomena that could not be dominated by the homogenous organisations of knowledge and society' (Noys, 2000: 33). The abject as it manifests in Manet's works provides a means by which to scrape against the heterogeneous. Kristeva's conception of abjection, which draws on Bataille for inspiration, provides a means by which to describe the presence of this painfully playful process of opening towards heterogeneity.

Sex uncertain

Clark condescendingly dismisses Bataille's reading of Manet as 'having little to do with the simpler narratives of modernist art history' (Clark, 1984: 139). In a practice such as Manet's, Bataille sees not the articulation of class uncertainties à la Clark, too reasoned an endeavour, but the expending of paint's potential as signifier, its tipping over into a substantial non-sense. In Manet's works paint is, at times, liberated and put to 'ends that cannot be subordinated to anything one can account for' (Bataille, 1985: 128). Clark strives to explain this paint through class. He rationalises it as a signal of uncertainty, an allegory of contingency. This reading is one readily available at the level of content. It is, however, less easy to reconcile with those formless marks which contribute to that content's production yet stubbornly exceed its compass.

Clark revels in the rich textures that mark Manet's surfaces, their variegated grain, yet he cannot admit their stirring meaninglessness. He must grasp them within a given vocabulary, make their meaning clear through his conformist syntax, their significance secure by way of his lapidary sentences.[13] Clark cannot acknowledge the semiotic content which gives them their revolutionary tenor as his conception of language is too limited. It affords no place for the semiotic, the drive-invested underside to language which brings it as close as is possible to base matter. The drives are, as Freud explains, internal pressures that operate at the borderline between the psyche and the soma (Freud, 1991a: 82–83). Language which liberates the drives makes matter proximate. It is therefore of a kind likely to appeal to Bataille. Kristeva, in fact, positions Bataille, along with Joyce, as a legatee of Lautréamont (1984: 82). He practices revolution through his own poetic language. This particular kind of language, however, because of its driven intensity, is painful to encounter. Freud explains in 'Beyond the Pleasure Principle' that excessive drive excitation, unbound or liberated energy, causes unpleasure (Freud, 1991b: 276).

Any artistic or literary practice that releases the drives from their symbolic prison, reducing sexual inhibitions, causes a degree of pain. It is this painful aspect to the modernist project that Krauss cannot countenance. She recognises how integral sadism is to Surrealism yet she is unwilling to embrace its unsettling effects. Her disavowal of the corporeal punishment at the heart of sadistic modernism leads Krauss to proclaim that the body is her 'phobic object' (Foster et al., 1994: 12). She refuses to confront the aesthetics of humiliation that runs through Manet and Bataille in its disfiguring literality. It is this refusal to recognise Surrealism's underbelly, its assailing of the body, which explains Krauss's desire to soften Bataille's Manet. She is therefore able to circumvent the painter's love of inflicting pain and elide the significance of his bodily aggressions for our understanding of the brutal psychic underpinning of his, and later artists, liberatory pictorial practices.

Manet's destructive assaults on language prompt a crisis in identity yet also liberate the subject from the constraints imposed by the assumption of a particular linguistic identity. This leads the patches of paint, of pain, in Manet to potentially simultaneously trouble and entice the spectator, holding promise by way of their hurting. The unfixing of language can also enable an unfixing of sexual identity. Jacqueline Rose has examined how language and sexuality go hand in hand (Rose, 1986: 228). Violent revolutionary practices such as those embodied in the pictorial language of Manet are capable of casting sexual certainties adrift. They are therefore postmodernist in Rose's understanding of the term. For Rose, postmodernism describes a bearing witness to the return of the referent but as a problem rather than a given. She writes of postmodern art: 'piles of cultural artefacts bring back something we recognise but in a form which refuses any logic of the same' (230). There is, in Rose's description, a sense of detachment, of an imperfect mirroring of the world, which is equally applicable to Manet's paintings.

The discomfort Manet cultivates calls subjectivity into question in a way comparable to the drawing of a couple engaging in coitus (attributed to Leonardo da Vinci). It is Freud's discussion of the drawing which prompts Rose to discern a connection between challenging a painting's powers of illusion and address and contesting seemingly self-evident beliefs about sexual difference (226).

Clark reads a drawing that was a precursor to Pollock's *Male and Female* (1942, Philadelphia, Philadelphia Museum of Art), in which copulation 'is portrayed as an upright and basically ludicrous sacrifice', as reminiscent of 'Leonardo's famous (inaccurate) notation of the same subject in his notebooks' (Clark, 1999, 358–359). Manet's use of paint, his production of occasional coarse zones of pigment coupled with smoother surfaces, his many-hued versification, operates to disrupt his work's semblances of reality and prompts a troubling of sexual surety in the vein of the Leonardo drawing. Through the rhythms of his handling the semiotic underside of language is revealed, carrying the spectator back to a time before their desires had been *fixed*. They are invited to encounter a moment in psychic life prior to their drives being directed, aimed at specific bodies or body-parts, at a specific (kind of) sex. The pictorial language provides a painful point of access for the subject to the state of polymorphous perversity that characterises early infancy.

The deconstruction of sexual difference present within the works is in keeping with the predilection for blurring which Krauss recognises to be at the heart of Surrealism. This blurring is not solely of visual matter but also of the concepts the visual usually concretises, the binaries it commonly articulates and perpetuates (Krauss, 1999: 1–50). The rhythms in the canvases open the spectator to an unrestricted aggression that existed in the early history of the subject. This violent impulse dominates the phase of sexual life which Freud called 'pregenital organization' (1991a: 111). At this stage of its existence, the child extracts pleasure from the infliction of pain without that pain being bound to a specifically sexed object. The ability of Surrealist works such as Manet's to tap into this sexless sexuality lends them a significant queer potential. They are able to undo socially accepted and expected models of sexual desire, such as that of penis-vagina, and open up an alternative libidinal geography.

The sexual world revealed by way of Surrealist practices such as Manet's is not utopic. The subject matter that accompanies their revolutionary pictorial poetics occasionally discloses the sadistic impulses that characterise periods of early infancy. The painter often depicts damaged bodies, individuals with the appearance of having been pitilessly attacked. Nochlin has described Manet as a painter of amputations. She was referring to the bodies which are 'cut in two' in *The Ball at the Opera* (1873, National Gallery of Art, Washington) (Nochlin, 1988, 14). It is, for her, violence directed solely at women. The male client in *Un bar*, however, with his ravaged face and fingers also appears injured. In Manet the effects of finding pleasure in the infliction of pain are graphically illustrated in depictions of both men and women.

Freud recognised that cruelty comes easily to young children because they do not posses a capacity for pity. In its polymorphous perversity, the infant is prone to mercilessness as it is prey to the drive to mastery (Freud, 1991a: 111). The revolutionary potential of Surrealism lies not in its exposure of this propensity to violence which existed as part of the multifarious sexual disposition which preceded the emergence of hetero-normative desire. It resides instead in the way disturbances in the field of vision of the kind perfected by Manet wipe clean the slate of difference, allowing for alternative attachments to then be developed. It permits the subject to return to language, to the source of sexual identity, on revised terms. The unchecked sadism of childhood is not to be embraced. The revelation of as yet undirected drives which accompanies it is, however, to be celebrated. In this light, the Surrealist investigations into sex can be read on one level as a debate over how to exploit the libidinal promise which was tied in with their literary and visual practices.

Aberrant fluids

The underlying sadistic dynamic to Surrealism, the aggressive disruptions of poetic and pictorial language it fostered, the aberrant recitations of familiar forms, led the idea of a fixed, pre-given sexual identity to be challenged. The discussions about sex conducted by various members of the movement between 1928 and 1932, in their argumentativeness, appear to mirror this contestation of hetero-normativity which was occurring within Surrealist artistic practice. The discussions share the concern with questioning identity which Lomas suggests 'resounds across the surrealist project' (Lomas, 2000: 1). This is not to say that reactionary beliefs were abandoned. The hetero-normative outlook signalled by Breton in 1924 in the first manifesto continued in his own contributions to the discussions. In the first paragraph of the manifesto he had stated that man, the 'inveterate dreamer', knows 'what women he has had' (Breton, 1972: 3). Later, in the discussions, Breton demonstrated a fierce intolerance of homosexuality (Lomas, 2000: 167). He had an abject fear of the topic, as is evident from his repeated threat to abandon debates on sex when the validity of same-sex relations was being examined. (Pierre, 1994: 27–28). The idea, however, obviously fascinated him as he was to return to it again in a subsequent discussion (54).

Breton's concerns about homosexuality can be understood, within the broader context of the investigations as a whole, to be related to the 'correct' destination for sperm. Many of the discussions involve ascertaining where members prefer to orgasm, in which situations, upon which parts of the body. For Breton, another man's body is not a suitable destination for seminal fluid. The Surrealist fascination with spunk is, perhaps, most obvious in Benjamin Péret's question: 'Would anyone allow himself to be seen by a woman with suspicious stains on his trousers?' (Breton, 1972: 42). Sperm haunts the periphery of many other lines of inquiry. The centrality of seminal fluid to the discussions can be explained by its psychic value as an abject material. Spunk traverses boundaries: moving from inside to outside the body and potentially crossing into another's body. Its viscidity also lends it an ambiguous relationship to the masculine.[14] Fluids have traditionally been associated with femininity and, by extension, the maternal. The stains Péret describes could therefore be said to expose the feminine in the masculine, to permit the woman within the man to be seen. Sperm forms a condensed disturbance in the field of vision.

It was for this reason that Surrealist artists embraced ejaculation and its result as a suitable subject. Salvador Dalí's *The Lugubrious Game* (1929, Private Collection), for example, depicts a statue in the background which is being stimulated. Dalí's drawing *Sperm* (1939, Private Collection), made using flesh-toned paper, displays the likely outcome of such an activity. Marcel Duchamp's *Faulty Landscape* (1946, Museum of Modern Art, Toyama) is made, in part, of seminal fluid. In this work the substance is literally employed as an artistic medium. The Surrealists left their suspicious stains not on their trousers but in their works. Oleaginous substances such as oil paint, however, often stand in for, figure, the aberrant fluid. The thick strokes of paint dispersed across Manet's paintings, for example, can be read as similarly spermatic. Through oily, unbounded ejaculations he cultivated interference, noisiness, in his paintings, enabling them to disturb the field of vision of the viewing subject, blurring 'the field of representation where our normal forms of self-recognition take place' (Rose, 1986: 228). In this context, Manet's lack of finish, a characteristic Michael Fried reads as inexplicable, becomes playful cruelty of an ejaculatory kind, a combining of pain and pleasure designed to unsettle and disquiet (Fried, 1996: 17). Some of Manet's paintings make the nature of Surrealism's creative expenditures particularly obvious. They openly embrace its aggressive impulses. The painter shares Bataille's desire to exploit sadism, to enact cruelty upon language, in order to make the matter of the body proximate.[15]

Manet's seminal works differ from, for instance, Pollock's spunky drip paintings because they continually contrast hard edges with patches of softening. Andrew Perchuk has read Pollock's works as exhibiting familiar, if critically elided, narratives of sexual reverie involving 'loss of individualization' (Perchuk, 1982: 33). As Louise Vigneault observes, his earthy approach, using a canvas laid upon the ground, lends Pollock's practice a telluric dimension (Vigneault, 2011: 298). It becomes a means by which to reaffirm beliefs in seed-soil.[16] In *Number 1, 1950 (Lavender Mist)* (1950, Washington, NGA), Pollock marks his territory through a balletic depositing of paint across the canvas, asserting that the canvas comprises his manly domain through a vigorous arabesque.[17] Kristeva suggests that in his intoxicating arabesques Pollock communicates a 'joy [*jouissance*] which is the dissemination of the other into me, of me into the other. A chromatic disappearance' (Kristeva, 2013: 68). Manet, however, maintains painterly control throughout, retaining a sense of boundary.

Pollock and Manet both toss paint yet the first does so with abandon, the last with restraint. The abject dimension to Manet stems from this restraint. He troubles boundaries but does not abandon them. There is no similar borderline quality to Pollock in his pomp. He tips into non-sense, enacting a violent loss of self. Pollock's inclusion of handprints in *Number 1A, 1948* and *Number 1, 1950*, a practice reminiscent of some Palaeolithic art, can be read as manifesting an abandoned appeal to the sanctity of symbolism, of signs. Writing of prehistoric handprints, Georges Didi-Huberman suggests they are produced by 'a gesture of clinging, holding, or gripping, which becomes a system of figuration, even of "precise" resemblances' (1997: 31). The act of making a handprint is touchingly figurative.

In both *Number 1a, 1948* and *Number 1, 1950* the prints were made early in the process of production. They are most in evidence in the top right corners of the canvases: figurations engulfed by a seeming maelstrom. *Number 1a, 1948*, where the prints are more numerous and visible, is particularly powerful. It is not Manet who, as Greenberg claimed, attacks 'subject matter on its own terrain by including it in his pictures and exterminating it then and there'. It is Pollock. In these works, his practice becomes an art of sacrifice. A premeditated commotion of dribbles and spatters gradually submerges Pollock's touching gestures, overwhelms them. The attack on the figure in each work is not frenzied. It comprises a gradual overwhelming through overlaying. This is ritualistic destruction through the cumulative pressure of abstract marks.

In the drip paintings, Pollock ultimately does away with the figurative. Vestiges of the figure are still visible in *Number 1a, 1948*, trace evidence. Clark describes the handprints as black and blood-brown in colour (Clark, 1999: 310). The impressions are reminiscent of the positive handprints in red ochre that were made by Palaeolithic hunters in caves such as Altamira and Fuente del Salín. The ruddy brown imprints also suggest blood residue at a crime scene: the last gestures of someone fatally wounded. Clark reads the colour of these prints coupled with their positioning as 'pure pathos' (311). This renders Pollock's handiwork in *Number 1a, 1948* as wholly anguished, despairing. In a Bataillean sense it can, however, also be read as triumphant. The death of figuration indexed by the painting with its tell-tale hands frees paint from its servitude. Paint as stuff finds itself again through compacting and obscuring the resemblances that Pollock chose to form *Number 1a, 1948*'s ground. In this sense, the work exhibits a jubilant baseness.

A painting such as *Number 1a, 1948* does not maintain that tension between abstraction and figuration upon which the enabling sadism of Surrealism is founded. It marks a rupture with Pollock's previous Surrealist-inspired works. Clark rightly reads paintings such as *Male and Female* as making good the main aspirations of Surrealism (356). The most powerful works from the early 1940s are, for Clark, 'as near as one gets in painting to a fulfilment of Surrealist hopes' (344). I would argue that Manet, in his unsettling brazenness, can also stake a strong claim to achieve this kind of realisation of the Surrealist project. Manet is able to reconcile Bataille's base desires with Breton's belief in lyricism. He does this in a way that simultaneously reveals the lie to Surrealism's hetero-normative façade. Underlying the movement there is a practical commitment to undoing sexual certainties. Manet calls into question such certainties through loosening the ties that bind paint to the figure yet studiously avoiding their undoing.

Notes

1 Pierre Bourdieu suggests that Manet's brutality can also be perceived through his use of a pictorial rhetoric that was steadfastly anti-Academy, one that flattens the figures in his paintings. This rhetoric is embodied in a particular approach to the treatment of light in the works. (Bourdieu, 2013: 4, 60).

2 Translation my own. All translations are mine unless otherwise stated.
3 This painting will henceforth be referred to simply as *Un bar*.
4 Adrian Rifkin suggests that the idiosyncratic composition can be explained by Manet's wish to combine the *salle de spectacle*, which had no bar, with the bar from the café's *jardin*. The iconography enables the depiction of two distinct spaces simultaneously (Rifkin, 1985: 493).
5 This practice of deforming can productively be linked to George Bataille's idea of the 'informe'. For an insightful exploration of this concept see Rosalind Krauss's essay '"Informe" without Conclusion' (1996).
6 Manet, by extension, also became rebarbative, a painter to be figuratively vomited upon by many in the Third Republic, hated and jeered by them (Bourdieu, 2013: 122).
7 For a discussion of Kristeva's analysis of Céline's abjection see my chapter Execrable Speech in *Auschwitz and Afterimages* (Chare, 2011: 11–44).
8 Krauss provides a formulation for the nature of this sadism (1996: 99–100).
9 Neil Cox also examines the influence of sadism upon Surrealism in his essay 'Critique of Pure Desire, or when the Surrealists were Right' (2001).
10 Emphasis in the original.
11 For Kristeva's definition of the thetic see p. 43.
12 Emphases present in the original.
13 For an analysis of Clark's style of writing see the introduction to my book *After Francis Bacon* (2012: 1–20).
14 See Murat Aydemir, *Images of Bliss* (2007: xviii).
15 Michel Leiris recognised the potential sadism holds as a means of producing a direct rapport with the body (Lomas, 2000: 140).
16 For a discussion of the seed-soil trope as a mainstay of patriarchal ideology see A. L. Jones's *The Gender Vendors* (2014).
17 In an inspiring reading of Lee Krasner's art practice, Griselda Pollock draws on Bataille's ideas about sadism to suggest that, contra-Jackson Pollock, Krasner gestures towards a space within performative abstraction for female creativity and 'the feminine' as it is theorised by psychoanalytic feminism (Pollock, 1996). Pollock's nuanced analyses of sexual difference in relation to modernism have held considerable importance for this study.

References

Ades, D. 1985. Web of Images. In Ades, D. and Forge, A. eds. *Francis Bacon*. London: Tate Gallery, pp. 8–23.

Aydemir, M. 2007. *Images of Bliss: Ejaculation, Masculinity, Meaning*. Minneapolis: University of Minnesota Press.

Bataille, G. 1955a. *Manet*. Trans. A. Wainhouse and J. Emmons. Geneva: Skira.

Bataille, G. 1955b. *Lascaux ou la naissance d'art*. Geneva: Skira.

Bataille, G. 1985. The Notion of Expenditure. In Stoekl, A. ed. *Visions of Excess: Selected Writings, 1927–1939*. Minneapolis: University of Minnesota Press, pp. 116–129.

Blanchot, M. 1982. *The Space of Literature*. Trans. A. Smock. Lincoln: University of Nebraska Press.

Bourdieu, P. 2013. *Manet: Une revolution symbolique*. Paris: Éditions Raisons d'agir/ Éditions de Seuil.

Breton, A. 1972. *Manifestoes of Surrealism*. Trans. R. Seaver and H. R. Lane. Ann Arbor: University of Michigan Press.

Callen, A. 2000. *The Art of Impressionism: Painting Technique and the Making of Modernity*. New Haven: Yale University Press.

Chare, N. 2011. *Auschwitz and Afterimages: Abjection, Witnessing and Representation*. London: IB Tauris.

Chare, N. 2012. *After Francis Bacon: Synaesthesia and Sex in Paint*. Farnham: Ashgate.

Clark, T. J. 1984. *The Painting of Modern Life*. Princeton: Princeton University Press.

Clark, T. J. 1999. *Farewell to an Idea*. New Haven: Yale University Press.

Cox, N. 2001. Critique of Pure Desire, or when the Surrealists were Right. In Mundy, J. ed. *Surrealism: Desire Unbound*. London: Tate, pp. 244–273.

Didi-Huberman, G. 1997. *L'empreinte*. Paris: Centre Georges Pompidou.

Foster, H. et al. 1994. The Politics of the Signifier II: A Conversation on the 'Informe' and the Abject. *October* 67, pp. 3–21.

Foucault, M. 2004. *Le peinture de Manet*. Paris: Éditions de Seuil.

Freud, S. 1991a. Three Essays on Sexuality. In Richards, A. ed. *The Penguin Freud Library Volume 7: On Sexuality*. London: Penguin, pp. 33–169.

Freud, S. 1991b. Beyond the Pleasure Principle. In Dickson, A. ed. *The Penguin Freud Library Volume 11: On Metapsychology*. London: Penguin, pp. 275–338.

Fried, M. 1996. *Manet's Modernism or, The Face of Painting in the 1860s*. Chicago: University of Chicago Press.

Gauthier, X. 1971. *Surréalisme et sexualité*. Paris: Gallimard.

Greenberg, C. 1946. L'art Américain au XXe siècle. *Le Temps Modernes* 2(10–15), pp. 340–352.

Greenberg, C. 1986. Towards a Newer Laocoon. In O'Brian, J. ed. *The Collected Essays and Criticism Volume 1*. Chicago: University of Chicago Press, pp. 23–37.

Greenberg, C. 1993. Modernist Painting. In O'Brian, J. ed. *The Collected Essays and Criticism Volume 4*. Chicago: University of Chicago Press, pp. 85–93.

Ishaghpour, Y. 1989. *Aux origines de l'art moderne: Le Manet de Bataille*. Giromagny: Éditions de la différence.

Jones, A. L. 2014. *The Gender Vendors: Sex and Lies from Abraham to Freud*. Lanham: Lexington.

Krauss, R. 1986. Antivision. *October* 36, pp. 147–154.

Krauss, R. 1996. 'Informe' without Conclusion. *October* 78, pp. 89–105.

Krauss, R. 1999. *Bachelors*. Cambridge, MA: MIT Press.

Kristeva, J. 1981. Giotto's Joy. In *Desire in Language: A Semiotic Approach to Literature and Art*. Trans. T. Gora, A. Jardine and L. S. Roudiez. Oxford: Blackwell, pp. 210–236.

Kristeva, J. 1982 [1980]. *Powers of Horror: An Essay on Abjection*. Trans. L. S. Roudiez. New York: Columbia University Press.

Kristeva, J. 1984. *Revolution in Poetic Language*. Trans. L. S. Roudiez. New York: Columbia University Press.

Kristeva, J. 2013. *Pulsions du temps*. Paris: Fayard.

Lomas, D. 2000. *The Haunted Self*. New Haven: Yale University Press.

Nochlin, L. 1988. *Women, Art, and Power*. New York: Harper & Row.

Noys, B. 2000. *Georges Bataille: A Critical Introduction*. London: Pluto.

Perchuk, A. 1982. Pollock and Postwar Masculinity. In Frascina, F. and Harrison, C. eds. *Modern Art and Modernism: A Critical Anthology*. New York: Harper & Row, pp. 31–42.

Pierre, J. ed. 1994. *Investigating Sex: Surrealist Discussions, 1928–1932*. Trans. M. Imrie. London: Verso.

Pollock, G. 1996. Killing Men and Dying Women: A Woman's Touch in the Cold Zone of American Painting in the 1950s. In Orton, F. and Pollock, G. eds. *Avant-Gardes and Partisans Reviewed*. Manchester: Manchester University Press, pp. 219–294.

Rifkin, A. 1985. Marx's Clarkism. *Art History* 8(4), pp. 488–495.

Rose, J. 1986. *Sexuality in the Field of Vision*. London: Verso.

Vigneault, L. 2011. *Espace artistique et modèle pionnier: Tom Thomson et Jean-Paul Riopelle*. Montréal: Éditions Hurturbise.

4

Juan Davila's abject after-image

Rex Butler and A. D. S. Donaldson

One hardly goes to Slovenian theorist Slavoj Žižek for aesthetic advice. As he admits, his interest in art is strictly 'machinic' (Žižek, 1999: viii), and even with works of art he clearly loves – the films of Alfred Hitchcock, the novels of Samuel Beckett and classical music of all kinds – he does not respond to them aesthetically, but merely interprets them for theoretical evidence. It is not so much these works in themselves that he is interested in – although he has obviously spent a long time watching, reading and listening to them – but for how they help him explain a particular Hegelian or Lacanian concept. Thus Alfred Hitchcock's *The Birds* is used to discuss the Lacanian notion of the gaze, Samuel Beckett's *Worstward Ho* is used to elaborate the Hegelian requirement to 'begin again at the beginning', and Richard Wagner's *Liebstod* is used to make sense of the Lacanian refiguring of the death drive. But in the middle of his latest book – well, almost his latest, for Žižek writes books almost faster than anyone can keep up with them – he pauses and criticises postmodern art. Moreover, he does so on aesthetic grounds; or, if not on actual aesthetic grounds, then at least by defending a position that, within contemporary art discourse, is understood to be conservative in its assertion of the integrity of the work of art and the distinctiveness of aesthetic experience.

On p. 255 of the 1,010-page *Less than Nothing: Hegel and the Shadow of Dialectical Materialism* (2012), Žižek argues that postmodernism is not an advance on modernism, but in fact marks a regression from it, insofar as it avoids grappling with the issue of 'medium'. To back up his view, he refers approvingly to philosopher Robert Pippin's advocacy of Michael Fried, an art historian for whom Žižek has expressed his admiration before and who is absolutely identified with a certain kind of modernism. Žižek writes, citing Pippin:

> There was no failure of modernism, no exhaustion by the end of abstract expressionism. Rather, there was (and still is) a failure to appreciate and integrate the self-understanding reflected in such art (a failure to appreciate modernism or the same kind of straw-man attacks, in what we call postmodernism). (Žižek, 2012: 255)

Žižek, as further evidence for his views, turns later to Fried's fellow art historian T. J. Clark and his now famous analysis of Jacques-Louis David's *The Death of Marat* (1793), which Clark argues – and Žižek agrees with him – is the first modernist painting. What Žižek is particularly interested in, following Clark, is the way that in David's image of Marat, the entire top half of the painting is wreathed in shadow. This has the uncanny effect for Žižek of somehow separating Marat from his background. Almost like an anamorphic portrait, we can focus either on Marat or on the wall behind him (which, according to Žižek, stands in for the People), but we cannot see both at once. Again, as Žižek writes:

> In *The Death of Marat*, it appears as if we see Marat in his bath tub in front of a dark screen onto which the fake background has not been projected… We see the figure, while the background remains an opaque stain; in order to see the background, we would have to blur the figure. But what is impossible is to get the figure and the background in the same focus (710–711).

Juan Davila is a Chilean-Australian artist, who, after coming to Australia in 1974, became well known in the 1970s and 1980s for showing it all. His art – absolutely at the forefront of the Australian version of postmodernism called 'Popism' – sought to overturn all repressions, all inhibitions, both sexual and political, which in many ways he saw as the same. First of all, Davila, a gay man, represented homosexual sex. His paintings are full of men copulating in full view of the spectator, exposing penises, anuses, the practices of fisting and fellatio. Thus, in a work like *Rat Man* (1980), we have a naked man on his hands and knees exposing his buttocks and exclaiming, in echo of a celebrated case of Sigmund Freud, 'Father, can't you see I'm burning!' Or, in *Painting* (1984), a muscled hunk in leather pants plays with himself while licking the leather glove of a man in high heels, who is himself sweating or dribbling in pleasure. But, alongside Davila's explicit representations of gay sex, there runs a certain practice of 'outing' a repressed homosexuality in both art and the wider culture. Thus, in *Portrait of Joshua Smith* (1990), Davila puts Joshua Smith, the subject of William Dobell's controversial Archibald Prize-winning portrait, in bed with Dobell's Billy Boy, a huge, tattooed and perhaps slightly simple-minded man, whose job it was to make meals for itinerant shearers. The combination is revealing, not only because such expressions of 'strong masculine labour' as the Billy Boy have an iconic (if not ironic) place in gay culture, but also because it is likely Dobell and Smith were lovers when they were billeted together during training in WWII; and this fact, although not raised, would have been material during the controversial court case brought by a disgruntled Archibald entrant, accusing Dobell's portrait of being a mere 'caricature' based on a lack of acquaintance with the subject, and thus ineligible for the Prize. Similarly, in *Nothing if Not Abnormal* (1991), Davila depicts the long-running rivalry between Prime Minister Bob Hawke and his brilliant if saturnine Treasurer Paul Keating, a rivalry that would eventually lead to Keating toppling Hawke as Prime Minister. In showing Keating in drag parting his buttocks and farting at the audience and having Hawke screw a blow-up representation of Australia with Keating waiting behind him, Davila seeks to reveal the hidden libidinal economy – put otherwise, homosociality – that led these two powerful men, who had once clearly been half in love with each other, to fall out so poisonously.

And throughout the 1980s and 1990s, Davila sought to 'revise' Australian history and culture and see it through the lens of a normally repressed homosexuality. There are images of an Aboriginal Ned Kelly with a bulging erection having his leather pants repaired by a hooded white man (*Sentimental History of Australian Art*, 1982), images of the iconic Mick 'Crocodile' Dundee being buggered by his creator Paul Hogan's comedic offsider 'Strop' (*Crocodile Dundee*, 1988) and images of the nineteenth-century explorers Burke and Wills lying naked in camp together with Burke having his anus licked by a kangaroo (*The Arse End of the Universe*, 1994). And there are couplings across all races, classes and even genders: a man with a man with a rose in his hair and indeterminate genitals in *Family Group* (1988), a man with breasts with a statue with an oversized green phallus in *Retablo* (1989) and even a man with the figure of death with his cloak and sickle in *[sic]* (1988). And, more generally, Davila seeks to destroy the whole decorum not only of art but of public space itself, in transposing 'the porn shop and the museum' (Foss 1985: 5). Thus we have, in some of his more violent or at least iconoclastic juxtapositions, the restaging of Michelangelo's *Pietà* as the Madonna cradling an enormous penis (*Holy Family*, 1985) or one man taking succour at the breast of another (*Pietà*, 1982). In the *Liberator Simón Bolívar* (1993–94), Davila depicts Simón Bolívar, the so-called 'liberator' of Latin America in his fight to free its indigenous populations from their Spanish colonisers, as a cross-dressing transsexual sitting atop a horse. And perhaps most notoriously, or at least programmatically, the huge, multi-panelled *Stupid as a Painter* (1981–82) features a toilet door graffito of cock and balls, an explicit figuring of the psychoanalytic concept of the vagina dentata and a small reproduction of Robert Mapplethorpe's infamous photograph of a man inserting his hand up to his forearm in another man's anus.

In all of this Davila directly tests not only the artistic but also the legal limits of image-making. His *Stupid as a Painter* when shown at the 1982 Biennale of Sydney was taken off the wall, only to be reinstated at a different gallery after an intervention by the liberal-minded Premier of New South Wales. Davila's depiction of Simón Bolívar, when the work was originally shown at the Hayward Gallery in London in 1994, led to a flurry of diplomatic protest, with the Venezuelan, Colombian and Ecuadorean governments writing to the Chilean government accusing Davila of defaming the 'father' of their country, and the Chilean Foreign Minister for his part expressing sympathy with their objections and outrage at Davila. And, of course, it is a supreme act of blasphemy to replace Mary and Christ with either Mary and a penis or two male lovers. It is a gesture that Davila – or, at least, a commentator writing on his behalf – likened to the vandalism wrought by the crazed Australian Laszlo Toth, who once physically attacked Michelangelo's real marble sculpture with a hammer (which is why the work is now to be seen only behind bullet-proof glass in the Cappella del Crocifisso of the Sistine Chapel) (Foss, 1985: 18–24). And as well as on the level of content, on the level of form or technique Davila seeks to transgress boundaries: the mimicking of bad or incompetent painting, the radical mixing of incompatible artistic styles (abstraction and figuration, expressionism and pop), the application of paint in smears or splashes to look like shit or sperm, the deliberate flouting of artistic copyright, the refusal of any apparent authorship or guiding intentionality. (As a summary of everything Davila rejects, we might think of his *This is Not* (1987), which in a kind of homosexual equivalent to René Magritte's *The Rape* simply substitutes a close-up of an anus for the sitter's face.)

And throughout the period both Davila and his critics spoke in polemical terms of not only the artistic but also the social and political consequences of this breaking of taboos. First of all, in *Art i$ ~~Homosexual~~* (1983–86), Davila points to some of the effects of the homosexual remaking of an assumed-to-be heterosexual art: the erasure of the image, the defetishisation of money and a conception of the homosexual subject as that which exceeds the symbolic economy (the dollar sign in the title recalls the Lacanian algebra for the split subject, just as the word 'Homosexual' with a line through it is an allusion to Jacques Lacan's conception of woman as not-all within the masculine order). Equally in the poster *Liberation of Desire = Social Liberation* (1982), which features the artist in drag with wig and make-up, Davila makes clear that the consequences of a gay sexual revolution would be a wider social revolution. (The connection between the sexual and the political is the theme of Argentine novelist Manuel Puig's *Kiss of the Spiderwoman*, which Davila uses as the basis of *Stupid as a Painter*. Puig's novel makes clear, through the figure of the repressed Marxist revolutionary Valentin Arregui – who is gradually seduced by the flamboyantly gay but apolitical window-dresser Luis Molina while the two spend time in jail together in Chile during Allende's regime – that there is no point in having a political revolution without having a sexual revolution, or indeed that it is not possible to have a political revolution without also having a sexual revolution.) As Davila states in an interview with the critic Paul Foss:

> [Art's] power of eruption, its creation of new possibilities, is located outside of the codes that constitute language itself. Art proposes the destruction of traditional cultural structures, not by idealist representations, but by exposing the materiality of the production of signs of culture. (Davila, 1985: 15)

There is nothing repressed here, nothing that is unsaid or unsayable. Everything can be shown, everything can be seen. But, to return to Žižek's analysis, there is only one thing that is missing in Davila, and that is any sign of struggle, any real evidence of the resistance of the medium. Ultimately in Davila's work of the 1980s and 1990s, there is a kind of unstated equivalence between all things: high, low, religious, secular, obscene, public. If we could put it in the form of a paradox, the only thing repressed is repression, the only thing hidden is the lack of anything to hide. And Davila is clear about this. For all of its explicit references to psychoanalysis, he rejects any idea of the unconscious in his work, of anything deeper than the surface of the painting. In the words of the Chilean critic Nelly Richard: 'Psychoanalysis is still located in an ideology of representation, as it interprets the artwork as an expression of content, be it a psychic one' (Richard, 1985: 29). And all of this puts interpreters of Davila's work in a difficult position because, in effect, there is nothing to interpret, or the work already performs its own interpretation (all of those signs pointing out Davila's artistic borrowings, all of those figurings of psychoanalytic symptoms). There is nothing left for the interpreter to do except retrace the argument of the painting itself. Indeed, interpretation – the desire for a 'deeper' meaning – is precisely one of the repressions Davila is seeking to free us from: liberation of desire = social liberation = liberation from interpretation.

But, as Žižek points out in *Less than Nothing*, the Real that Davila's art aims at is not to be directly attained. As he writes, admittedly somewhat parodically, of postmodern art: 'Suffice it to recall recent trends in the visual arts: gone are the days of simple statues or framed paintings – what we see now are the frames themselves without painting, dead cows and their excrement, videos of the insides of the human body, the inclusion of odours in the exhibition, and so on' (Žižek, 2012: 256).[1] In fact, what Žižek is getting at here, while he does not say it in so many words, is that postmodernism is defined by the separation of the frame and what it frames. Although he mentions only 'frames themselves without paintings', what is to be seen in the rest of the list he compiles is a series of objects without frames, presented as such: dead cows and their excrement, videos of the insides of the human body in which we (or at least the camera) are immersed, odours that cannot in any way be confined or contained. And what we have in the postmodern Davila – for all of its putative emphasis on the sign – is the same attempt directly to present the Real. We have not only, to follow the terms of Žižek's argument, a series of frames that frame nothing, but also, as the strict correlate of this, a series of objects without a frame: body parts and actions upon them that, as in pornography, seek to come at us unmediated; paint that attempts to go beyond its status as representation and actually be shit or sperm; the liberation of social desire through a painting that is properly performative.

However, Žižek's point is that this Real is not to be directly achieved but only through an act of sublimation. This is exactly his argument concerning David's *Portrait of Marat*: the full horror of Marat's death (both the horror of his assassination and also that of the Terror he represents) can be represented only through a certain minimal distance from the subject. And Žižek means this not merely in the sense that David did not paint the 'real' subject (the actual Marat suffered from a terrible skin disease that required him to spend prolonged periods in water, whereas in David's depiction of him he is clear-skinned), but more profoundly in the sense that through the structure of his painting what David represents is *an object out of its place*. That is to say, the effect of David shrouding the top half of the painting in darkness is, as Žižek suggests, like anamorphosis: we can see either Marat in the foreground or the background behind him. As a result, a certain minimal gap is opened up between foreground and background. Unlike a conventional portrait in which background and foreground are intended seamlessly to blend together, here it is as though Marat comes to occupy a hole opened up in reality, exactly equivalent to our gaze upon him. And, again, it is this that makes David's painting modernist (and, indeed, Žižek will go on to relate David's portrait to Malevich's *Black Square*, by most accounts the first truly modernist, that is, abstract, painting) (Žižek, 2012: 711–712). If, as against postmodernism, it is not a matter of asserting some real object, it is also not, as with pre-modernism, that painting is cut off from some 'transcendent Truth'.[2] In both cases, there would be some pre-existing reality outside of the painting that it either can directly capture or forever falls short of. Rather, in modernism the object can be represented, but only through the mediation of the medium. Indeed, in some way it *is* the artistic medium.[3] We might say, then, that the real subject in modernist painting is neither the individual in the foreground nor the People in the background, but the very gap between them.[4]

And it is in this sense that we must understand a shift in Davila's practice that occurred some time in the early 2000s, in which he transformed himself from a postmodernist into a modernist. We can see this change figured in many ways in his work. There is a shift from iconoclasm and transgression to an iconicity and what the critic Kate Briggs calls an 'act of faith' (Briggs: 2010: 1). There is a shift from the destruction and pulverisation of the picture plane to the attempt to produce a unified tableau (as figured by the artist's 'studio' as a location for the painting). There is a shift from a kind of indoors self-referentiality and enclosedness to a *plein air* naturalism or even impressionism. There is a shift from gay men being the chief protagonists of the painting to women (although there is still the relative absence of straight men). There is a shift from mid- to late twentieth-century predominantly American, Australian and South American references (Andy Warhol, Arthur Streeton, Roberto Matta) to mid- to late nineteenth-century French references (Gustave Courbet, Édouard Manet, Gustave Caillebotte). There is a shift from the easy mastery and clarity of the grid to the irresolvable struggle and blur of the brushstroke. There is a shift from the image to what we might call the after-image, which comes not merely at the end of painting as a conclusion but at the beginning, opening up a permanent break.

But, more specifically, how is all of this to be seen in Davila's work? Where is this new necessity for sublimation to be found and in what does it consist? We might date the change in Davila's work to a series he undertook in 2002 entitled *The Origin of the World*. The series was based on Courbet's notorious painting of the same name, which features a close-up of a woman's genitals, and we might say that Courbet's painting fulfils the same role for Davila as *The Death of Marat* does for Clark as the first modernist painting (although Davila speaks of his version of the work as reversing Courbet's 'modernist solution') (Davila 2006: 216). How is this so for Davila, and how, perhaps despite his own understanding, does he repeat the lesson that David puts forward for Clark? Davila in an essay entitled 'Courbet's Curtain' makes the point that he was inspired to make his series in response to an incident he witnessed at the Musée d'Orsay in Paris, where Courbet's *Origin* now hangs, in which a mother forced her young son to look at the painting, in what Davila describes as a virtual episode of 'rape'. And he goes on to speak of the 'anxiety' that the sight of a woman's genitals can provoke in men. This is why, he suggests, the Courbet original was always hung with a curtain across it, and why perhaps, in another Courbet painting of a naked woman, *Woman with a Parrot* (1866), Courbet added a bird: to provide a 'cut' within the realm of the picture, to distract our gaze, as a 'displacement' of our anxiety in front of a naked woman. But, if at times 'too much' is offered to the gaze, on other occasions 'too little' is offered.[5] This is the case, we suggest, with Davila's *Two Women on the Bank of the Yarra* (2003), his version of Courbet's *The Young Women on the Banks of the Seine* (1856–57), in which the two young women's genitals are deliberately pointed away from the viewer, equally provoking a kind of anxiety, which is that of a certain loss. As Davila writes in his essay, summarising the lesson of his two series of images in response to Courbet: 'Whereas in *The Origin of the World* too much is offered and the gaze has to be averted, here there is too little. Viewing is no longer placid when modernism sets in. If cropping is disturbing, so is slippage of the image' (Davila 2006: 217). In fact, the real point here – and this is why we might say that Courbet serves the same purpose for Davila as David does for Clark – is that in both cases a *gap* is opened up between the genitals and where they are meant to be. Each set of genitals is either too much or too little, or even, insofar as both excite a sense of anxiety, both too much *and* too little. That is, the paradox is that even when female genitals are right before our eyes they are missing (this is, of course, Freud's insight and undoubtedly why the young boy was so disturbed 'seeing' a woman's genitals for the first time) and when they are missing they are everywhere or everything stands in for them (this is the case with *Woman with a Parrot*: the parrot can distract our gaze or draw it away from the naked woman only by standing in for her genitals).[6] To put all this another way – and this is exactly Lacan's formula for anxiety – the most desublimated (woman's genitals as such) relies upon a certain effect of sublimation, and sublimation produces something desublimated (which is why the process of sublimation can never come to an end).[7]

Again, we might say that the 'transcendent' does not lie out there as that from which we are excluded – as some 'infinite Reality' or 'divinity too sublime to be grasped by the human mind' – but in here. It is not a noumenal that cannot be thought, but arises as a result of the gaze of the subject upon it, and in some ways *is* this very gaze. In Pippin's words, the medium of abstraction 'thematises and renders conscious components of sensible meaning that we traditionally would not see and understand as such' (cited in Žižek, 2012: 255).[8] This for Žižek is the distinction between Immanuel Kant and Georg Wilhelm Friedrich Hegel and why it is only with Hegel that modernism is properly achieved. And it is something like this that we see in an exhibition by Davila entitled *The Moral Meaning of Wilderness* (2010). It is in the work assembled there that Davila continues his earlier exploration of the portraiture of women. Along the lines of his earlier renaming of his version of *The Origin of the World* after the woman whose genitals Courbet depicted, he produces a series of images of *named* subjects. But there is also in each of them a certain disjunction between these women and their place, the painting and what it names. Thus in *Maria* (2009), a woman stares intently out at the viewer standing in front of an unidentified background made up of smeared and cross-hatched brushstrokes. In *Nina Sers* (2008), the subject stares sideways away from us while before her a literal slit or split opens up in an indeterminate space. And in *Guacolda del Carmen Gallardo* (2007), a naked woman floats in outer space, the pink of her flesh melding with the cold blue of the cosmos. In each case – even *Guacolda del Carmen Gallardo* – there is a void not so much out there as in here, a space that is not so much outer space as the space between figure and ground, a void that we might say is equivalent to their gaze on to the world. And this gap is to be seen also in other of

Davila's works from the exhibition, such as *Albert Street* (2007), which is a quickly sketched landscape in the Heidelberg style, in which towards the right-hand side of the canvas the brushstrokes simply peter out, giving way to bare canvas. However, the point here is that we cannot see this canvas as such, but only through these brushstrokes (and it is just this 'in betweenness' that is figured in the series by the term 'wildness', for this wildness, as with the Heidelberg School, is never simply 'out there', but always a location on the outskirts of Melbourne, a non-place between the urban and the rural.)[9]

It is perhaps in this sense that we might understand Davila's series of works entitled *After Images*. These are images that 'accompany' other images, being reproduced on the right hand side of the catalogue after them, as though they can be seen only through them. Thus for *A Man Renounces Love* (2010; Figure 2), which features a shirtless middle-aged man sitting down in a desert-like wilderness, staring into the void, there is an *After Image* consisting of a streaky blue and white background with patches of red, yellow and pink floating on top. For *This is No Man* (2010), which features a stern-looking woman in jeans and brown jacket looking at the viewer while the disembodied head of a man floats to one side, there is an *After Image* consisting of an out-of-focus grey background and thinly painted black-and-white clouds on top. And for *A Man is Born without Fear* (2010), which features a man, woman and child standing nervously before the viewer while what appears to be a giant gold nugget hovers behind them, there is an *After Image* consisting of a broadly stroked black background on which something like a blue cartoon thought bubble sits. In some ways, as we say, these *After Images* can appear to be the literal after-image or visual echo of their 'originals'. Thus the vertically brushed green to the left and right and the blue at the top centre of *After Image: A Man Renounces Love* (Figure 3) can appear to be based on the eucalypts and blue sky of the original *A Man Renounces Love*. Or the greys around the edges and the white highlights of *After Image: This is No Man* can appear to be based on the rain-soaked streets and approaching headlights of the original *This is No Man*. More abstractly perhaps, these *After Images* can appear to reveal a certain symbolic truth to the original that would otherwise remain unspoken. Thus, as Briggs argues in her catalogue essay for *The Moral Meaning of Wilderness*, the yellow patches at the bottom and centre of *After Image: A Man Renounces Love* recall the strange yellow halo that surrounds the man in *A Man Renounces Love*, which is the sign of his forsaking human connection for power and money. Or the floating blue thought bubble and ominous black foreground of *After Image: A Man is Born without Fear* point to the lure of earthly riches in the form of the gold nugget and the temptation to dark despair that have to be overcome if we are truly to live without fear (Davila, 2010: 51–52, 65–66).

But against this – and against any idea that these 'after images' are in any

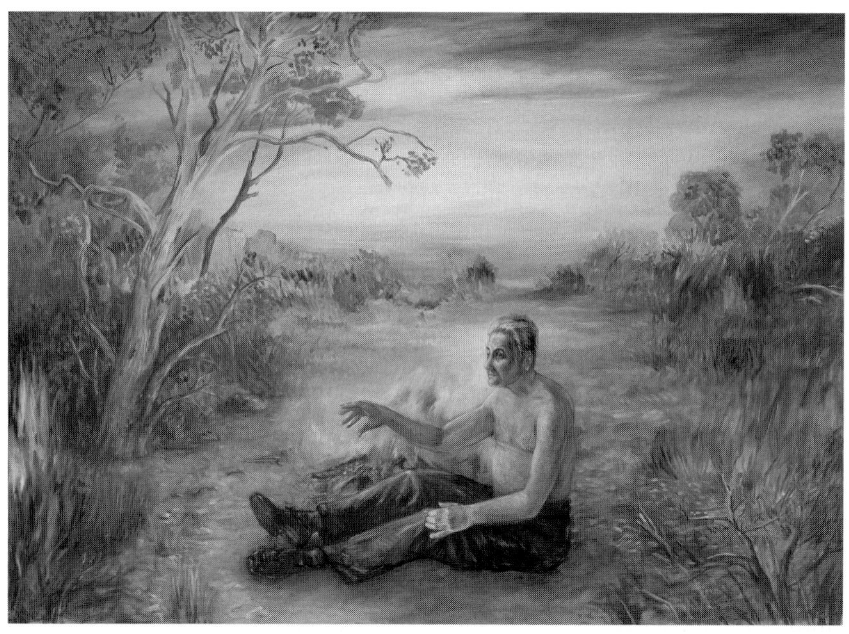

2 Juan Davila, *A Man Renounces Love*, 2010. Oil on canvas, 200 × 280 cm. © Juan Davila. Courtesy of Kalli Rolfe Contemporary Art.

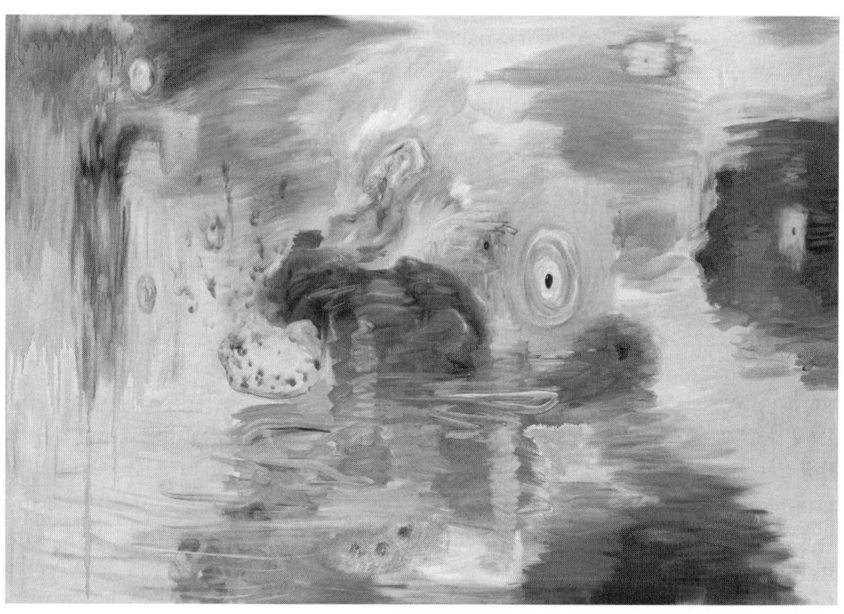

3 Juan Davila, *After Image. A Man Renounces Love*, 2010. Oil on canvas, 200 × 280 cm. © Juan Davila. Courtesy of Kalli Rolfe Contemporary Art.

way a further abstraction of the strange mollusc-like forms of *Wilderness* (2010) or the sleek aerodynamic shape that sits on the riverbank in *Pulp Mill on the River Tamar* (2009) – we would want to suggest that these 'after images' come not so much after as *before*. That is, what Davila is staging here – it is that 'zero point' Žižek speaks of with regard to Malevich that must be passed through before we can begin again at zero (Žižek, 2012: 712–713) – is the fundamental act of sublimation, the opening up of that gap or distinction between figure and ground brought about by the gaze for which all subsequent images stand in. But, to the extent possible, in this series of 'after images', Davila does not try to fill in this void. He does not seek to reduce or make sense of the essential mediation of the medium out of which art arises. He does not attempt to 'tame' the gaze, the gaze of the subject or spectator that introduces a gap and in a way even *is* this gap. In the words of Žižek in *Less than Nothing*: 'Keep the screen empty!' (Žižek, 2012: 708) And, in fact, we would say that we have something like this in Davila's earlier work in those moments where he leaves the canvas blank: *Self Portrait* (1991), *The Painter's Studio* (2006) and, most importantly, *The Australian Republic* (2000), which repeats the gesture of David in representing the People not directly but only as the 'disappearance' of the figure in front of them (Žižek, 2012: 711). (Indeed, perhaps the real equivalent to *The Death of Marat* in Davila's oeuvre is *Untitled* (2010), whose subject is the politician Kevin Andrews, the hard-line Minister for Immigration and Citizenship under Prime Minister John Howard, whom Davila similarly holds up against a blank or obscured surface.) But this blankness, like that of the *After Images*, can last only a moment. We are always too late for it; it is fading away even as we look at it, taking the form of those 'original' images on which it appears to be based. Like Courbet's *The Origin of the World*, it is almost immediately curtained, with something coming to stand in for it. It is undoubtedly only a 'utopian' possibility – another topic of Davila's art – seen through its very loss.[10]

And to turn finally to the title of this collection, it is in this way that we might say the *abject* is figured in Davila's work: not as the undoubtedly abject faces and bodies on display, but as a kind of effacement or blankness. For the point of Julia Kristeva's abject is that the object is not abject in itself but only by reason of what it stands in for. More precisely, the abject is the disjunction between the object and its place. But, indeed, the true paradox of the abject object – this is Kristeva's ultimate point and the profound innovation of her book – is that it is not simply an object without a place or a place without an object, those pre- and postmodern alternatives Žižek outlines. Rather, repeating the terms of Žižek's description of the modernist medium, Kristeva makes it clear that the abject object is never seen as such but only as the gap between the object and its place. That is, abjection refers not so much to something desublimated as to the very process of sublimation itself: abjection is literally the 'medium' between object and place. The identification of the object as abject is already to bring about its sublimation, its passing over into the symbolic. The criticisms of Kristeva's book for falling short of a real abjection are, therefore, only to make the argument Kristeva wants to make. This is her very contention in *Powers of Horror*, in which she takes up Freud's notions of negation and sublimation (and Kristeva reads Freud through Lacan, so that, if the desublimated is always sublimated, the process of sublimation also can never come to an end, insofar as it gives rise to what again has to be sublimated – and this, of course, is Žižek's Hegelian point concerning to ongoing process of modernist 'mediation'). Kristeva writes there:

> If the abject is already a wellspring of sign for a non-object, on the edges of primal repression, one can understand its skirting the somatic system on the one hand and sublimation on the other. The symptom: a language that gives up, a structure within the body, a non-assimilable alien … *Sublimation*, on the contrary, is nothing else than the possibility of naming the pronominal, the pre-objectal … In the symptom, the abject permeates me, I become abject. Through sublimation, I keep it under control. The abject is edged with the sublime. (Kristeva, 1982: 11)

In a sense, Davila's later work operates as a 'critique' of his earlier. As opposed to the polemical openness and incompletion of the earlier postmodernism, which is actually just another form of mastery, implying a certain meta-position outside of the techniques he employs, with the later work there is a real failure from which nothing is exempt. Put simply, it would not be a reflection upon failure, but a kind of practice of it. Failure would not be the subject of the work but the medium in which it takes place. And perhaps – in a gesture admittedly absolutely against the 'non-criticality' of this second period – we might actually re-read Davila's earlier work in the light of his later. Where in Davila's postmodernism might we see a true resistance of the medium that is unable to be made to speak? In other words, where is something of the 'after-image' in it? Where something of the abject? It is a small detail in the earlier work that is so easily overlooked; indeed, it is almost intended to be overlooked, whether consciously or unconsciously, because Davila does not signpost it, unlike so many of the other references in his work. It is not the subject of the work and, in some ways – like the after-image and the abject – is unable to become a subject. In the multi-panelled work *Fable of Australian Painting* (1982), Davila offers us several 'scenes' from the history of Australian painting, each featuring – in a precursor to the later Courbet-derived 'studios' – an image of someone painting. In the first panel, an Albert Tucker-like Antipodean Head paints a Tom of Finland-style male hunk humping a spindly gum tree. In the second panel Nolan's Ned Kelly paints a hawk-faced man by John Brack. In the third panel, a hysterical-looking

Arthur Boyd 'half-caste' paints the elongated figure from Drysdale's *Man Feeding the Dogs*. And in the fourth and final panel an amorphous Jedd Garet paints Dobell's Joshua Smith, who at the same time is seemingly being fellated by a dog. However, although each of our painters stands before their subject, what ends up on their easels appears to bear little relationship to what they see. In the first panel, before the Tom of Finland, we have a blank canvas with the words 'A Republic for Australia' along the bottom; in the third canvas, before the man feeding the dogs, we have a pound sign; in the fourth canvas, before Joshua Smith, we have a David Aspden lyrical abstract; and in the second panel, before the Brack, we have a strange painting made up of irregular multi-coloured squares and rectangles. And, significantly, while almost all of the details of these paintings (the painter, their subject and frequently their easel) are labelled after their artistic sources, this curious multi-coloured patchwork is named, in an apparently autobiographical touch, and against the attack upon authorship of the rest of *Fable*, 'Davila'.

And, in fact, if we look closely, we can find this motif throughout any number of Davila's other works, almost like a watermark or, indeed, artist's signature. We see it, for example, towards the left centre of *The Barricade* (1989), at the centre of *Bottle* (1993), at the centre of *Modern Ex-Voto* (1994) and making up the horse in the two versions of *The Liberator Simón Bolívar* (1993 and 1994). We have variants of it in *Monogram* (1989) and *Mexicanismo* (1990), and it is behind the design of the political poster *Woomera* (2002). It also forms the underlying grid-like armature and right-hand framing panel in Davila's enormous *Wuthering Heights I* (1990), which was shown as part of the exhibition *Transcontinental: Nine Latin American Artists* in Manchester in 1990. The critic Guy Brett, writing in the catalogue for the 2006 retrospective of Davila held at the Museum of Contemporary Art in Sydney, identified no fewer than fifteen artists whose work Davila was playing on there, including some seven South American artists; but he fails to identify the real source for this image, which is *Marco recortado No. 2* (*Structural Frame No. 2*) (1946) by Juan Melé of the Argentine artist group Asociación Arte Concreto-Invención, whose activities intersected but also broke with those of Madí, the other Buenos Aires-based group of abstract artists then emerging in the years immediately after the war (Brett, 2006: 244, fn. 37). Indeed, Davila even made a large wood and canvas construction entitled *Madí* in 1991, in which Melé's form recurs, along with – importantly for our argument – a scrap of the Australian flag.

We might perhaps offer here a brief history of Madí to conclude, both to think what it might mean for Davila to include Melé's work in *Fable of Australian Painting* and to hold up a section of the Australian flag next to it in *Madí*. Undoubtedly, the greatest contribution of the Madí artists was their establishment of the irregular frame or shaped canvas as a problem in the history of painting, part of what Argentine painter and writer César Paternosto calls their 'radical removal of the acquired traditions of geometrical abstraction' (Paternosto, 2011: 33–4). Gathered together in their preliminary form by the Uruguayan Joaquín Torres Garcia, it was these South Americans who first broke with the right-angle in painting and began to explore the possibility of the shaped support – in particular, as in Davila's version of it, involving non-parallel edges and non-regular geometry – and not at all such Americans as Frank Stella and Kenneth Noland, as we have been taught to believe in the Anglosphere.

The Madí group itself, following the pioneering efforts of Torres Garcia, was officially brought together in Buenos Aires in 1946 by the Hungarian-Austrian artist and poet Gyula Kosice and the Uruguayans Carmelo Arden Quin and Rhod Rothfuss. Of course, like many significant art movements, the story behind the formation of this group of abstract artists is contested. Kosice later claimed that the name of the movement was derived from the republican motto in the Spanish civil war of the 1930s: 'Madí, Madí, no pasarán' ('Madrid, Madrid, they will not pass', that is, the forces of the fascist Franco will not take Madrid). For his part, Quin asserted that the name of the group was an acronym of his complete name: CarMelo Alveo ArDen QuInn. The name of the group is most commonly understood, however, as deriving from the acronym for Movimento, Abstracción, Dimensión, Invención (Movement, Abstraction, Dimension, Invention). Like the word Dada, whatever its origins, Madí gave its name to an expansive practice, characterised by both a playfulness and a politics, whose legacy is still relevant and, indeed, in whose name there are still artists practising into the twenty-first century, including such foundational figures as Arden Quin and his fellow Uruguayan Volf Roitman.

Now, in its first catalogue, Madí declared itself a universal art movement, and it reproduced its essays in Spanish, French and English. And under the leadership of Quin, Kosice and Rothfuss, the artists began publishing in 1947 the bilingual Spanish-French *Arte Madí Universal*, the journal continuing until 1954. However, not long after this first issue, the group split and divided itself between Quin and others, including the German-born Argentine Martin Blaszko, and Kosice and others, including the Argentinian Diyi Laañ. Nevertheless, with his deep roots in France, Torres Garcia, who was eventually to take Quin's side, had already been instrumental in the organisation of abstract artists in Paris in the late 1920s and early 1930s in their fight against the other dominant art movement of the time, Surrealism. Certainly, it can be seen that his chance meeting with the great Belgian writer, artist and art historian of abstraction Michel Seuphor at Friedrich Vordemberge-Gildewart's exhibition in Paris in 1929 was a pivotal moment in the formation of a united bloc of abstract artists against Surrealism in France. And this meeting typified, in its bringing together of the Polish with the Belgian, German and Uruguayan, the cosmopolitanism of abstract art between the wars in France – and it was an internationalism that was to continue in Paris in the years following the war, with the united exhibition of the Madí artists within the Salon des Realités Nouvelles, the post-war reconstitution of the earlier Abstraction-Création group of the mid-1930s, which had itself been born out of the collapse of Dutch artist Theo van Doesberg's Art Concret and Seuphor and Torres Garcia's Circle et Carré around 1930.

In 1992, the French artist Roger Neyrat, a member of Madí from the late 1940s – as we say, the group eventually went beyond the countries of South America in finding its members – recalled the Madí workshops of the early 1950s in Paris in his essay 'De la creación del Centre d'Études et recherches MADÍ', published in the catalogue for the exhibition *Arden-Quin-Roitman*, held in Paris in 1995. They were held, Neyrat recalled, in French painter Marcelle Saint-Omer's large studio overlooking the Montparnasse cemetery, with each member hanging the particular work they were engaged in on the wall and a poem-object by Quin, a transparent plexiglass cube on which was inscribed the line: 'Tout visiteur nait d'un éclat [Every visitor is born out of a thunderclap]', installed at the entrance. For Neyrat, it was all a 'formidable optical manifesto', and in the space the group also showed films, held dinners and gave or listened to lectures (Neyrat cited in Borràs, 1997: 298). And, according to Neyrat, with studios open all week and artists always being present, the centre had a constant stream of visitors, from curators and art historians, representatives from both the better-known and less-well-known galleries and 'famous artists' from all around the world, including Georges Vantongerloo, Auguste Herbin, Marcelle Cahn, Viera da Silva, César Domela, Alexander Calder and Wilfredo Lam (Neyrat cited in Borràs, 1997: 298)

Now we come to the speculative part of our brief history here and our attempt to think what Davila might be said to mean by including the Australian flag as part of his sculpture *Madí*, for among the 'famous artists who came to see others less important than themselves' mentioned by Neyrat is Mary Webb, a Sydney-born painter and collage artist, who moved to Paris in 1949, was represented by Galerie Collette Allendy (where Madí artists showed) for most of the 1950s and showed as a *sociétaire* with the Realités Nouvelles from 1950 until 1957. A founding member of the Club International Féminin, she was awarded the Médaille d'Argent de la Ville de Paris in 1958, the year of her death aged 57. Immediately after her passing, Seuphor, the author of the monumental *Dictionary of Abstract Painting* (1957), wrote to Webb's friend and colleague Grace Crowley back in Australia, expressing the hope that at least 'a few paintings of Mary Webb will now enter the museums and collections of Australia'. It would in fact take over 50 years for Seuphor's wish to come true, when in 2012 her work was finally acquired by the Queensland Art Gallery and the Art Gallery of New South Wales, where it now rightly hangs besides that of her fellow abstractionists Crowley and Ralph Balson. And perhaps the second Australian with whom the Madí artists intersect is J. W. Power. Power had been essential to the formation of Abstraction-Création in the early 1930s, the group that, as we say, was the immediate forerunner to the Salon des Realités Nouvelles, the umbrella organisation that sheltered Madí during its initial appearances in Paris immediately after the War. It was in the Abstraction-Création annual *cahier* – in all likelihood, funded by Power, who inherited a considerable fortune that allowed him to move to Europe to become an artist – that Power's second-generation Cubist abstracts could be seen alongside the work of such South Americans as Juan del Prete in 1933 and Lucio Fontana in 1935. And it is Webb's and Power's careers that Davila is able to make us recognise in his *Madí.*

Davila in his artist notes for the MCA retrospective writes of *Fable of Australian Painting*:

> The coincidence between the imperial ideology and the present economic rationalism has produced a linear visual representation as our art history, a sort of comic strip. We as artists can mock the dependence of our art history, as I have done in this *Fable*. It does not alter past ills or propose an Australian national identity. It aims to create a flicker of a doubt but no revisionism. (Davila, 2006: 97)

And this is what Davila does in *Fable* and *Madí.* To think about the Madí artists and perhaps even to think about them in the context of Australian art is to think art history not in the linear, progressivist sense of ineluctable advances and singular creative geniuses, but neither is it to offer a simple revision or reversal of this modernism from either a postmodern or postcolonial perspective. Madí was not a 'first order' art movement from the centre, but neither is Davila in his treatment of Madí in his work proposing a simple parody or revision of it. There is not here the necessary critical distance, the unambiguous standing outside of tradition that characterises revisionism or postmodernism. This is the meaning of Davila identifying Madí with himself in *Fable*, insofar as he is unable to separate it from himself, insofar as he still understands himself as in some way belonging to its tradition. Madí is essentially the name for a series of ongoing, unresolved formal problems in the history of art, the 'minor' issues of framing, colour and figure-ground relations that continue to open up new possibilities in painting. (All of this, incidentally, along the lines of the Madí allegiance, is to suggest a shift from Surrealism to abstraction as the ruling problematic in Davila's work.) And a history of 'Australian' art that thinks its relationship to Madí is neither nationalist nor a postcolonial critique of nationalism (always in the name of another nationalism). Instead, we might describe it in that sense we have been trying to develop here as 'abject': open, inclusive, unfinished, unresolved, always out of place or always in between places. Again, as Kristeva puts it in *Powers of Horror*:

> The 'sublime' object dissolves in the raptures of a bottomless memory. It is such a memory, which, from stopping point to stopping point, remembrance to remembrance, love to love, transfers that object to the refulgent point of dazzlement in which I stray in order to be. (Kristeva, 1982: 12)

Notes

1 It is notable that the artworks Žižek uses to speak of the separation of the frame from what it frames – identifiably those of Damien Hirst, Mona Hatoum and Helen Chadwick – are conventionally understood as abject. In this essay, we argue for a different conception of abjection in art, although one still indebted to Žižek.

2 Žižek writes: '[A new possibility for art] is not to be grounded in any limitation of Reason, of reflexive mediation: the modernist break has nothing to do with the reassertion of the unsurpassable horizon of finitude. There is no transcendent Truth from which we, as finite humans, remain forever cut off, either in the form of an Infinite Reality, which art cannot properly represent, or in the form of a Divinity, too sublime to be grasped by our finite mind' (Žižek, 2012: 254).

3 Žižek writes: 'This is what "abstraction" means: a reflexive questioning of the very medium of artistic representation, so that this medium loses its natural transparency. Reality is not "out there", reflected or imitated by art; it is something constructed, something contingent, historically conditioned' (Žižek, 2012: 254).

4 On the destiny of David's *Marat*, we might think of another great representation of political 'assassination', this time from the end of modernism: Gerhard Richter's series on the Baader-Meinhof gang, a number of whom hanged themselves on the same day in Stammheim prison, *October 18, 1977* (1988). Here, too, we would say that Richter's technique of brushing the final layers of paint across themselves opens up a certain gap between the painting and itself, which could also be seen to figure the gap between the Baader-Meinhof gang and the People they were trying to reach. This disconnection would obviously be a 'failure' of the ideals of modernism, and as David's painting shows it is a failure that runs from the beginning of modernism itself. See on this Benjamin Buchloh, 'A Note on Gerhard's Richter's *October 18, 1977*' (1989).

5 All previous quotes from 'Courbet's Curtain' (Davila, 2006: 214–221). And Davila's subtle point throughout the essay is that the name of Courbet's *The Origin of the World* is the work's first sublimation, the first 'curtain' Courbet draws over it. That is to say, the work's title is precisely the *lack* of the proper name of these genitals, which is why Davila gives them the name of their sitter in his own version of the work, *Portrait of Joanna Heffernan* (2003).

6 The other great example of this in art history, of course, is Manet's *Olympia* (1863), where the covering over of her genitals by Victorine Meurent leads to her genitals being seen everywhere else in the picture: in the gap between her fingers, her hair, the tassels on the pillow, her bracelet, the flowers, the bow around her neck, the cat, her servant …

7 See on this Lacan's remarks on the vase as the first work of art: '[The vase] creates the void and thereby introduces the possibility of filling it. Emptiness and fullness are introduced into a world that by itself knows not of them. It is on the basis of this fabricated signifier, this vase, that emptiness and fullness as such enter the world, neither more nor less, and with the same sense' (Lacan, 1992: 120).

8 Žižek is referring here to Jackson Pollock and Mark Rothko, and we would certainly add Rothko, along with David and Malevich, to the genealogy of Davila's 'after-images'. For Davila's comments on the kind of 'abstract' painting Žižek, after Pippin and Fried, is speaking of, see 'A Conversation Between Juan Davila and Kate Briggs', in *The Moral Meaning of Wilderness* (Davila, 2010: 52–53).

9 This 'non-space' or space between can be seen earlier in Davila's work in such paintings as *On the Fringes of Melbourne* (2003), which features the infamous 'cheese-stick' or giant yellow beam that hangs over the Melbourne International Gateway on the Tullamarine Freeway connecting the city to the faraway airport in Melbourne.

10 Indeed, this 'filling in' has come to pass: in *After Image, Kreon* (2013), exhibited at the National Gallery of Victoria's *Melbourne Now* show, Davila has 'filled in' the void with a pair of shoes seen from above, a 'Sorry' poster and the torso of a young man staring at the viewer.

References

Borràs M. L. 1997. Madí in Paris in the 1950s. In Borràs, M. L. ed. *Arte Madí*. Madrid: Museo Nacional de Arte Reina Sofia, pp. 1–33.

Brett G. 2006. Nothing Has Been Settled. In Brett, G. and Benjamin, R. eds. *Juan Davila*. Melbourne: Miegunyah Press, pp. 2–23.

Briggs, K. 2010. Painting: An Act of Faith. In Briggs, K. ed. *Juan Davila: The Moral Meaning of Wilderness*. Canberra: Drill Hall Gallery, Australian National University, pp. 1–40.

Buchloh, B. 1989. A Note on Gerhard's Richter's *October 18, 1977*. *October* 48, pp. 88–109.

Davila, J. 1985. A Question of Im-Pertinence: Interview between Juan Davila and Paul Foss. In Taylor, P. ed. *Hysterical Tears*. London: GMP Publishers, pp. 10–12.

Davila, J. 2006. Courbet's Curtain and *The Fable of Australian Painting*. In Brett, G. and Benjamin, R. eds. *Juan Davila*. Melbourne: Miegunyah Press.

Davila, J. 2010. A Conversation between Juan Davila and Kate Briggs. In *Juan Davila: The Moral Meaning of Wilderness*. Canberra: Drill Hall Gallery, Australian National University, pp. 45–65.

Foss, P. 1985. *The Mutilated Pieta*. Sydney: Artspace.

Kristeva, J. 1982 [1980]. *Powers of Horror: An Essay on Abjection*. New York: Columbia University Press.

Lacan, J. 1992. *The Ethics of Psychoanalysis 1959–60: The Seminar of Jacques Lacan, Book VII*. London: Routledge.

Paternosto, C. 2011. Irregular Frame/Shaped Canvas: Anticipations, Inheritances, Borrowings. In *Cold America: Geometric Abstraction in Latin America 1934–1973*. Madrid: Fundación Juan March, pp. 33–42.

Richard, N. 1985. Love in Quotes: On the Painting of Juan Davila. In Taylor, P. ed. *Hysterical Tears*. London: GMP Publishers, pp. 17–33.
Žižek, S. 1999. *The Žižek Reader*. Oxford: Blackwell.
Žižek, S. 2012. *Less than Nothing: Hegel and the Shadow of Dialectical Materialism*. London: Verso.

5

Animals, art, abjection

Barbara Creed and Jeanette Hoorn

This essay will explore the representation of the animal in contemporary art in relation to Kristeva's theory of abjection, in particular the way in which this concept is employed to define what it means to be 'human' – as distinct from animal – as well as the association of animal, abjection and woman. It will discuss the journey of the female artist into the abject, as distinct from the male. It will also draw upon George Bataille's concept of *informe* to argue that when the human subject is represented as an animal, or the lines between the two are sufficiently blurred, what follows in many works is a disturbance at the level of the signifier itself.

Kristeva: animals and abjection

Animals, or rather all non-human species, have a special relationship to the abject in human culture and artistic representation. In *Powers of Horror: An Essay on Abjection* (1982), Julia Kristeva defines the abject as that which 'disturbs identity, system, order' (4). Kristeva argues that the abject plays a crucial role in the creation of meaning, the establishment of the whole and proper self and the functioning of civilised human society. This is because the abject is that which threatens meaning. The abject 'draws me toward the place where meaning collapses' (2) and as such is perversely alluring but in the end it must be 'radically excluded' (2) in order to enable the proper functioning of self and society. In confronting, and then excluding the abject, the individual is able to re-define what it means to be 'human' and to function anew as a fully symbolic member of society. Without such encounters, once provided by religious ritual, and now by art, the abject forms a kind of underside to society and culture – horrifying but absolutely necessary. Kristeva draws particular attention to the role of woman and the non-human animal as abject beings that play key roles in social and cultural renewal. As she represents the roles of woman and animal as interrelated, it is necessary to explore these together before concentrating on the animal and its representation in abject art. Given this interconnection, it is not surprising to discover that female artists in particular explore abjection and the animal in their work. Artists discussed will include Louise Bourgeois, Julie Heffernan, Kiki Smith, Jenny Saville, Julie Rrap, Patricia Piccinini, Janet Laurence, Marian Drew and Vanessa Barbay. Furthermore, this essay argues, female artists who confront the abject embark on a different journey compared to male artists, in that the female artist must confront herself as an abject being.

Kristeva defines abjection both in relation to 'the threatening world of animals' and the world of the 'maternal entity' whose power is as secure as it is stifling.

> The abject confronts us, on the one hand, with those fragile states where man strays on the territories of *animal.* Thus, by way of abjection, primitive societies have marked out a precise area of their culture in order to remove it from the threatening world of animals or animalism, which were imagined as representatives of sex and murder. The abject confronts us, on the other hand, and this time within our personal archeology, with our earliest attempts to release the hold of *maternal* entity even before ex-isting outside of her, thanks to the autonomy of language. It is a violent, clumsy breaking away, with the constant risk of falling back under the sway of a power as securing as it is stifling. (Kristeva, 1982: 12–13)

These references to the abject nature of the animal and the maternal entity ('on the one hand' and 'on the other hand') single out the importance of 'areas' and 'borders' which should not be traversed. This is a risky business because the lure of the abject animal and maternal entity beckon and entice the subject who runs the 'constant risk of falling back'. Kristeva sees all literature, for instance, as an exploration of borders or liminal, fragile states where the subject's identity is directly threatened by the abject which has the power to settle within the subject, to threaten identity from within as well as from without, through the processes of metamorphosis.

> On close inspection, all literature is probably a version of the apocalypse that seems to me rooted, no matter what its socio-historical conditions might be, on the fragile border (borderline cases) where identities (subject/object, etc.) do not exist or only barely so – double, fuzzy, heterogeneous, animal, metamorphosed, altered, abject. (Kristeva, 1982: 217)

Borderline cases experience a powerful assault on their identities, which come to signify the various states – 'heterogeneous, animal, metamorphosed'. In some instances Kristeva speaks directly of the 'human animal', which suggests that she sees the boundary between human and animal (the animal in the human) as particularly fragile.

> This means once more that the heterogeneous flow, which portions the abject and sends back abjection, already dwells in a human animal that has been highly altered. I experience abjection only if an Other has settled in place and stead of what will be 'me' (Kristeva, 1982: 10).

Kristeva describes the Other as a being which 'precedes and possesses' her, 'a being there of the symbolic that a father might or might not embody' (10). Kristeva refers to Sigmund Freud who argued that during the period when religions evolved, the father came to be substituted for the totem animal. As Kelly Oliver points out, Lacan, in his reading of *Totem and Taboo*, proposed that Freud's 'primal father "originally" must have been an animal'.

> So the 'father' in this primal scene, the father on whom the Oedipal situation, the laws of civilization, and the possibility of representation that makes us human are founded was 'originally' an animal. (Oliver, 2009: 249).

If this was the case, then the animal was once a powerful figure in the imagination of early human subjects. The animal, along with woman, it would appear had the power to disturb 'identity, system order'.

> What will concern me here is … the alterations, within subjectivity and within the very symbolic competence, implied by the *confrontation with the feminine* and the way in which societies code themselves in order to accompany as far as possible the speaking subject on that journey. Abjection, or the journey to the end of the night. (Kristeva, 1982: 58)

Kelly Oliver, one of the few theorists to analyse the animal's role in abjection, argues that in Kristeva's theory, animals function as substitutes for the mother and as such do not exist in their own right. 'Furthermore, because animals and animality in her texts are reduced to stand-ins for the mother and the maternal body, she erases animals, as they exist outside human imaginary or symbolic systems' (Oliver, 2009: 178). Oliver also argues that in Kristeva's theory 'animals are symbols through which humans become speaking beings' (178). In other words the human subject separates itself from the non-human animal, and its culture from the cultures of animals, in order to define itself as civilised and exceptional – a specially created being with language. The animal is the ultimate 'other' that enables the human and its symbolic order of law and language to come into being. 'In other words, abjection is a disavowal of the essential dependence on animals (or mothers) that enables separation or autonomy, which in turn enables imitation, and through which we become speaking beings, human beings' (282).

Throughout her essay, Kristeva aligns the animal with woman and the abject. The interesting question is whether Kristeva herself endorses this double abjection (as Oliver would maintain) or whether she is accounting for the way in which patriarchal human societies have come into existence.

Having presented the animal as signifying one face of abjection, Kristeva then focuses on the figure of the archaic mother who in her role as the maternal authority is both powerful and frightening. She is the one who gives birth to all life. Through abjection, Kristeva by implication aligns the archaic mother with the (female) animal in that both signify the abject body – fecund, primitive, and belonging to the natural world. 'The body must bear no trace of its debt to nature: it must be clean and proper in order to be fully symbolic' (Kristeva, 1982: 102).

Citing *Leviticus*, Kristeva notes that apart from the gash of circumcision, the proper (male) body should not bear any other mark. 'Any other mark would be the sign of belonging to the impure, the non-separate, the non-symbolic, the non-holy' (102). Woman (marked by blood and childbirth) is both impure and non-symbolic. Although Kristeva does not say this, the animal's body too is marked – primitive, dirty, furry and scaly. In particular, the proper symbolic body should not signify the natural order: the bodies of women and non-human animals have a contaminating power that is at its strongest in relation to blood – blood of the slaughtered animal (forbidden in some religions) and of the menstruating, birthing woman (also taboo in many religions).

Woman's body perpetually signifies its debt to nature. Kristeva draws particular attention to the abject nature of woman and her procreative functions such as menstruation, pregnancy and childbirth. These are abject in that they threaten identity and form. The reproductive female body, human and animal, is inherently malleable – it exudes fluids, changes shape and generally signifies the basic instability of form; it is this instability that threatens a breakdown in meaning. It also brings us to George Bataille's idea of *informe*, which we will discuss shortly. Through their shared identities as the bearers of the next generation, women and female animals are rendered abject. A number of female artists have explored this relationship. It is important to point out that if we think of Kristeva's abject animal as a female animal then we might posit a special bond, grounded in procreation and abjection, which is shared by the two. It is also important to note that when the female artist explores the nature of abjection she, unlike the male artist, must confront herself and her specific relationship with the abject. The journey for her is essentially different.

Griselda Pollock draws attention to a related difficulty – the difficulty of such a journey, of all journeys that the feminist artist faces:

> In 'feminist interventions in art's histories', we have to confront the problem of how to 'see' what artists who are women produce. Their works come to us already 'framed' by existing art historical discourses that define the meaning of the period and practices within which the artists worked. … Art historical discourse already inscribes its own privileging of the masculine in art as the norm,

> leaving us feminists to fit women in, against the grain of what has been validated as the centre of the artistic movement. (Pollock, 1996: 223).

In a sense the artist who explores the abject, explores herself. Kiki Smith's sculpture, *Born - Deer Birth* (2002), emphasises the shared abjection of woman and the female animal. *Born* depicts a comparatively small deer giving birth to a fully-grown woman. The woman lies on the ground, her legs still emerging from the deer's uterus. Their mutual bodily entanglement emphasises both their procreative functions as well as the deep connection between woman and animal, once represented through the figure of Diana, Roman goddess of the hunt, who is frequently depicted in the company of a deer. The sculpture is confronting because of the way our eye is drawn to the woman's feet which remain inside the animal's body – the blood and flesh of the two are joined together giving them the appearance of a single extended body. In Smith's sculpture, the bodies of woman and animal offer visible evidence of their debt to nature.

Jenny Saville, for whom Kristeva's writings were an important influence, is noted for her paintings of the female body as large and fleshy, often to the point where the flesh threatens to fall over or enfold the body's borders. Her female figures interrogate the conventional representation of the female nude. There is also a strange defiant majesty about Seville's bodies, which some critics describe as perversely abject. Saville's *Host* (2000) deliberately merges woman's body with that of an animal. The female figure, with its head off-canvas to the left, is represented in the pose of a reclining Venus – except that the flesh is marked and scarred. At first sight the torso blurs the boundary between woman and animal because it displays a set of teats rather than breasts. Saville's *Torso* creates a similar confusion, as the slain animal's open legs, that extend beyond the frame and presumably are hanging from hooks, could be those of a woman with a pubic mound. *Host* was inspired by the novel, *Pig Tales* by Marie Darrieussecq (1996), which tells the story of a woman who begins to metamorphose into a pig as she becomes more aware of her sexual desires. The woman's large belly with its erect nipples suggests a pregnancy, which may explain the title – *Host*. She is Kristeva's fertile, voluptuous earth mother whose abjection is shared by female animals of other species. She clearly transgresses the borders between human and animal to the point of metamorphosis. This is not the smooth, unmarked body of the symbolic order. It is abject in that its ambiguous appearance entices and beckons the viewer while also holding the viewer at bay – the woman's animal-like voluptuousness is too threatening, possibly invoking disgust in some spectators. This body is very clear about its debt to nature – but this is not necessarily represented as a negative state of being. These two artists draw on abjection in positive and empowering ways in relation to the fecund female body, human and animal, to challenge the gaze of the proper symbolic (male) subject.

It is in woman's power to signify the fluid and evolutionary nature of the human body that reminds man of his animalistic origins. The subject may desire to re-experience his origins but ultimately those things that remind him of his primitive past must be excluded. Hence the male desire to separate himself from the female when she is in her most animal-like state, when her reproductive body loses its discrete form, emits secretions, such as blood and milk, and swells with pregnancy before subsiding after birth. The potential of the term 'animal' to remind us of the animal nature of the human, the human-as-animal, is ever present yet perpetually repressed. Human culture is founded on the absent-presence of the human being who ironically is also a human animal.

The artist

It is the role of the artist, Kristeva argues, to embark on a journey into the world of abjection, a journey to 'the end of the night' in order to purify the abject.

> The various means *of purifying* the abject – the various catharses – make up the history of religions, and end up with that catharsis par excellence called art, both on the far and near side of religion. Seen from that standpoint, the artistic experience, which is rooted in the abject it utters and by the same token purifies, appears as the essential component of religiosity. That is perhaps why it is destined to survive the collapse of the historical forms of religions. (Kristeva, 1982: 17)

In discussing the journey of the artist Kristeva refers to both sexes.

> If 'something maternal' happens to bear upon the uncertainty that I call abjection, it illuminates the literary scription of the essential struggle that a writer (man or woman) has to engage in with what he calls demonic. (208)

In Kristeva's view, feminine language is forged in the pre-oedipal period when the mother–child union is at its most intense. The mother teaches the infant about the boundaries of the clean and proper through touch and sounds. She described this period as the semiotic chora – it signified a maternal feminine language. Some theorists are highly critical of Kristeva's theory of the maternal semiotic, arguing that it is based on conventional and binary notions of femininity and masculinity, which fail to examine the idea of gender as a social construction. Domna Stanton argues that 'Kristeva's model for engendering the poetic does not then deviate fundamentally from the patriarchal oedipal script' (Stanton, 1986: 166). Her critics, however, do not explore Kristeva's alignment of woman and animal and the way in which her journey into the abject becomes fundamentally different from that of the male artist who is not asked to confront the abject nature of his reproductive body.

When a female artist, however, journeys into the abject she – unlike her male counterpart – encounters herself and her abject animal body. In focusing on the place of the animal in Kristeva's theory of the abjection, it becomes possible to see how the journey of the female artist differs from that of the male. Contrary to Kristeva's concept of the artist as one whose task it is to purify the abject, female artists who explore the abject, in relation to the animal, often do so for reasons unrelated to purification. Some appear to embrace the condition of the abject subject, the one who, in Kristeva's words, is 'double, fuzzy, heterogeneous, animal, metamorphosed, altered, abject' (Kristeva, 1982: 207): others use the abject in powerful ways in order to question what it means to be a woman and an animal in a patriarchal world. Although Kristeva does not explore what abjection means for the animal at the mercy of anthropocentric societies, many women artists, as we have seen, have taken this task upon themselves. Theirs constitutes a different, uniquely female journey.

One interesting approach is to 'play' with the abject. Some female artists engage in witty and subversive ways with the so-called abject nature of woman and her reproductive functions, particularly when 'she strays on the territories of the animal'. Julie Rrap's *Horse's Tale* (1999) plays with the abject, porous and malleable nature of the female form. It depicts a naked woman bent forward, her buttocks facing the camera, revealing the long strands of a horse's tail flowing down between her parted legs. The tail seems to fall from between her buttocks, and out from her anus. Is she human or animal? Although abject there is something uncannily seductive about Rrap's enigmatic equine woman: the skin is smooth, the horse's hair sleek and flowing, the woman/horse offers an enigma.

Other artists focus directly on the image of the animal and the animal/woman in order to raise ethical questions about the treatment of animals, insects and other species, including those that have been genetically engineered. Patricia Piccinini's sculptures such as *The Young Family* (2002; Figure 4) are particularly confronting in that they dissolve boundaries between woman and animal yet they also seem to defy species classification – even in terms of hybridity. The creatures are uncannily abject. *The Young Family* displays a human/animal/porcine figure, a mother lying on her side feeding a litter of babies. She possesses a human body with teats instead of breasts and a porcine face with long floppy ears. Her skin and that of her babies, is human – bare and pink. Her contemplative expression indicates that she is worried, concerned. Piccinini states that the mother, knowing her infants to have been bred for organ transplantation into humans, is deeply concerned about what will happen to them. She says that her work raises questions not

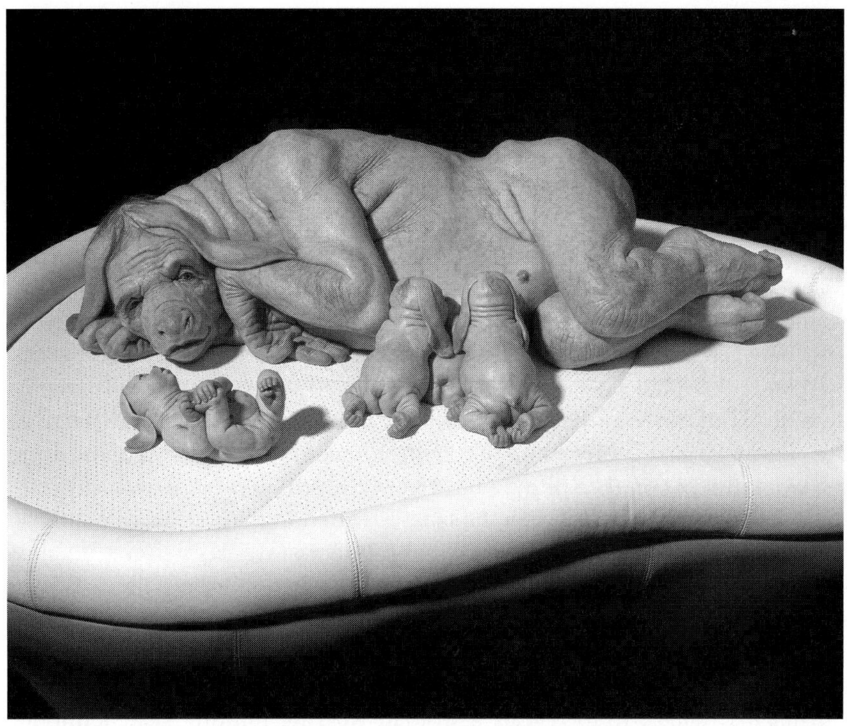

4 Patricia Piccinini, *The Young Family*, 2002. Silicone, fibreglass, leather, human hair and plywood, 85 × 150 × 120cm approx. Courtesy of the artist, Tolarno and Roslyn Oxley9 Galleries. Photograph: Graham Baring.

so much about 'the mother's humanity, but the 'animalness' in us' (Piccinini, 2003).

Kristeva argues that the abject plays a crucial role in the creation of meaning, the establishment of the whole and proper self and the functioning of human society. This is because the abject is that which threatens meaning. The abject 'draws me toward the place where meaning collapses' and as such is perversely alluring but in the end it must be 'radically excluded' (Kristeva, 1982: 2) in order to enable proper functioning of self and society. The abject is slippery in that it 'does not respect borders, positions, rules.' It signifies 'the in-between, the ambiguous, the composite' (4). The notion of the 'in-between' is central to many works by female artists who encounter themselves as abject and animal. In her essay, Kristeva acknowledges her debt to Bataille and his writings on abjection particularly the ambiguous nature of the abjection – its relationship to prohibition, its power to attract yet also repel. Bataille links abjection to 'the inability to assume with sufficient strength the imperative act of excluding' (Kristeva, 1982: 64). The attraction of the so-called abject animal, and all it signifies, is overwhelming, finding expression through a play with ambiguity as in Emily Burns' paintings of deer-headed women, Julie Heffernan's flora and fauna self portraits and Julie Rrap's photographic works such as *Camouflage #3 (Elizabeth)*, 2000.

Burns' *Deer Girl* (2013) series of paintings depict a woman's body, usually positioned in a self-conscious and sensual pose, wearing the head of a deer with large antlers. The latter suggest a once-powerful buck rather than a female deer as the only female that grows antlers is the reindeer or caribou. Burns' painting blends the two together artlessly. The vibrant pose of the woman helps to bring the head of the deer alive thus creating a symbiotic alliance between woman and buck that endows her with animal powers. What the woman and animal share in common is that both are conventionally trophy animals – but not so in Burns' works. Here the deer looks out of the frame at the viewer, its gaze is direct and self-assured. In donning the head of the deer, the woman takes on the animal's intelligence, emotions and desires, suggesting a seamless alliance between the two. The merging of woman and animal seems to take place naturally and the hybrid figure assumes a strange quality of beauty. The deer girl of these works is an uncanny sexualised figure whose image suggests an uncanny metamorphosis beyond rational understanding.

Julie Rrap's series of photographs that blend together woman (Rrap herself) and animal are similarly surreal, ambiguous and abject. In *Camouflage (Elizabeth)* (2000), Rrap reveals a woman wearing hunting gear, jodhpurs and red coat, but instead of hands and feet she possesses hooves. The woman stands with one arm resting on a lattice board, her face turned towards the viewer. There is no suggestion that she is uncomfortable with her two sets of hooves. Although she stands upright the temptation is to imagine her galloping on her equine limbs. The portrait of Elizabeth asks us to consider whether or not the woman is still in the process of evolving or whether she has achieved her evolutionary destiny. Is she human or human/animal? Central to the surreal portraits of Burns and Rrap is the woman's body, which unlike the male body is malleable, animalistic, and capable of changing shape and giving birth to the other. It is the so-called abject nature of woman's body that makes these surreal and confronting works of art possible in the first place.

According to Kristeva the most abject thing of all is the corpse. The corpse signifies 'the most sickening of wastes, is a border that has encroached upon everything. It is no longer I who expel. "I" is expelled' (Kristeva, 1982: 3–4). The possibility of reducing or transforming a body with form into matter without form, a state of formlessness, produces a powerful and uncanny form of abjection. According to Kristeva, the subject is drawn to the abject, that which is taboo, such as the corpse, but in the end must exclude the abject in order to secure the integrity of the self and the proper functioning of society. In discussing the abject nature of the human corpse, Kristeva refers also to the equally abject nature of the animal corpse. 'Impure animals become even more impure once they are dead (*Leviticus* 11: 24–40), contact with their carcasses must be avoided' (118). The dead animal reminds the human of its own abject and borderless future. In recent years a number of contemporary female artists have been exploring animal death in their artistic practice. Yet these artists do not exclude the animal, even the dead animal, as abject – rather they approach the animal with respect, even tenderness, exploring its significance for their own shared identities with the animal. If anything unites the approach of these artists it is that each one engaged empathetically with the bodies of the animals that will become a part of their artistic works.

In her decomposition prints such as *Female Eastern Grey Kangaroo* (2009) Vanessa Barbay places the animal's body on to a canvas, which she covers with plastic until it has decomposed. Barbay then uses the kangaroo's physical impression as a basis for the artwork. Using earth pigments she paints the bones back into the shape of the animal's decomposed body. Barbay writes that 'I evoked the maggots by stitching amid the remaining fur and stains'. To Barbay the disintegrated form of the kangaroo is not in any way abject, as defined by Kristeva, but represents a 'sublime beauty'. Barbay refers to this as the 'shroud process'. *Female Eastern Grey Kangaroo* reminds the viewer of her/his own mortality and the evolutionary cycle of death, decomposition and rebirth through the earth. By using a variety of materials (stains, fur, bone, earth pigments) Barbay's compositions are grounded in the natural world. Barbay's shroud art-works include a series of animals such as *(Harefield) Summer Hare* (2013), *Foxground (Autumn Fox)* (2013), and *Lamb of God* (2011–12). In a sense the animal is an active agent in Barbay's re-creation of its decomposing form because the animal's own form, and sometimes its fur or bones, dictate the shape and texture of the painting.

Marian Drew, a photographic artist, pays tribute to animal death, and the beauty of animals, through her *Australiana/Still Life* series (2003–9). Drew's animals have died as a result of human environmental intrusion – loss of habitat, introduced predators or a collision with a car. Drew arranges their bodies with meticulous care, usually on a white tablecloth alongside objects such as fruit, a serviette, or lighted candle. In *Kingfisher with Fancy Work* (2009) the body of a brilliant blue bird with a black head and white chest lies on an embroidered cloth beside two ripe, red strawberries. The bird and fruit lie along the bottom of the frame, thus unsettling the line of vision. Drew pays particular attention to the way she arranges light to fall on her still life compositions so as to create an eerie almost uncanny sense of stillness. In *Bandicoot with Quince* (2005) the body of a small animal lies on its back with its head facing the viewer and its paws raised to reveal its white furry underbelly, the impression is one of vulnerability combined with a strange serenity. A yellow quince lies on the white cloth alongside the bandicoot. In the almost empty background the silhouette of a tree and dark horizon rhymes visually with dark clouds gathering overhead. Drew writes of her work:

> By imitating the historic painted forms of the 'Still Life', but replacing paint with photographic verisimilitude, and familiar European animals with Australian native species, a discord is exposed. This work aims to overlay the historical and the present, the European with the antipodean and photography with painting, while exploring contemporary notions of death and a changing relationship to animals. (Drew, 2012)

Although dead, the animals are strangely and uncannily beautiful.

Janet Laurence similarly explores the idea of transformation through animal death, taxidermy and the extinction of species in her multimedia installations. To achieve her goal she has worked in the depths of natural history museums studying inventories and living and extinct species. In her exhibition *Muses* (2000) she presented glass cases filled with carefully arranged bodies of birds, decontextualised, but with their identification tags attached to their feet. The overall effect is one of human cruelty and needless loss of life – the inevitable price of the human compulsion to attempt to control death through the imposition of systems, order and control. Although the animal bodies signify abjection, they nonetheless appear strangely beautiful, almost sculptural in their stillness. In their own private encounters with dead animals, none of these artists shy away from the abject nature of death *per se,* but rather pay tribute to the way in which animal death reminds us of the passage of life and the evolutionary fate of all creatures – human and animal.

Georges Bataille's *informe*

Theorists such as Yve-Alain Bois and Rosalind Krauss argue that Kristeva's theory of abjection is grounded too heavily in images of the body and bodily wastes (Krauss et al., 1994). They also level the same criticism at much abject art of the 1980s, which they see as focusing on images at the expense of form. They contend that Bataille's notion of formlessness offers a more radical strategy than abjection with which to undermine meaning. Bataille defines *informe* as 'a term that serves to bring things down in the world'. Bataille's definition of *L'informe* (1929) appeared in the 'Critical Dictionary' section of *Documents,* an art magazine which ran from 1929–1930, and which he co-edited. Bataille's aim was to overturn all forms of hierarchy – social, political, artistic, moral. It is worth quoting in full:

> A dictionary begins when it no longer gives the meaning of words, but their tasks. Thus formless is not only an adjective having a given meaning, but a term that serves to bring things down in the world, generally requiring that each thing have its form. What it designates has no rights in any sense and gets itself

> squashed everywhere, like a spider or an earthworm. In fact, for academic men to be happy, the universe would have to take shape. All of philosophy has no other goal: it is a matter of giving a frock coat to what is, a mathematical frock coat. On the other hand, affirming that the universe resembles nothing and is only formless amounts to saying that the universe is something like a spider or spit. (Bataille, 1985: 31)

Bataille's examples of *informe* are all gathered from the most vulnerable end of the creaturely world, such as earthworms, spiders – anything that can be squashed or rendered formless. In this context, abjection is arguably aligned with lowly creatures, woman and her abject body, a body that disturbs its own boundaries, undermining form, while the 'frock coat' shouldered the male philosopher. The concept of things that can be 'squashed' disturb the nature of signification in relation to the symbolic body and formation of human identity. Rosalind Krauss defines *informe* in this way:

> I take the *informe* to be structural. I take it to be a way for Bataille to group a variety of strategies for knocking form off its pedestal. The word coins the notion of a job, a process; it is not merely a way to characterize bodily substances so that the formerly disprivileged becomes the privileged – as is the case now with art that invokes 'abjection'. That seems a childish move, one Bataille wouldn't support. But the permission to make such a move is there, deep in the heart of Kristeva's project, because her whole effort seems to be about returning to the referent. (Krauss, 1994: 4)

Arguably, Kristeva's approach is more sophisticated than Krauss allows. Both Bataille and Kristeva draw metaphorically on the animal body to explore the collapse of boundaries in relation to things, which in Bataille's discussion oppose form, and in Kristeva's theory disrupt boundaries and subjectivity. Whereas both writers are concerned with traversing of boundaries, Bataille is more interested in that which is operational, which 'serves to bring things down in the world'. The animal or insect as represented in the art works discussed above, has this potential. In anthropomorphic discourse, the animal is not so much a subject in its own right, but a representation of abjection designed to produce its imaginary opposite – the 'human'. Female artists undertaking their journey into the night, represent themselves and the animal as a way of undoing form. This may help to explain why a number of contemporary artists who represent animals focus on the dead (the utmost form of abjection in Kristeva's view) and the decaying, stuffed, formless and 'squashed' bodies of non-human creatures who in Bataille's words have 'no rights' but who nonetheless threaten the frock coats. In discussing de Kooning's series of paintings entitled *Women*, which she found 'savage, explosive, funny', Kristeva raised the question of what it might mean if a woman has painted these. 'But what if they had been created by a woman? Obviously she would have had to deal with her own mother, and therefore with herself, which is a lot less funny' (Kristeva, 1986: 297–298).

Artist and sculptor Louise Bourgeois turns to her own mother, exploring the form of the spider in her *Maman* series. Here she reacts against the patriarchal abjection of the spider and its association with woman as witch through her creation of a sculptural form that cannot be squashed. Bourgeois created an amazing series of spider sculptures, entitled *Maman* ('Mummy'). *Maman* (1999; Figure 5), which stands over four metres, is a steel and marble sculpture which stands in sharp contrast to Bataille's notion of the creature as 'squashed' and rendered formless. Yet the potential to be squashed is firmly present in the sculpture's design. *Maman* plays on both the power and fragility of spiders through focus on its enormous body, which is held aloft on its eight long spindly and delicate legs. The sculpture is so large it can only be installed in a very large building or outdoors. Bourgeois, whose work is intensely autobiographical, has said that the spider sculpture with its connotations of spinning and nurturing refers to the endurance and protectiveness of her mother who ran the family business of tapestry restoration. 'The spiders were an ode to my mother. She was a tapestry woman and, like a spider, was a weaver. She protected me and was my best friend' (Bourgeois, 2007). Traditionally spiders are associated with witches and other abject places and creatures. Spiders quietly invade human domains, crossing boundaries established between nature and culture. Bourgeois uses its form, its long hairy legs and black body and egg sac (sculpted high enough for people to walk underneath) both to repel yet entice. The hanging egg sac is filled with seventeen marble eggs nestled inside a wire mesh sac that allows viewers to see them hovering above their heads. *Maman* is defiantly female and aggressively abject. Here the artist has taken one of Bataille's lowly creatures, capable of being squashed, and transformed it into its opposite – a gigantic abject creature that signifies both Kristeva's concept of abjection in the threat it offers to symbolic boundaries and Bataille's notion of *informe* in relation to its perceived form and potential for formlessness. Artists interested in the border between abjection, woman and animal, such as Bourgeois, use their art to make it clear that the symbolic body cannot erase the traces of it debt to nature.

The journey of the female artist into the abject world of the reproductive body, human and animal, is essentially different from that of the male artist whose fertility does not align him with a loss of form or formlessness. Although women, and animals, are more likely to find themselves squashed in Bataille's world of academic men and frock coats, it is the lowly but metamorphosing and transformative nature of their bodies and lives that in the end offers resilience, resistance and a degree of hope.

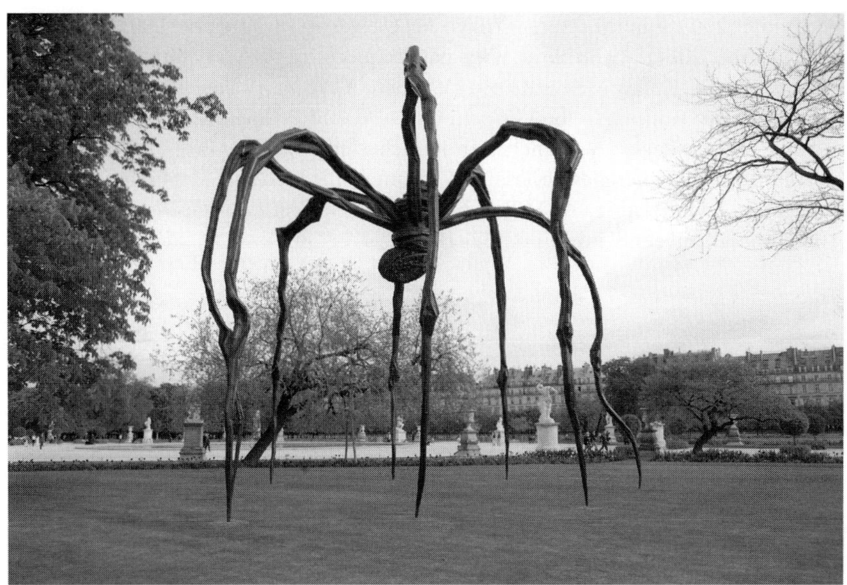

5 Louise Bourgeois, *Maman*, 1999. The 9.1m steel spider is the largest of a series of spider sculptures by Louise Bourgeois. It has travelled to various cities and is seen here in Paris on a spring morning. Courtesy of the Art Archive / Manuel Cohen. Photograph by Manuel Cohen.

References

Barbay, V. In My Eyes. [Accessed 28 October 2014]. Available at: http://drss.anu.edu.au/inmyeyes/Barbay.php.

Bataille, G. 1985. Formless. In Stoekl, A. ed. *Visions of Excess, Selected Writings*, 1927–1939. Trans. A. Stoekl with C. R. Lovett and D. M. Leslie. Minneapolis: University of Minnesota Press, p. 31.

Bourgeois, L. 2007. My Art is a Form of Restoration. Interview with Rachel Cooke. *Observer*. [Accessed 28 October 2014]. Available at: www.theguardian.com/artanddesign/2007/oct/14/art4.

Drew, Marian. HSC Visual Art Resources. 2012. [Accessed 28 October 2014]. Available at: http://hscvisualartresources.wordpress.com/2012/07/29/marian-drew/.

Krauss, R., Foster, H., Buchloh, B., Bois, Y-A., Hollier, D. and Molesworth, H. 1994. The Politics of the Signifier 11: A Conversation on the *Informe* and the Abject. *October* 67, pp. 3–21.

Kristeva, J. 1982 [1980]. *Powers of Horror: An Essay on Abjection*. Trans. L. S. Roudiez. New York: Columbia University Press.

Kristeva, J. 1986. A New Type of Intellectual: The Dissident. In Moi, T. ed. *The Kristeva Reader*. New York: Columbia University Press, pp. 292–300.

Oliver, K. 2009. *Animal Lessons: How They Teach Us To Be Human*, New York: Columbia University Press.

Piccinini, P. 2003. Public Lecture – Tokyo Art University, 8 December 2003. [Accessed 28 October 2014]. Available at: www.patriciapiccinini.net/essay.php?id=27.

Pollock, G. 1996. Killing Men and Dying Women: A Woman's Touch in the Cold Zone of American Painting in the 1950s. In Orton, F. and Pollock, G. eds. *Avant-Gardes and Partisans Reviewed.* Manchester: Manchester University Press, pp. 219–294.

Stanton, D. 1986. Difference on Trial: A Critique of the Maternal Metaphor in Cixous, Irigaray, and Kristeva. In Miller, N. K. ed. *The Poetics of Gender.* New York: Columbia University Press, pp. 157–182.

6

The fragmented body as an index of abjection

Rina Arya

In this essay I want to explore abjection in the work of Hans Bellmer and Francis Bacon, and will begin by providing an overview of abjection as it relates to the fragmented body. Abjection is a theoretical concept and 'a pervasive cultural code' (Arya, 2014: 2) that addresses boundary crossings between the subject and the source of threat. In Julia Kristeva's account of abjection in *Powers of Horror* (1982) abjection is staved off by a practice that involves safeguarding the boundary of the self (or system in question) and ensuring that the subject is not under threat. If the boundary is transgressed however, then this leads to an experience of abjection, thus necessitating the reinstatement of the boundary again in order to maintain order. Hal Foster identifies this dual aspect of abjection which involves two distinct senses and operations – *to abject* and *to be abject*; while the operation (of abjection) seeks to stabilise, the condition (of the abject) is inherently disruptive, meaning that there is a constant tension between drives (Foster, 1996a: 114, italics added). The need for the boundary arises in order to keep the subject away from the potential source of disruption. Ordinarily that which is other to the subject can be objectified and distanced from the subject, thereby not posing a threat to its subjectivity. In cases of abjection, however, the source cannot be objectified and it threatens the subject with engulfment and dissolution. This is one of the unrelenting features of the abject as defined by Kristeva: it is not a subject nor is it an object but it displays features of both. It exists in between these two states, where it cannot be discretely separated from the subject (as an object would be) and where it lurks objectlike but without becoming an object. The non-object impresses on the subject's stability and hovers 'at the boundary of what is itself assimilable, thinkable …' (Kristeva, 1982: 18) but is itself unassimilable, which means that we have to contemplate its otherness in its proximity to us but without it being able to be incorporated.

The boundary outlines the edges of the structure or system, which may refer to something particular and concrete such as one's body or self, or an organisation, institution or society, and is responsible for protecting the system from rupture. Threats to the boundary come in different forms and are divided into those that come from outside (external) and those that are issued from within (internal), each bringing about a state of abjection. As danger increases in magnitude or draws near, fear mounts and the possibility of dissolution or collapse becomes more pressing. The abject 'does not respect borders, positions, rules' (Kristeva, 1982: 4) and for this reason '[t]hat which threatens identity must be jettisoned from the borders and placed outside' (Oliver, 2003: 47). And while it does not respect the boundary, abjection does not cut itself off from it, and brings about its reinforcement, thereby conveying the proximity of transgression and the taboo (Jenks, 2003: 2).

The body is the most ubiquitous symbolic system of societal drives, and bodily rituals are devised in order to maintain its workings. Mary Douglas (1970) argues how the physical body is socially mediated, and in its unrelenting materiality it is also 'the primary site of the *abject*' (Foster, 1996b: 149).[1] Various theorists, such as Lyotard, Deleuze, Irigaray and Kristeva have demonstrated ways in which the body is managed and controlled by the individual, society and the state. There has been a general trend since medievalism to curtail the anarchism of the body and to 'civilise' human identity as part of the project of modernism. Metaphorically, the body went from being open and collective to being closed and individualised. This did not eradicate the need for Dionysian expression, where individual identity dissolved into the collective but these moments were marginalised in mundane life. But even in the closed body metaphor, boundaries are under threat of contamination from normal organic processes.

The leaking body

In the non-fragmented, whole body, boundaries are situated between the points of exchange between inner and outer, where the point is to ensure that there are no visible traces of the natural body. Kristeva states that '[t]he body must bear no trace of its debt to nature: it must be clean and proper in order to be fully symbolic' (1982: 102). The discomfort that the natural body with its seepages and flows continues to instill in our socialised and cultural understanding of the body conveys the conflict between our organic bodies, which operate according to the laws of nature, and our desired cultural projections of the body. Colin McGinn reinforces the revulsion that we have at our irreducible physicality and the practices that we undertake to cleanse the body:

> The living body is a rich repository – a factory – of dischargeable disgust materials. On a daily, even hourly, basis we must manage and contain the polluting substances generated by our own organic existence, as the body leaks and expels its natural products. The body spews forth its organic materials, what it needs to flourish and survive – and meanwhile we recoil. These vital substances are the objects of our steady revulsion, biologically necessary as they are. Semen, say, without which human life is impossible, is regarded with distaste, or even outright disgust – as if there were something *wrong* with the stuff. Why should we be revolted by something so harmless and so vital to life? Isn't semen something to savor and celebrate? Much the same can be said of menstrual blood, another source of intense taboo and revulsion. We seem as disgusted by the body in the full flight of life, squeezing and pumping, as we are by its quiet dissolution in death. (McGinn, 2011: 19)

Our paradoxical attitude to the body is apparent in McGinn's account – we despise the body when it is at its most vital but also in the complete absence of life. McGinn contends that we are divided between ourselves where we applaud and celebrate the aspects of human life that reveal our sophistication as a species and yet are metaphorically uncomfortable in our own skins. He is here building on Ernest Becker's dualistic notion of the physical and symbolic worlds as expounded in *The Denial of Death* where the latter claims that we construct a symbolic world of meaning which is self-sustaining, as a way to counteract the physical world of death (Becker, 2011). McGinn states that we cannot accept the materiality of the body in its limits and mortality, although it is precisely the body that makes possible all the achievements that we want to celebrate. This is one of the great ironies of human life. In its natural state the organic body cannot be trusted to remain intact and whole and is instead prone to secretion, excretion, breakdown, decay and ultimately death. In spite of the continual turbulence of the body and the routines and rituals that we undertake to keep ourselves freed from its outpourings, which include the labours of washing, dressing and grooming, we feel repelled by the forces of our corporeal roots. Kristeva outlines the relentlessness of bodily regimes: the body 'extricates itself' from 'the border of my condition as a living being' and 'Such wastes drops so that I might live, until, from loss to loss, nothing remains in me and my entire body falls beyond the limit – *cadere*, cadaver' (Kristeva, 1982: 3). The corpse is the ultimate abject thing: the negation that is contained within the body and is its ultimate destiny. To recognise the death that lurks within and makes itself known in the process of life itself is 'to accept the rejection which is the abject' (Piper, 2003: 104).

In these accounts it is not the diseased body that is despised but the healthy and flowing body that is feared and scrutinised.[2] Its partial impermeability means that there is an exchange between inner and outer. Echoing Douglas, the body's boundaries need to be protected as they are constantly under threat. The places of greatest vulnerability are the orifices, some of which elicit the highest level of disgust and, ironically, since they are also erogenous zones, also the greatest level of desire. Bodily waste products, from the most odorous and offensive to our sensibilities (for example excrement) to the less indecorous (for instance nail clippings), threaten the inviolability of the body's boundaries but also help establish the boundary itself as well as thus reinforcing the distinction between internal and external. These traces of abjection are both 'me', and 'not me', and threaten the stability of the bodily boundaries and the sense of self. Ritualistic practices involving health and hygiene are used to maintain a sense of the social propriety of the body and to prevent it from becoming seen in terms of its animalism, which is the primal fear at the root of body-abjection.

In the relatively recent literature on disgust, much has been discussed about bodily fluids as indicators and components of the instability of the body. Bodily wastes, especially those of others, represent danger because they are boundless and are seen as carriers of dirt and infection. They remind us of our animality – the fact that we are decaying and that once life has been taken away our bodies will putrefy. For this reason they, particularly sexual fluids such as semen and menstrual blood, are the subject of taboos. The mere sight of these substances makes us contemplate the insides of our bodies, a journey which starts with the specific fluid, continues with disease and illness and ends with death.[3] Bodily fluids cannot be homogenised in their 'disgust quotient' as certain fluids may cause a greater sense of unease because of their liability to be controlled and their polluting properties – mucus is more acrid and ghastly to think about than tears, which is largely because the clearness and odourlessness of tears can be translated into poetic terms, and seen as purifying without being polluting. But the overriding feature is the out-of-placeness; in the body they are essential to normal physiological functioning but outside of the body they signal something else, often carrying the threat of disease and vulnerability. In fact even by 'issuing forth' from the orifice, bodily fluids 'have traversed the boundary of the body' (Douglas, 2002: 150). As Kristeva remarked when speaking about a corpse, within the desired and prescribed parameters, the meaning can be controlled but outside of it, it takes hold of us – 'seen without God and outside of science, [it] is the utmost of abjection' (Kristeva, 1982: 4). Being neither human nor non-human, the corpse epitomises the horror that abjection gives rise to. Its ambiguous status and creeping putrefaction means that as living subjects we need to escape from its treachery, which we do in the form of appropriate funerary rituals, either by burial or cremation.

Outside of the body, bodily fluids, and indeed any other body parts cannot be wholly separated from us, and are reminders of our inability to extricate ourselves from our organic being. As discussed earlier, we cannot view these fluids and substances dispassionately or treat them as we would objects.

Elizabeth Grosz remarks that '[n]o part of the body is divested of all psychical interest without severe psychical repercussions' and that '[t]here is still something of the subject bound up with them'; they are abject and inspire disgust and desire (Grosz, 1994: 81). When thinking about the level of disgust there is also a positive correlation between the amount of bodily fluid generated and the degree of pollution caused. Consider the following experiment by Gordon Allport, where he examines how, once across a boundary, bodily fluid becomes alien and foreign to us:

> Think first of swallowing the saliva in your mouth, or do so. Then imagine expectorating it into a tumbler and drinking it! What seemed natural and 'mine' suddenly becomes disgusting and alien. Or picture yourself sucking blood from a prick in your finger; then imagine sucking blood from a bandage around your finger! What I perceive as separate from my body becomes, in the twinkling of an eye, cold and foreign. (Allport, 1955: 43, in Miller, 1997: 97)

It becomes apparent that disgust increases with increased activity of expectoration so that as more and more spit is expelled into the tumbler, the proposition of drinking it becomes increasingly uninviting. This is because as the volume increases so does the mounting threat of abjection – we fear that our insides are being turned out.

Unbounded: the fragmented body

In the ordered body, abjection occurs at its margins, which corresponds to points of the greatest vulnerability, and the body is regulated accordingly. Abjection is harder to establish in the case where the body is fragmented and does not conform to being an organically ordered and functioning body. How are we to think about the boundary when it is not clear where the body starts or ends? This essay considers this situation with a study of the fragmented bodies of Hans Bellmer and Francis Bacon.[4]

In the twentieth century, visual artists (including performing artists) started to experiment with the metaphor of the body by breaking it up into fragments or parts which were assembled together in various ways that provoked questions about identity and representation. In his Cubist and Surrealist phases, and particularly in his paintings of figures on beaches executed in 1927 and 1928 in Cannes and Dinard, Picasso distorted the human form. Olivier Berggruen identifies two strategies of experimentalism: 'one is predominantly anatomical, in which different parts of the body are given an unusual prominence, without compromising the verisimilitude of the anatomical model. Another, more radical one features the notion of "assemblages" in which different body parts are taken out of context and reassembled in a seemingly random way' (Berggruen, 2003: 76).

The grotesque was a visual strategy and aesthetic that enabled the body to be reconfigured in interesting and inventive ways, where the normal structure of the human form became the site of experimentation and exaggeration, threatening the stability of form. It became used to challenge notions of classical beauty by describing images and entities that exhibited the following characteristics: the combination of incongruous parts, the decomposition of reality, the metamorphosis from one reality into another and the disproportionality of form. In the combination of different parts or transformation from one into another, the grotesque, like abjection, involved disrespecting the boundary and was 'defined by what it does to boundaries, transgressing, merging, overflowing, destabilizing them…' (Connelly, 2003: 4). This contrasts with the beautiful which maintains clear and discrete boundaries (Burke, in Connelly, 2003: 4). The grotesque invited new idioms of the body, which involved reconfiguring the body from inside out in its abject and base state. Georges Bataille's concept of base materialism was highly influential among artists who wanted to distort the innate tranquility of representations of the nude that had persisted throughout centuries of Western art. Base materialism involved reconfiguring the human body away from that which is 'external and foreign to ideal human aspirations' (Bataille, 1985: 51) and towards the brute and irreducible materialism of the anarchic body in its baseness. This body ruptured the representation of dualism in which the body had been relegated to a subordinate position in relation to the mind and involved a leveling out of the human with the animal. Base materialism also involved depicting the realism of the body which entailed recognising that the body was not an external static representation but was instead prone to breakdown, fragmentation and dissolution, where the body-part was used to explore questions of identity, sexuality and death. In its fragmented state, 'lacking its customary wholeness and unity', the body tested our own sense of stability. 'This [was] not the healthy normal body, intact and functioning, but the body as damaged and sundered; it accordingly prompt[ed] the shudder we feel when the body is otherwise falling to pieces' (McGinn, 2011: 16). Two artists that took fragmentation to its extreme are Bellmer and Bacon. In each case the body was not depicted as whole and complete but was instead defined in terms of its highly charged fragments.

Bellmer's fragmented dolls

Hans Bellmer is best known for his constructions of life-size pubescent female dolls – *Die Puppe* – that were dismembered and distorted in various ways and then photographed. Influenced by the realistic life-size doll Olympia in Jacques Offenbach's final opera *The Tales of Hoffmann* (1881), Bellmer constructed his first doll in 1933, which consisted of a moulded torso, a masklike head and a pair of legs. A few years later (in 1935) he made a second doll, which was less naturalistic, more deformed but also more mobile. He kept the head from the first doll and then added four legs, four breasts, three pelvises, an upper torso and a spherical belly (Taylor, 2000: 73). These various body parts were used interchangeably in assemblages and the movable ball joints at different points across the body meant that Bellmer could be inventive and increase the grotesqueness of the doll as well as explore the 'fluidity between internal and external properties' (Semff and Spira, 2006: 10). Bellmer stated how he wanted to 'construct an artificial girl with anatomical possibilities which are capable of re-creating the heights of passion, even of inventing new desires' (Green, 2005: 16).

Although the dolls themselves are sculptures, they were always only presented to us through the medium of photography. This enabled Bellmer to control the context in which they are set but also the perspective from which they are seen. Bellmer relays the misadventures of the doll to the viewer via photography. There are a number of photographs featuring two pairs of legs arranged around the belly, where one pair evokes the presence of the young girl/doll, if only because of the presence of black patent Mary Jane shoes; provoking the disturbing question regarding the identity of the other pair, and conveying the defenceless nature of the doll without arms, a point made by Sue Taylor (2000: 32). In spite of the numerous parts, a sense of wholeness is not achieved and the dolls are disarticulated, in a state of mutant and insectoid metamorphosis, which is exaggerated by the doubling up of limbs. Hal Foster comments on how Bellmer 'manipulates the [dolls] excessively [and] photograph[s them] in different positions, [where] each new version is a "construction *as* dismemberment" that simultaneously signifies castration (in the disconnection of body parts) and its fetishistic defense (in the multiplication of these parts as phallic substitutes)' (Foster, 1991: 87).

Bellmer stages elaborate backdrops for his photographs of the dolls, which include deserted locations in woods, suspended from a ceiling, draped on a bed, or in a forest with Bellmer emerging from behind a tree. All these scenes are deeply disturbing and convey the sinister, paedophilic and violent quality of his images, that are suggestive of rape scenes.[5] In other examples Bellmer reduces the doll to a series of stumps, which look like bulbous and tumorous growths. He also adjoined random body parts in incongruous combinations, which adds to the ambivalence of the body as we do not know how to read them. In addition to the photographs of the dolls, Bellmer was also an accomplished draughtsman and produced a number of drawings, etchings and books, all of which were part of his 'quest for a "monstrous dictionary" dedicated to the ambivalence of the body' (Semff and Spira, 2006: 10). His work can be explained by a lifelong motivation to liberate himself from the dictates of 'adult' behaviour and from certain constraining powers in his life, such as his overpowering father and prevailing fascist ideals (Taylor, 2000: 4–5)[6] as well as an overwhelming need to express one's instincts and explore his perverted misogyny. The doll has been interpreted in various ways: as an alter ego, a fetish, and a transitional object 'that protects the artist from an overwhelmingly terrifying maternal imago' (Taylor, 2000: 6). Couched in terms of abjection, his work can be read as a re-enactment of maternal abjection where we are surrounded by bulbous maternal forms – a breast, a spherical belly – that we loathe but cannot annihilate. Like Bataille he was also directly parodying the classical tradition of the nude, and fashions instead an aberrant and corrupt materiality. Whilst Bellmer's work was regarded as degenerate and antithetical to the ideals of human strength and power in Nazi Germany, his ideology was in sympathy with the Surrealist spirit of exploring irrational desires and the incongruous pairing of different realities, a feature that originated with the tradition of the grotesque.

Bellmer was intrigued by the gifts of childhood including imagination and play and wanted to recreate them as 'a pre-Oedipal moment before castration' (Foster, 1991: 87) but, through the eyes of a grown man, his images instead conjure up psychosexual disturbance and the nightmarish. His erotomania, which was directed at pubescent dolls, would be regarded by many as distasteful, as was his need to articulate polymorphous perversity. Bellmer corrupts the innocence of childhood toys with the existential fear of death. The crisis of subjectivity articulated in his dolls was actualised in world events in the collapse of Western civilisation in the rise of fascism.

Bacon's bodies without organs

Francis Bacon too was interested in exploring the expressive possibilities of the body. His representations of bodies blur boundaries in multitudinous ways resulting in various states of fragmentation and distortion where the body is featured as unstable and anarchic. The boundaries between outer and inner are in tension, as conveyed by the relationship between the structure of the body and the matter, where they are often pulled in opposing directions, which contributes to the effect of torsion (or twisting). Visually this is conveyed by smears and smudges that are wiped across the body. Michel Leiris (1988: 13) uses the term 'liquefaction' to refer to this process of turbulence, which many of Bacon's figures are subject to, and which results in overspill, where the inner contents flow into the foreground, causing confusion as to whether we look at the external or internal, a fact compounded by the overspilled material being more opaque than the boundaries of the body. In *Portrait of John Edwards* (1988) we are left questioning where the body begins and ends as the toes of Edwards dissolve to form a pool on the floor that flows to the chair leg, thus doubling up as the shadow of the chair. The 'indefinable form of the figures in some cases, seems to lose their bone structure to become strange fluxes or whorls of matter in fusion' (Leiris, 1988: 11).

Another boundary that is blurred in Bacon's figures is that between the human and animal. Bacon merged them in order to explore the extremes of human psychology and as a further comment about the godless state of the world.[7] He was familiar with Bataille's writings and would have encountered the spirit of base materialism presented in the latter's journal *Documents*. During experiences of extreme pain and suffering, the human is reduced to the position of the animal to express its torment. This often takes the form of a cry or scream, expressions that can be found in the three biomorphic and Picasso-inspired forms in *Three Studies for Figures at the Base of a Crucifixion* (c.1944). Dawn Ades observes how the figure in the central panel, bearing gritted teeth, and the figure in the right-hand panel, with its open mouth, vent frustration and rage that seems to stem from their inverted positions in the genital region. The displacement of mouth or teeth to the genital area contributes to the bestiality of the imagery (Ades, 1985: 16). By merging the human and animal in these forms, Bacon conveys the desperate nature of these creatures and uses these figures to represent the dysfunctional nature of humanity. Their bestial outlets provide channels for the ravening appetites of the figures, which are insatiable and destructive. One of the reasons that these three figures caused such uproar when first put on show, and still continue to shock even today, is that, in spite of their resemblance to the human form, they are still de facto fragments and not whole bodies, which is enhanced by their placement on podiums. Another example, *Fragment of a Crucifixion* (1950) displays similar tendencies. We are faced with a form that is organic and deeply suggestive of the body without being an actual body part. In the 1970s and 1980s, Bacon did a number of figure studies that focus on the fragment as body part. *Triptych – Studies of the Human Body* (1970) consists of three undifferentiated bulbous figures on a rail that resemble the fragmented sculptural forms of Hans Bellmer . *Diptych: Study of the Human Body – From a Drawing by Ingres* (1982–84) consists of two fragments that are like trunks sprouting body parts – hands and legs that are strapped with cricket pads in the 'male figure', and breasts and legs for the 'female figure'. Not all the fragments are recognisable parts of the body. But what they do in all cases is to evoke the physicality of their part. In their fleshy colour palette and mass they resemble what Armin Zweite describes as 'the flatlands of shapeless matter' (Zweite, 2006: 9), or, to use a Deleuzian phrase, 'a mass of ambulating flesh' (Deleuze, 2003: 24).

In his study on Bacon, Deleuze describes the Baconian body as a body without organs (Deleuze, 2003: 44–45). The body without organs, a term coined by Antonin Artaud in his radio play, *To Have Done With the Judgement of God* (1947), does not, within this context, mean that the body is literally without organs but rather that the structure of organs is irregular, chaotic even, and, following on from that, that the organs do not operate functionally. This renders the body more malleable and prone to dissolution. In fact, the force of his figures causes them to want to exit their bodies through any available aperture or orifice, whether through the mouth or the anus. The spasmodic or paroxysmal potential of the body often manifests itself as a force that cannot be contained and where the body attempts to escape through one of its polyvalent orifices into the outside world. In *Figure at a Washbasin* (1976), the figure clings 'to the oval of the washbasin, its hands clutching the faucets, the body-Figure exerts an intense motionless effort upon itself in order to escape down the blackness of the drain' (Deleuze, 2003: 15). In some examples, such as *Portrait of John Edwards* discussed earlier, the body exits the human form via a different point, such as through the left foot. The bodies of the dolls of Bellmer also operate dysfunctionally in that there are 'various body schemes in which various body parts are valorised, doubled or multiplied by others, or elided' (Green, 2005: 23) like the two pairs of adjoining legs.

Bacon's idiosyncratic representation of the body is a reaction against the conventions of narrative representation that were governed by figuration, which he believed distracted from the aesthetic properties of artworks. In a figurative portrayal the viewer's immediate identification of the form, for example, may detract from (or minimise the effect of) paying close attention to the power of the aesthetic. Bacon's figures are instead *figural*, which in its Deleuzian sense refers to a form that pertains to the figurative (but does not resemble it) and is also abstract.[8] Bacon uses distortion to bring about the *figural*, which involves abstracting from the figure and distorting the figurative appearance of the photograph that he works from in the process of image-making. He approached the human body via the flesh rather than the external figurative form. In his explorations, the body was prone to dissolution, fragmentation and distortion, and he conveyed in powerful terms what it feels like to *be* a body rather than simply *having* a body.

Abjection and the fragmented body

The body fragment takes many forms in Bellmer and Bacon. In some instances the body is featured as an assemblage of disparate parts that do not form a seamless whole, and where the parts are interchangeable. In other cases one fragment stands for the whole body, drawing attention to its sentience. Fragmenting the body renders it unstable and vulnerable, both for the viewer, who is uncertain how to read it as it subverts conventional understanding, and also because it takes on an indeterminate form with ambiguous boundaries. Bellmer and Bacon employ fragmentation for different ends, which can be couched in general terms as their assault on the hierarchy of the organic human body. Bellmer's doll was built primarily as a plaything, companion and symbol of revolt against castration.[9] The numerous configurations that the dolls are photographed in conveys the range of movement and expression. In the hands of a young child, the doll replete with satin hair bows and other accessories would be viewed innocently, and as in child's play, the doll is dismantled and distorted. These associations become sinister in the knowledge that the doll is created and owned by a grown man who forbade public access to his inventions except through the screen of photography. The distortions of the doll now are seen as attempts to increase arousal and perverse fantasy. Bacon drew on fragmentation as his strategy of realism. His aesthetic idiom challenged established practices of representing the external body. Bacon turns the body inside-out thus giving the viewer access to a heightened sensory experience. As well as being inside-out the body is also fragmented, and this fits in with his desire to dismantle the artificial represented body and to show the lived body which is in motion.

Their fragmented bodies can also be discussed within the discourse of abjection. Kristeva defines the maternal body as the first abject object that the infant must reject before it can become a subject in the Symbolic order. This necessitates the imposition of boundaries that denote clearly differentiated limits and render one's body 'clean' and bounded. The subject must disavow part of itself in order to gain a stable self, and this form of refusal marks whatever identity it acquires as provisional, and open to breakdown and instability' (Grosz, 1990: 86). Such a body corresponds to the social norm for what is permissible in 'civilised' society. The perpetual need to rid ourselves of our corporeal traces is part of the unspoken agreement that exists between socialised adults; this explains the paradoxical nature of the duality of glory and shame that McGinn identified as the strange position of humanity that, on the one hand, can celebrate its achievements whilst, on the other hand, is disgusted by its origins. By being unable to delineate the boundaries of the body, both Bellmer's and Bacon's representations of boundaries remain in the pre-Symbolic state of being, where they are incomplete subjects that are trapped in various states of narcissism and psychosis that is symptomatic of the impulses of the Kristevan semiotic. Their inability to stand apart as autonomous subjects reflects on the viewer who experiences dislocation in viewing (see van Alphen, 1992). The violence is carried out at one remove from the spectator; in Bellmer the distortions to the doll's body, which include horrific amputations and dismemberments, where women are 'reduced to stumps' (Green, 2005: 23) occurs behind the scenes, and the effects are mediated to us via the slickness of photographic (and pornographic) documentation. Violence in Bacon is not actual, in the sense of the actual violence of bodies, but is created in the struggle of aesthetic depiction, 'a violence that is involved only with line and colour: the violence of a sensation … a violence of reaction and expression (Deleuze, 2003: x).

Civilisation is a campaign against abjection. Although we may take great pains to avoid abjection by purifying it and safeguarding boundaries, it dominates a large part of our existence on an individual and societal level. Kristeva's claims for it are profound: it is foundational to both the production and maintenance of society: '[f]or abjection, when all is said and done, is the other facet of religious, moral, and ideological codes on which rest the sleep of individuals and the breathing spells of societies' (Kristeva, 1982: 209). In an interview with David Sylvester, Bacon declares as one of his aims the desire to look behind the veneer that he claims society operates under and to expose the instinctual sensibilities that we are governed by, and which justify his ideological formula that places the human on the same level as an animal, neatly conveyed in his phrase 'we are meat', 'we are potential carcasses' (Sylvester, 1993: 64). Continuing in this vein he wanted to 'unlock the valves of feeling' to bring about a more violent and immediate perception of reality (7). This sensibility is also apparent in Bellmer. In his experimental work with his dolls he sought to tap into the 'body's unconscious representations' (Green, 2005: 7) in order to 'help people lose their complexes, to come to terms with their instincts' (Taylor, 2000: 3).

Notes

1 Douglas does not actually use the term 'abject' in her analyses but describes what it is.

2 Disease and illness also bring the body's stability into question, which causes fear and distrust of the body. In today's Western culture ageing has also become loathsome and people take great pains to slow down the process in various ways.

3 According to Kristeva menstrual blood provokes disgust because it is a further reminder of the archaic mother who has been made abject. This is witnessed in the numerous rites particularly in pre-modern religions about menstruation.

4 Many of the ideas discussed in this essay have also been explored in *Abjection and Representation*; see Arya, 2014.

5 Peter Webb picks out the 1935 photograph of the second doll with two sets of legs, one set belonging to a young girl crossed coyly on a bed, and the other set belonging to a man dressed in trousers with his flies open as being an 'intimation of rape' (Webb and Short, 1985: 70).

6 Therese Lichtenstein viewed the construction of the dolls as a virulent attack on National Socialism and its promotion of an idealised race (Lichtenstein, 1991: v). Bellmer's cultivation of the abject in the form of the orifice-laden body that invited the overflow of impurities undermined the totalised and fascistic body.

7 Matthew Gale and Chris Stephens argue that: 'In a world without God, humans are no different to any other animal, subject to the same innate urges; transient

and alone, they are victims and perpetrators of meaningless acts'. They suggest that the godless world provides the theoretical context in the 1940s for what can be described as Bacon's animalistic humanoid figures, where there is a melding between human and animal forms (Gale and Stephens, 2008: 27). The context can be expanded here to encompass Bacon's worldview. In a godless world the human is levelled with the beast, and the hierarchy separating the two is suspended. See also Rina Arya's *Francis Bacon: Painting in a Godless World*, 2012, for an extensive discussion about this subject.

8 Deleuze adopted the term 'figural' from Jean-François Lyotard's *Discourse, Figure* (1971). See J-F. Lyotard, *Discourse, Figure*, trans. A. Hudek, M. Lydon, Minneapolis: University of Minnesota Press, 2011 [1971].

9 Sue Taylor claims it is also an instance of Donald Kuspit's category of 'the modern fetish' (Taylor, 2000: 58).

References

Ades, D. 1985. Web of Images. In Ades, D. and Forge, A. eds. *Francis Bacon*. Exhibition catalogue. London: Tate Gallery and Thames and Hudson, pp. 8–23.

Arya, R. 2012. *Francis Bacon: Painting in a Godless World*. Farnham: Lund Humphries.

Arya, R. 2014. *Abjection and Representation: An Exploration of Abjection in the Visual Arts, Film and Literature*. Basingstoke: Palgrave.

Bataille, G. 1985. *Visions of Excess: Selected Writings, 1927–1939*. Ed. A. Stoekl. Trans A. Stoekl with Lovitt, C. R. and Leslie, D. M. Jr (trans.) Minneapolis: University of Minnesota Press.

Becker, E. 2011 [1973]. *The Denial of Death*. London: Souvenir Press.

Berggruen, O. 2003. Picasso and Bacon: Painting the Other Self. In Seipel, W., Steffen, B. and C. Vitali. eds. *Francis Bacon and the Tradition of Art*, Exhibition catalogue. Milan: Kunsthistorisches, Skira Editore, pp. 71–83.

Connelly, F. S. 2003. *Moden Art and the Grotesque*. Cambridge: Cambridge University Press.

Deleuze, G. 2003. *Francis Bacon: The Logic of Sensation*. Trans. D. W. Smith. New York: Continuum.

Douglas, M. 2002 [1966] *Purity and Danger: An Analysis of Concepts of Pollution and Taboo*. London: Routledge.

Douglas, M. 2003 [1970]. *Natural Symbols: Explorations in Cosmology*. Abingdon, Oxon: Routledge.

Foster, H. 1991. High/Low Art: *Art and Mass Culture. October* 56, pp. 64–97.

Foster, H. 1996a. Obscene, Abject, Traumatic. *October* 78, pp. 106–124.

Foster, H. 1996b. *The Return of the Real: The Avant-Garde at the End of the Century*. Cambridge, MA: MIT Press.

Gale, M. and Stephen, C. eds. 2008. *Francis Bacon*. London: Tate.

Green, M. 2005. *The Doll*. Trans. M. Green. London: Atlas Press.

Grosz, E. 1990. The Body of Signification. In Fletcher, J. and Benjamin, A. eds. *Abjection, Melancholia, and Love: The Work of Julia Kristeva*. London: Routledge, pp. 80–103.

Grosz, E. 1994. *Volatile Bodies: Towards a Corporeal Feminism*. Bloomington, IN: Indiana University Press.

Jenks, C. 2003. *Transgression*. London: Routledge.

Kristeva, J. 1982 [1980]. *Powers of Horror: An Essay on Abjection*. Trans. L. S. Roudiez. New York: Columbia University Press.

Leiris, M. 1988. *Francis Bacon: Full Face and in Profile*. Trans. J. Weightman. London: Thames and Hudson.

Lichtenstein, T. 1991. The Psychological and Political Implications of Hans Bellmer's Dolls in the Cultural and Social Context of Germany and France in the 1930s. PhD thesis, City University of New York.

Lyotard, J-F. 2011 [1971]. *Discourse, Figure*. Trans. A. Hudek and M. Lydon. Minneapolis: University of Minnesota Press.

McGinn, C. 2011. *The Meaning of Disgust*. New York: Oxford University Press.

Miller, W. I. 1997. *The Anatomy of Disgust*. Cambridge, MA: Harvard University Press.

Oliver, K. 2003. The Crisis of Meaning. In Lechte, J. and Zournazi, M. eds. *The Kristeva Critical Reader*. Edinburgh: Edinburgh University Press, pp. 36–54.

Piper, K. 2003. The Signifying Corpse: Re-Reading Kristeva on Marguerite Duras. In Lechte, J. and Zournazi, M. eds. *The Kristeva Critical Reader*. Edinburgh: Edinburgh University Press, pp. 98–112.

Semff, M. and Spira, A. eds. 2006. *Hans Bellmer*. Ostfildern: Hatje Cantz Verlag.

Sylvester, D. 1993. *Interviews with Francis Bacon: The Brutality of Fact*. London: Thames and Hudson.

Taylor, S. 2000. *Hans Bellmer: The Anatomy of Anxiety*. Cambridge, MA: MIT Press.

Van Alphen, E. 1992. *Francis Bacon and the Loss of Self*. London: Reaktion Books.

Webb, P. and Short, R. 1985. *Hans Bellmer*. London: Quartet Books.

Zweite, A. 2006. Foreword. In Zweite, A. ed. in collaboration with Maria Müller. *Francis Bacon: The Violence of the Real*. London: Thames and Hudson, pp. 9–27.

7

Skin, body, self: the question of the abject in the work of Francis Bacon

Ernst van Alphen

Based on a common sense understanding of the abject and of abject art – which I will complicate later – the paintings of Francis Bacon can easily be understood as abject. The effect of the abject on the viewer is usually seen as discomfort, repulsion or even nausea. This is an aesthetic judgment. To many viewers Bacon's work is repulsive or frightening, which could imply that his paintings are abject. His works have, however, other characteristics, themselves of an aesthetic nature, that complicate such a judgment. To begin with, his paintings always have a vertical format, and the figures in his paintings are usually represented vertically; they are standing or sitting. This vertical format mirrors the viewer's own bodily dimension. It functions as a Gestalt, 'a whole body from the outlines of which nothing is missing' (Krauss, 1997: 240). This counters a consideration of Bacon's work as abject. But, of course, and in support of the position that his work is abject, it is precisely the wholeness of Bacon's figures that is under siege. His figures are losing their contours; it is as if their bodies dissolve into the space that surrounds them.

Other elements support these paintings and their figures to function as perfect Gestalt, however. Bacon was very outspoken about how he wanted his works to be shown. He wanted his paintings to be covered by glass. To hide paintings by glass is a kind of curse in the art world. It is only done in the case of extremely valuable paintings, which need to be protected, as required by the insurance. But Bacon thought that his paintings looked best when they were covered by glass. The glass in front of the painting tends to mirror the viewer's body. It is as if the paintings' potential functioning as a Gestalt for the viewer is emphasised, or made easier. The viewer has difficulty seeing the painting as paint. The glass dissolves the materiality of paint and what can be recognised is only the represented figure and space. It is only after some effort, after the viewer has positioned herself at the right spot and angle, that she can look through the glass and see the skin of the figure as well as of the paint.

But this Gestalt effect, too, is reversed. It is the skin of the represented figure as well as of the paint that undermines, in turn, the functioning of Bacon's paintings as Gestalt. Whereas the spaces in which the figures are located are usually painted in flat, uniform paint, the figures are tooled and worked on. Bacon often used all kind of tools to belabour not the surface of the whole painting, but just that of the figures. As a result the skin of the paint as well as of the represented figure becomes ambiguous. The distinction between the two can no longer be made. The materialities of paint and of the represented body are undifferentiable. The fact that the boundary between matter and representation has been crossed produces yet again the affect of abjection.

So far, the works' leaning towards the abject, after all, is based on a somewhat simple notion of what abject is. In order to assess if Bacon's work is a prime example of the abject or not, we first have to understand what the abject entails more precisely. Julia Kristeva's notion of the abject developed in her book *Powers of Horror: An Essay on Abjection* has been the most influential, so I will discuss hers (Kristeva, 1982). The abject is what the subject-in-becoming must get rid of in order to become an I. According to Kristeva the protection of the boundaries of the body is the main function of abjection. The anxieties triggered by the abject are first of all anxieties resulting from the end-products and by-products of the body, such as body fluids, blood, urine and fecal matter. What defines these end- or by-products of the body is that they are neither subject nor object. They embody the transition between the body and what is outside it. Although we treat them as objects outside of us, they were once inside or part of our body but we got rid of them. And while we distance ourselves from these bodily discharges they remain a constant threat to a consistent body identity. It is through socialisation that we learn to mark the boundaries of our self. By removing waste and creating a clean, obedient body we safeguard these boundaries. This happens at the cost of, or thanks to, abjection.

According to Kristeva, abjection can be traced back to the first rejection, that is, to the separation from the mother helping her baby to establish him/herself in the symbolic order. Abjection preserves some of that pre-objectal relationship and some of the ambivalence that is experienced by the subject when it becomes an independent body separated from the mother. Kristeva's psychological notion of the abject has, however, social ramifications and has been developed further into a theory of abjection. Abjection, no longer referring to an ambiguous object but to a process or activity, refers to cultural mechanisms that exclude certain groups of people or individuals by stigmatising them with loathing. Xenophobia is usually fuelled by abjection. But not only foreigners, also other marginalised groups within a society are often considered to be ugly, dirty or frightening, which evoke aversive responses in the rest of that society. Homophobia, racism, sexism and ageism are also structured by the mechanism of abjection. Subjects react to the abject with repulsion and loathing in order to restore the border separating self and other. The other is 'abjected' from the self, because the abject is seen as not respecting borders, rules and positions of a society. These abject others are not only abjected by means of exclusionary mechanisms but they are simultaneously needed and produced by societies. This is so because subjects are formed by the exclusion of what they are not. In the words of Judith Butler: 'the subject is constituted through the force of exclusion and abjection, one which produces a constitutive outside to the subject, an abjected outside, which is after all, "inside" the subject as its own founding repudiation' (Butler, 1993: 3).

This short account of the abject and abjection reveals a slippage between the condition to be abject and the operation of abjection, in other words, to abject. In Hal Foster's words: 'To abject is to expel, to separate; to be abject, on the other hand is to be repulsive, stuck, subject enough only to feel this subjecthood at risk' (Foster, 1996: 156). This distinction makes clear that the work of Francis Bacon has little to do with abjection, even though it can possibly be understood in terms of the condition of being abject. For, it is clear that the figures in his paintings demonstrate subjecthood at risk. Bacon is then representing figures from the experience of having no boundaries, that is, from the position of being abject.

Especially in the 1980s and 1990s, not long after Bacon had become one of the most prominent international artists, the abject became an important notion in the understanding of contemporary artworks. Foster has argued that abject art of those days has tended in two directions:

> The first is to identify with the abject, to approach it somehow – to probe the wound of trauma, to touch the obscene object-gaze of the real. The second is to represent the condition of abjection in order to provoke its operation – to catch abjection in the act, to make it reflexive, even repellent in its own right. (Foster, 1996: 157)

An example of the second direction is the work of Andres Serrano, whose *Piss Christ* (1987) represents the condition of abjection, provoking evangelical senators like Jesse Helms to complete the work of abjection negatively. The first direction, identification with the abject, has developed, according to Foster, a division of labour according to gender. Artists who probe the maternal body repressed by the paternal law tend to be women. Examples are Kiki Smith, Maureen Connor, Rona Pondick and Cindy Sherman (after her turn to the grotesque in the mid-1980s). Artists who assume an infantilist position to mock the paternal law tend to be men. Examples include Mike Kelley, John

Miller and Paul McCarthy (Foster, 1996: 159). In spite of this difference, the art objects of both female and male artists embody the abject and the feelings raised by the abject such as loathing or disgust. Those feelings are imposed on the viewer.

Francis Bacon is not part of this generation of artists from the 1980s and 1990s obsessed with the abject and abjection. And, although some viewers consider his works as horrifying and repulsive, it is not so evident that the feelings raised by the abject are imposed on Bacon's viewers. In the introduction to my argument I pointed out how Bacon's work functions in some respects as Gestalt of and for viewers, which opposes the possibility that abject feelings are imposed on them. Perhaps we should make a more precise distinction between horrifying and repulsive: the fact that the tormented look of many of Bacon's figures can be horrifying does not imply that they are repulsive in the way the abject can be. If the viewer is horrified by his figures, this affect is not the result of the sight of something abject, but rather of identification with figures who experience themselves as abject, in the sense that their subjectivities are at risk. For the viewer, Bacon's figures are not an abjected outside, or abjected others, but they represent an abjected condition viewers can identity with. This identification is stimulated, rather than undermined, by their Gestalt form.

This is a problematic statement because identification is in many ways the opposite of horror or repulsion. How is it possible that the viewer will identify with figures who look horrifying or repulsive; in other words, what kind of sinister case of identification is this? What is the point of identifying with figures that seem to lose their self and whose subjectivities are in the process of dissolution? This identification is not only remarkable in its target, but is also qualitatively different from the common understanding of identification. But as Kaja Silverman has argued, identification takes one of two forms (Silverman, 1996). One form involves taking the other into the self on the basis of a (projected) likeness, so that the other 'becomes' or 'becomes like' the self. Features that are similar are enhanced in the process; features that remain irreducibly other are cast aside or ignored. Silverman calls this idiopathic identification. The other form is heteropathic. Here, the self doing the identification takes the risk of – temporarily and partially – 'becoming' (like) the other. This is both exciting and risky, enriching and dangerous, but at any rate, affectively powerful. This distinction can help to get more clarity about the relation between Bacon's paintings and the abject. When the viewer of Bacon's work identifies with figures that experience themselves as abject, the kind of identification that is at stake is heteropathic identification. The viewer takes the risk of temporarily and partially putting her or his subjectivity at risk.

If the viewer of Bacon's paintings identifies (or not) with figures from the position or experience of being abjected and as a result having no clear boundaries, we must assess how this dissolution of boundaries in Bacon's paintings is realised. As remarked earlier, this dissolution concerns the skin of the represented figures as well as of the paint. In the former case we remain within the representational domain: it is as if the figures dissolve or fall apart within the represented space that surrounds them. In the latter case the materiality of the paint and that of the represented body become nondifferentiable. The boundary between matter and representation is being blurred, or crossed. A good example of such boundary crossing can be found in the triptych *Three Studies for a Portrait of John Edwards* (1984). As the title announces, we see Bacon's friend John Edwards on each panel, sitting on a stool, but from different angles: the left hand panel from the right, the middle panel frontally, and the right hand panel from the left. The space in which Edwards is located is ambiguous: it can be an empty room, but the curved edge between wall and floor also suggests that it is open space. The curved line is then an allusion to the horizon of an open landscape. The space in which the three figures are represented is painted in thin paint, covering the canvas with homogeneous colour fields.

The figures are in sharp contrast with the space that surrounds them, especially their faces. The three figures are not just representations. We notice how they are built, constituted by paint, hence, matter. The paint is sometimes wiped or whisked away. This belabouring of the paint does not result in a representational illusion. It does not transform the paint into representation; the paint remains matter. The skin of the face of all three figures is covered with regular stripes, usually pink but also in dark grey, almost black. These stripes look like footprints, the sole consisting of a striped pattern. The patterned surface of the figures' skin can also be the result of a kitchen tool used for the treatment of meat. Whatever the tool has been that Bacon has used for making this striped pattern on the face of the three figures, the pattern never crosses the border of matter to representation. It remains paint.

This example demonstrates the importance of skin in Bacon's work. Bacon's notion of skin is grounded in a phenomenological and psychoanalytical view of skin, although not limited to such a view. I invoke this view to complicate the standard conception of abjection. French psychoanalyst Didier Anzieu explains this view in his book *The Skin Ego: A Psychoanalytic Approach of The Self* (1989). According to Anzieu the skin serves the purposes of containment, protection and communication:

> The primary function of the skin is as the sac which contains and retains inside it the goodness and fullness accumulating there through feeding, care, the bathing in words. Its second function is as the interface which marks the boundary with the outside and keeps that outside out; it is the barrier which protects against penetration by the aggression and greed emanating from others, whether people

> or objects. Finally, the third function – which the skin shares with the mouth and which it performs at least as often – is as a site and a primary means of communication with others, of establishing signifying relations; it is moreover, an 'inscribing surface' for the marks left by those others. (Anzieu, 1989: 40)

Anzieu is not speaking of the physical properties of the skin but of the metaphoric qualities of flesh. His concept of 'skin ego' articulates this beautifully. By 'Skin Ego', Anzieu explains, 'I mean a mental image of which the Ego of the child makes use during the early phases of its development to represent itself as an Ego containing psychic contents, on the basis of its experience of the surface of the body' (Anzieu, 1989: 40). The skin's functions of containment, protection and communication are the result of a dual process of interiorisation. Two spatial aspects of the skin need to be internalised. First of all, the subject needs to internalise the interface between the bodies of the child and the mothering figure (what Anzieu calls the 'psychic envelope'), and second, the mothering environment itself with all its verbal, visual, and emotional properties. Anzieu articulates this concept of skin ego and this dual interface by means of the somewhat odd word combination 'the goodness and fullness accumulating there through feeding, care, the bathing in words'.

Clearly, this psychoanalytic notion of skin is closely related to Kristeva's psychoanalytic notion of the abject. They presuppose each other. The skin's functions of containment and protection can only be realised by means of exclusion and abjection of that which threatens the safety of this bodily and psychic envelope. This view of a psychoanalyst can surely not be unproblematically brought to bear on works of art. But to the extent that it represents a philosophical conception as well, it can be brought into dialogue with art. And that is exactly what happens here, so that Bacon, not Anzieu or Kristeva, complicates the notion of abjection. I contend that Bacon's work engages a dialogue with this rich conception of skin. The artist's work 'on the skin' seems to propose a notion of the subject, which is not 'contained' to use Anzieu's term, nor does it need abjection in order to establish its borders. The condition of the abject is not seen as repulsive, but as a mechanism that is needed for maintaining 'open borders' between self and (abjected) other.

This assessment implies a paradoxical re-evaluation of the abject. When the skin is not the body's envelope, then skin and body can no longer adequately be distinguished from each other. Body and skin permeate and sink into each other. This seems to be the condition of most of Bacon's figures. Elsewhere, I have explained the relationship between body and self of Bacon's figures by the difference between the form in which a human subject experiences her or his body and the way it is perceived by others.[1] Simply stated, one does not see oneself as one is seen by others. While others see the subject's body as object and as whole, the subject has only inner experiences or fragmented views of her or his body. This view complicates Kristeva's notion of the abject. Within her theory body and self are seen as self-sufficient. She does not take the visual dimension of existence into account. Instead, by means of the mechanism of abjection the subject is itself able to maintain and safeguard its wholeness and borders. In this alternative view, inspired by the ideas of Mikhail Bakhtin and Roland Barthes, the relationship between self and other is a new element, and so is its visual dimension. As Bakhtin writes:

> The body is not something self-sufficient: it needs *the other*, needs his recognition and form-giving activity. Only the inner body (the body experienced as heavy) is given to a human being himself; the other's outer body is not given but *set as a task*: I must actively produce it. (Bakhtin, 1990: 51)

Others create an external shape and form for the string of inner sensations of self: they create a perception of the body as 'whole'.

If we look at Bacon's images in light of this understanding of the self/other relationship, it becomes immediately clear that the subjects/figures in Bacon's paintings are all represented as trapped in a solely inner sensation of self. Again and again we see bodies as series of fragments, dangling on the string of the inner sensation of self. Bacon's subjects seem to lack the wholeness the self-other relationship would produce. This lack is particularly strongly foregrounded in *Three Studies for Portraits including Self-Portrait, 1969*. While in most cases the fragmented bodies are clearly distinguishable from the space that encircles them, in the three panels of this triptych it is not exactly clear where the body ends. The faces are fragmented in such a way that we cannot decide whether the formless appendices belong to the subjects' faces or not. Even in the middle and left panel, in which the appendices are directly contiguous with their faces, differentiating the subject from its context is not easy. Subject and non-subject become one visual field constructed upon contiguity, making it impossible to speak of a subject or self.

Similarly, although in a less radical manner, the faces in *Studies of George Dyer and Isabel Rawsthorne, 1970* are not clearly delineated. This painting, belonging to the genre of the diptych that Bacon practised less frequently, shows two figures facing each other. Bacon makes here ironic use of a genre in which husband and wife, facing each other, are traditionally represented to preserve for posterity the identity of the bourgeois couple in early capitalist Europe. While in the conventional couple each partner derives his or her identity from the allegiance to the figure they face, in Bacon's diptych the visual relationship is not defining but undoing the characters. Facing each other with blind eyes, these figures seem to lose their boundaries from the confrontation. Dyer's face is extended by a strange pointed element that seems to be reaching toward Rawsthorne; she, on the other hand, displays one of the characteristic substantial shadows, characteristic because occurring in

Bacon's work almost systematically.[2] Here, again, Bacon's representation of the inner experience of self ends up deconstructing the idea of self: if there is only an inner-self there is in fact no self at all.

If we try to describe these two examples of Bacon's work in light of the abject and abjection, the only way is then to contend that Bacon has represented the figures from the position of being abject, from the experience of having no boundaries. The question is then if we should consider this as a negative or a positive experience. The conventional idea of the abject would suggest it to be negative, because subjectivity depends on boundaries, distinctions and differences. I will argue, however, that Bacon's figures do not suffer from their loss or lack of self. Their abject condition is privileged above the wholeness of a contained self.

In order to make this argument I will first provide another dimension to Bakhtin's account of self-other relationship by adding the one of Roland Barthes. In the case of Barthes self-other relationships are not seen as form-bestowing, as in Bakhtin's account of these relations, but rather as the cause of the loss of self. At first sight Barthes' view of the self-other relationship is very similar to the early Bakhtinian position.[3] In both accounts the subject's experience of self is determined by the position of her body in the world and by the very limited perspective she has on her body. In both stories about the creation of self the other has a strong hold over the subject through her ability to represent the body of the subject, an ability the subject herself lacks. While in Bakhtin's account, however, this relationship of dependence on the other is sweet, loving and desirable, in Barthes' account the subject is sentenced to this dependence.

In *Roland Barthes par Roland Barthes* (notice, in this title, Barthes' effort not to be defined, represented by the other: par Roland Barthes) he expresses the pain of this dependence: 'You are the only one who can never see yourself except as an image …: even and especially for your body, you are condemned to the repertoire of its images' (Barthes, 1975: 82). In *Camera Lucida* he even describes the dependence on the form-bestowing relation with the other as mortifying: 'I feel that the photograph creates my body or mortifies it, according to its caprice' (Barthes, 1982: 11).

In Barthes' view the objectification of the subject is not the work of another individual subject. For him the other is discursive. The objectification of the subject that bestows on her or him the experience of wholeness is a discursive transformation that translates the subject into the terms of the *doxa*, the already-said, the platitudes of public opinion (Jefferson, 1989: 170). The dependence on the other to achieve wholeness is unbearable for Barthes, because

> it is through the other that the subject falls prey to a representation that constructs him in terms of the stereotype. The Barthesian subject is alienated not

> merely by becoming an image in the eyes of the other but through this assimilation into the *doxa*. (Jefferson, 1989: 170)

There is no longer a question of a loving and shaping self-other relationships, but of a grim conflict between discourses.

The only thing the subject can do in order to fight the mortifying images of the doxa is to try to undo the objectification and mortification of the self through the practice of writing or representing. But the assertion of an alternative discourse that would be her or his own is impossible because the subject cannot avoid using the elements of the discourse which preceded it to build up a 'private' one. Even behind a very particular style or discourse, developed by the subject itself, the doxa will be lurking. Only the practice of representation as an ongoing bodily activity with no special object as its goal besides this movement, succeeds in destabilising the objectifying transformations of the other, of discourse: 'In this practice the body's relationship to language is altered from being the object of its representation to becoming the support and condition of a certain linguistic activity' (Jefferson, 1989: 170).

Instead of allowing the doxa to objectify the body, Barthes proposes to keep the body in a movement that asserts its resistance against, even if through the use of, the doxa. This movement re-subjectifies the body, thus escaping total colonisation through full awareness of the dependence on the discourses of the other.

Barthes' account of the self–other relationship as a conflict between discourses makes it possible to reconsider Bacon's paintings as so many efforts to unsettle representations of the self (of the body) that mortify any experience of the self. In his interviews with David Sylvester Bacon's incessant emphasis on the need for distortion in order to represent the 'real' appearance of somebody can be understood as a fight against stereotypical representations of the body:

> FB: What I want to do is to distort the thing far beyond the appearance, but in the distortion to bring it back to a recording of the appearance.
> DS: Are you saying that painting is almost a way of bringing somebody back, that the process of painting is almost like the process of recalling?
> FB: I am saying it. And I think that the methods by which this is done are so artificial that the model before you, in my case, inhibits the artificiality by which this thing can be brought back. (Sylvester, 1987: 40)

It seems that Bacon wants to represent the self of a subject without the mediating, form-bestowing role of the perspective that the other, here meaning discourse, offers.

His remarks about the effect on the viewers he strives for, and very incessantly too, shows that he aims for the opposite of an objectifying discourse:

'It's an attempt to bring the figurative thing up onto the nervous system more violently and more poignantly' (Sylvester, 1987: 12).

His paintings try to avoid offering the objectifying, healing effect that makes the onlooker's self feel whole; instead his images should evoke a violent, *direct* response in the onlooker.

The gaze of the other, represented, embodied in the image, is not allowed by Bacon to offer an image of the subject's self as whole. The presented image should cling to the fragmentation and shatteredness that the subject previously knows as inner-self experience. By calling on the nervous system, Bacon tries *to fragment again* the experience of self in order to 're-call', 'bring back' the real 'appearance' of a subject. And that real appearance is the condition that people have called abject because it is lacking in boundaries. And like Serrano who provokes evangelical senators like Jesse Helms to complete the work of abjection negatively, Bacon provokes his viewer to complete the mechanism of the abject. He re-shatters the viewer's sense of self by refusing to offer the projections of whole bodies that enable the onlooker to experience her- or himself as whole.

This refusal manifests itself, of course, literally by representing bodies *as* clearly fragmented. Bacon's recurrent subject matter of disfigured people like the paralytic child or the dwarf, can, however, also be understood in this light. The strange posture of the paralytic child in *Paralytic Child Walking on All Fours (From Muybridge)* (1961) has a very uncanny effect. It is as if his limbs do not fit his body. Bacon's choice for this subject could be explained by arguing that the paralytic child is already fragmented by nature. There is in fact no need to fragment this body by representation. The short legs and big head of the dwarf in *Portrait of a Dwarf* (1975) make up a body which is already not 'whole.' The shortness of his legs is even emphasised by his being depicted as sitting on a barstool. His limbs do not 'fit' together, so the body remains fragmented. At the same time there is no radical difference between the dwarf, the paralytic child, and the 'normal' figures in Bacon's paintings. All figures are fragmented as if they were dwarfs or paralytics. Every figure, deformed or not, is disfigured.

Bacon's position, then, appears highly ambivalent. On the one hand, he militates against the mortification of the subject by the objectifying force of the gaze of the other, folding the subject back on to itself and endorsing the resulting fragmentation as the inevitable consequence of this denial of the power of the other. His statements in the interviews emphasise this denial. This is the side of mortification, the price to pay for this autonomy undeniably present in the painted figures. Struggling his way out of the either/or mechanism of discourse, Bacon fights the domination of the other by drawing the other in. The viewer cannot resist the violently powerful figures whose wholeness is lost but whose presence is absolute. The endorsement of the loss of self bestows on these figures a power of absorption that accounts for the strong responses they solicit.

Notes

1 See the chapter 'Bodyscapes' in my book *Francis Bacon and The Loss of Self*, Cambridge MA: Reaktion Books, 1992.
2 For shadows in the work of Bacon, see the chapter 'Perception' in my book *Francis Bacon and the Loss of Self*.
3 Jefferson argues that Barthes' view is also strongly influenced by Sartre in this respect of self-other relations. He has, as she calls it, 'an undeniably Sartrian streak' (p. 153). This is made explicit by Barthes himself in his dedication of *Camera Lucida* as homage to Sartre's *L'Imaginaire*.

References

Anzieu, D. 1989. *The Skin Ego: A Psychoanalytic Approach of the Self*. Translated from the French by Chris Turner. New Haven: Yale University Press.

Bakhtin, M. 1990. Author and Hero in Aesthetic Activity. In Holquist, H. and Liapunov, V. eds. *Art and Answerability. Early Philosophical Essays by M. M. Bakhtin*. Austin: University of Texas Press, pp. 4–256.

Barthes, R. 1975. *Roland Barthes par Roland Barthes*. Paris: Éditions du Seuil.

Barthes, R. 1982. *Camera Lucida. Reflections on Photography*. London: Fontana.

Butler, J. 1993. *Bodies that Matter: On the Discursive Limits of Sex*. New York: Routledge.

Foster, H. 1996. *The Return of the Real. The Avant-Garde at the End of the Century*. Cambridge, MA: MIT Press.

Jefferson, A. 1989. Bodymatters: Self and Other in Bakhtin, Sartre and Barthes. In Hirschkop, K. and Shepherd, D. eds. *Bakhtin and Cultural Theory*. Manchester: Manchester University Press, pp. 201–228.

Krauss, R. 1997. The Destiny of the Informe. In Bois, Y-A. and Krauss, R. eds. *Formless: A User's Guide*. Cambridge, MA: MIT Press, pp. 235–252.

Kristeva, J. 1982 [1980]. *Powers of Horror. An Essay on Abjection*. Trans. L. S. Roudiez. New York: Columbia University Press.

Silverman, K. 1996. *The Threshold of the Visible World*. New York: Routledge.

Sylvester, D. 1987. *The Brutality of Fact: Interviews with Francis Bacon*. London: Thames and Hudson.

Van Alphen, E. 1992. *Francis Bacon and The Loss of Self*. Cambridge, MA: Reaktion Books.

8

Abjection, melancholia and ambiguity in the works of Catherine Bell

Estelle Barrett

This essay examines the work of several artists including that of Australian artist Catherine Bell. These seemingly different practices provide a framework for understanding Julia Kristeva's multi-layered conception of abjection. Moreover I will demonstrate how artistic practice can help to extend and re-articulate notions of abjection put forward by both Kristeva and Georges Bataille. I suggest that accounts by art commentators and historians that have generally remained within referential approaches to criticism have failed to grasp the critical implications of abjection for understanding aesthetic experience in both the making and viewing of art. This has been the result of a tendency to engage with the artwork, referentially and as a text to be read rather than as an encounter with an object engendering an experiential encounter that implicates both biological/material as well as cognitive processes. Bell's works to be considered here not only operate through the forces of attraction and repulsion that characterise abjection, but also articulate abjection as a more nuanced process that ambiguously positions the viewer as both a critical and distanced observer whilst at the same time evoking direct sensory, affective and empathetic engagement.

Previously I have discussed the way in which Bell's engagement with the scatological and criminality exerts affective forces that articulate the workings of abjection (Barrett, 2014). For example, the works for the *Making a Baby* series (2006) and the work *Waste Not Want Not* (2011) are multi-modal, in that whilst they may appear repugnant, they also invite 'collusion' by structuring the gaze so that it strays towards what is forbidden. Abjection is related to prohibition, because the demarcation or separation from objects that are forbidden, dangerous and unclean is founded upon it. In art, abjection can also turn on a desire to look even though we may be afraid or repelled and it is also in this sense, that abjection and art can be related to perversion. Kristeva tells us that abjection is also related to melancholia and that art can act as an assuaging of grief through a commemoration and partial recuperation of the lost object (Kristeva, 1989: 43). Indeed understanding grief as a bridge between melancholia and abjection helps to illuminate the more complex and ambiguous workings of abjection as process. In this essay I would like to explore the relationship between grief and abjection and demonstrate how abjection is also aligned laughter since the latter operates through the rupture and/or refusal of customary meaning.

In this essay, Bell's work will also be considered within the context of George Bataille's notion of a dualist materialism that presents bodily pleasure and sensation as the ultimate measure of good and evil. This mode of thought underpins literary genres that graphically explore issues such as incest, aberrant sexual practices, mutilation and other taboo behavior. Transgressive fiction is based on the premise that knowledge emerges from extreme or borderline experience and that the body operates as site for transgression and the expansion of human knowledge and experience. I want to suggest that commentators on abjection as it is elaborated by Bataille and Kristeva, including Rosalind Krauss and Hal Foster, have tended towards a literal or selective interpretation of Kristeva's work and have thus overlooked her accounts of more nuanced operations of abjection that would allow us to appreciate *how* abjection produces transgressive discourse and is also an *alteration* and expansion of language itself – therefore, also of thought. Bell's work operates in various ways as a visual counterpart to transgressive literary genres engaging with the disturbing subject matter to confront and explore grief and 'criminality' both within and outside the conventional socio-cultural domain. In order to provide a backdrop and framework for a further analysis of Bell's practice as an articulation of the functioning of abjection, I will first trace how Kristeva and Bataille's notions of abjection differ, and also look at some of the debates and misconceptions that have centered on abjection as it relates to art.

Abjection: Kristeva and Battaille

A fundamental difference between Bataille and Kristeva's thinking is that Kristeva views abjection as a 'primer of culture' (Kristeva, 1982: 2). In creative production, it operates at the crossroads of phobia, obsession and perversion. However, the abject as psychic figure is not excreted, 'vomited' or expelled, but occurs completely within being and the being of language as material process that does not end in solipsistic repetition or a decent into obscenity and perversion. Hence in Kristeva's theorisation, the subject of abjection is 'eminently productive of culture; its symptom is the rejection and reconstruction of languages' (Kristeva, 1982: 45). Kristeva's account of abjection goes beyond a concern for the socialising impetus of abjection to a revelation of the way in which, as a psychic process, it brings about alterations within subjectivity and extends symbolic competence. Her departure in this direction starts with an emphasis on the fragility of the law and its prohibitions as an effect of the beckoning force of the archaic mother or the body of the mother from which the child must separate in order to live. She argues that confrontation with the feminine is not a confrontation with a primeval essence, but with an unnameable other that can engender both fear and *jouissance*. This ambiguity is the basis for creative production in literature and art. It is what structures both the aesthetic image and the audience's affective responses in ways that rupture language and meaning and dissolves the split between subject and object. As Kristeva observes: 'The abject has only one quality of the object – that of being opposed to *I*' (Kristeva, 1982: 14). It simultaneously beseeches and pulverises the subject. All abjection is recognition of want on which, being, meaning, language and desire are founded. This is the basis for *jouissance* or ecstasy that attends the drive toward non-meaning. However, because want is preliminary to being and the object, the infant has a sense of the abject even before things *are* – and drives them out even before they are signifiable. What is abjected in this first separation, is the biological body of the mother as a means of resisting the death drive, a drive related to the tendency of matter or life to return to a state of entropy in which everything is the same. After entry into language, abjection as *process* takes hold when there is a failure of the capacity to identify with something outside that would constitute the subject as a separated entity. For the ego or subject who has entered language, brushing up against the unnameable thing collapses meaning; what is unnameable must therefore be excluded because it threatens the emergence of self. The fluctuation of forces of attraction and repulsion of abjection constitute negativity or 'expenditure' as productive material process. This is an indication of how the body acts as a filter for incoming stimuli through direct encounter of objects in the world, including language directly experienced as sensation. Thus abjection in Kristevan thinking has survival value – this, rather than undirected or chaotic drive towards death or insanity underpins aesthetic experience and the making and viewing of art. I will return to this in more detail with reference to Bell's work from the exhibition *The Gathering*.

Because abjection is an ambiguous border, it attracts even as it repels. Even whilst releasing hold on the subject's entry into language, it does not radically cut the subject off from what threatens it, but rather demarcates a space from which signs and objects arise. In this sense, abjection is an indication of our being alive in the world – a physiological and psychic functioning or responsiveness that allows us to make sense of our encounter/enfoldment in and with the world. This conception of abjection provides a means of accounting for revolution and change, both in terms of society, as well as within visual and verbal language *itself* as expansion of literary and artistic style. It is also crucial to understanding why certain examples of abject art are ambiguously disgusting, obscene or violent in terms of content – and yet give rise to a sense of beauty or the sacred.

Whilst acknowledging the liberating role of abjection and its capacity to bring forth the 'sacred' as stylistic invention or the revelation of truth, Bataille's conception is predominantly nihilistic: ultimately abjection produces only more of the same: a shattering of meaning and a return to nothing. Though there are some implied contradictions across his various writings, Bataille maintains the view that art does not produce anything of use to society, but rather, it transcends prohibitions by opening up on to a realm of sublimity and excess. Through art, or specifically through poetry, being escapes rationality by entering a heterogeneous realm. In *Literature and Evil* (1973) he states:

> The isolated being *loses himself* in something other than himself. What the 'other thing' represents is of no importance. It is still a reality that transcends the common limitations. So unlimited that it is not even a thing it is nothing. (Bataille 1973: 26)

Bataille's comment is at odds with his assertion in an earlier work, *Inner Experience* (1954), in which he suggests that something does emerge from Dionysian excess. Though non-knowledge gives rise to ecstasy or rapture, as soon as one emerges from it, the loss of self is arrested. 'I have ceased to abandon myself – I remain there but with new knowledge' (Bataille, 1988: 53). Notwithstanding this qualification, Bataille's opposition to all systems leads him to stop short of explaining how this 'knowledge' might be deployed and of positioning what is retrieved from loss of self within a social or cultural context. This slippage or erasure is characteristic of commentaries on so-called abject art, perhaps because the operation of abjection in the viewing of art creates multiple layers of signification that challenges any closure of interpretation. The effect of this is evident in discourses for example, of Rosalind Krauss and Jon-Ove Steihaug that have focused on Bataille's notion of abjection and the *informe* as a basis for interpretation.

Another crucial difference in the thinking of Bataille and Kristeva is related to their respective conceptions of the homogeneous and heterogeneous. For Bataille, writing as heterology emerges through a descent into brute materialism or animality – to base matter which is regarded as heterogeneous. By this Bataille is referring to the entropic nature of matter, whilst anything related to culture, society and systems of thought remains within the realm of the homogeneous. Fred Botting and Scott Wilson point out that this is so for Bataille, with the exception of beggars, vagabonds, warriors, lovers or poets who can exert a sovereign force and subversive potential by constituting the negation of the principal of utility, so refusing all subordination (Botting and Wilson,

2001: 57). Paradoxical and intrinsic to this position is the implication of a binary at work in a thinker who would refuse all binaries. Bataille's critique of social codes is above all, a critique of binaries that result in the dominance or privileging of one pole above the other. The issue here is that Bataille starts out with a conception of abjection that is linked to the notion of social abjection, that which is low and obscene; consequently there is a tendency in his work to view abjection referentially rather than as a process that is located within the subject and within language. This applies not only to an obsession with excrement, filth and the obscene, but also to members of *lumpenproletariat*, those belonging to the lowest social order that Bataille claims are abjected by bourgeois society as the excremental product of capitalist production (Hollier, 1989: 25). Although Kristeva acknowledges Bataille's illumination of abjection in terms of prohibition and as a way of conceiving the subject/object relation (Kristeva, 1982, 64), her account of the productive operation of abjection reveals a blind spot in Bataille's thinking by demonstrating that both the human subject as well as all systems of culture, including science and language, are ineluctably heterogeneous. In her thinking there is a sustained and more profound refusal of binaries since she views the subject, language and the body as inextricably enfolded and co-emergent.

Kristeva explains that abjection is a primary separation from the mother that instantiates psychic demarcations that remain throughout life as precursors of language; the fluctuating expenditure of energy and negativity that are founded on abjection constitute the semiotic or biological dimension of the subject and the materiality of language as it is heard and directly experienced – *as process*. The semiotic in verbal language is made up of articulatory or phonetic effects that shift the language system back towards the sensory and drive-governed basis of sound production. The choice and sequencing of words, repetition, particular combinations and sounds that operate independently of the communicative function of language also constitute the semiotic function, a function which has the capacity to multiply the possible meanings of an utterance or text – it is what constitutes the structuring of the aesthetic image as *style*. In visual language, the semiotic is made up of articulatory effects that shift the system back to the drive-governed basis of *visual* production. This functioning is related to sensations and affects evoked by colour, visual marks and formal elements that operate independently of figuration or the communicative and referential elements of images. Again, for Kristeva, both the human subject and all systems of language are heterogeneous.

Two important points should to be taken from this. The first is that, for language to have any meaning or effect on us at all, it has to be spoken and or 'heard' – it has to be put into *process*. Secondly, this putting-into-process of language must connect with our biological processes, affects and feelings in a vital way in order for language to take on particular meanings or to *affect* us.

Hence the *subject* and *practice* are crucial to Kristeva's account of language as material process. The 'by product' or 'fallout' of this process – renewal and recuperation of the subject or, in Deleuzian terms, re-territorialisation – is necessary for alteration of language and production of new codes that challenge established systems of thought. This expansion and revolution does not necessarily rely on encounters with what is commonly understood as the abject – filth, excrement, the obscene and so on – but is rather, a process that occurs in all forms of creative production as a result of negativity expenditure, an operation that is intensified through a striving to subvert, move beyond the limits of what is already given in an established system. Creative practice or 'performance' of language maintains the link between the semiotic and the symbolic, between language and our lived and situated experiences and thus it is a basis for subversion and resistance. The operation of the semiotic and by extrapolation, of abjection, is intensified in aesthetic experience whether it be in the making or viewing of art. As I have discussed in detail elsewhere (Barrett, 2011) this is fundamental to understanding how and why art is performative, and to appreciating the difference between abjection as process and abjection as abjection – that is as *representational* demarcation between what is considered as obscenity and filth as opposed to what can be assimilated by society. So why this obsession with the scatological and the obscene in Bataille's work that subsequently found its way in to so-called abject art?

Rosalind Krauss and Imogen Tyler suggest that the answer lies in understanding the operational function triggered by an encounter with the abject and they draw directly from Bataille's work to demonstrate this. For example Krauss suggests that it is the bringing together of the political and the psychosexual that produces a 'scandal of identification between two heterological untouchable elements, thereby unsettling the repressive forces that determine established meaning' (Krauss, 1996: 100). Here she is drawing on Bataille's idea that bringing together the very high and the very low – politics and anality/sadism (an indication of the binary operating again in Bataille) – leads into an inversion of the two and a collapse of the terms into a single couplet that unsettles or inverts the binary so that politics and anality/sadism occupy a level footing (Krauss 1996: 100). Krauss turns to the scatological works of Mike Kelley, such as *Arena #1* (1990) to further demonstrate, via Bataille, that abjection as an operational function comes about through transgression from beneath. That is to say, and according to the artist himself: contiguity with filth and the obscene causes a 'repression' of the high that triggers the 'jesuvian' process, a process that involves a reversal of attraction and repulsion and a confounding of the high and the low that collapses (customary) meaning. Krauss suggests that Kelley's earlier scatological works influenced the later production, *Lumpenrol* (1991), a floor installation that evokes optical ambiguity through formalist arrangement of volume, colour and line.

Kelley's first work presents abjection as abjection; it uses recognisable abject or 'degraded' objects, excrement and soft toys made by women in order to convey an ideological position. I suggest that the later work is primarily conceptually driven. Further, I suggest that this need not negate the *process* of abjection as a function in the making of the work. This functioning can be evoked again in the viewing of it, but the articulable subversion and conceptual innovations identified 'after the fact' are the 'fallout' of abjection as a process that is often triggered through discomforting encounters with abject objects or what is not assimilated within culture or its pre-established codes. Hence, I would argue that that the *informe* is the first phase of a movement or straying towards abjection. Abjection as process is not an object that can be seen or a meaning that is deciphered, for example, a squashed worm, a spider or spit (*pace* Bataille!), but is rather an experience of 'shock' and/or *jouissance* that is engendered by aesthetic experience in the making and viewing of art. I would go as far as to say the intensity of its effects is an indicator of innovation and the new. It is this aspect of abjection that fails to be clearly articulated in Bataille's account perhaps because of his primarily political/social focus as opposed to Kristeva's explication that is founded from psychoanalytical perspectives. Imogen Tyler's observations on Bataille's conception of abjection illustrate this distinction further.

Tyler explains that in order for a prohibition to function, it must be seen to be practised and experienced as disgusting, and it must also be continually transgressed (Tyler, 2014). Because society's disciplinary regimes of inclusion and exclusion produce sectors of society as 'waste' that cannot be fully expelled, this poses a threat to society from within. Waste populations are an inevitable product of dominant discourses that result in their *presence* and therefore inclusion. It is upon this paradoxical logic that Bataille sees the possibility of revolt. This aspect of Bataille's explication of abjection is thus rooted in the social and the political. The abject that is the site of poetry (and art) on the other hand, arises from inner experience of pure carnality and excess; it returns the subject to a heterogeneous world where there is an absence of limitations, and (paradoxically) the realm of the sacred, 'all that is sacred is poetic and all that is poetic is sacred' (Bataille, 1973:18). Bataille's unproductive expenditure is not a celebration of recovery of plenitude, but is an imperative that arises out of insufficiency as the basis of life. Unlike Kristeva, Bataille elevates poetry and art precisely because, like Dionysian excess they serve no utilitarian or instrumental purpose. For Kristeva on the other hand art is not merely an internal and momentary recovery of plenitude (of the subject) but is a means of realising it anew through creative production that also has potential for revolution or change in culture.

In an essay entitled 'Violence and Representation in the Works of George Bataille and Michel Leiris' Peter Poiana (2013) draws on Michel Leiris to question the notion of raw unadulterated experience derived from the force of carnality or physical drives. He suggests that Bataille's claim of arriving at a state of unreflective innocence or animal purity is merely a mask since it is unattainable: 'There is no cure for this symbolic contamination, no solution that will remove the indelible stain of language and thought from consciousness' (Poiana, 2013: 6). Alan Stoekl (1985) points out that despite the potential for some synergies between the ideas of the Surrealists and Bataille's work, André Breton, author of the *Second Surrealist Manifesto* (1969) dismisses Bataille as an 'excremental philosopher' and suggests that there is a profound contradiction between Bataille's embrace of the heterogeneous – animality, excrement and other forms of filth as a means of eradicating consciousness – and his ability to reason: 'This very fact proves that he cannot claim, no matter what he may say, to be opposed to any system like an unthinking brute' (Stoekl citing Breton, 1985: xi). The application of Bataille's work as it relates to art and interpretation adds credence to this assertion.

Jon-Ove Steihaug's observations concerning different approaches to interpretation – those that posit a structural against a referential reading – as well as the vexed issue of relating form and content are also pertinent here. The work of Andres Serrano, for example *Piss Christ* (1989), and Cindy Sherman's *untitled #177* (1987) can be read as direct polemic and abjection as abjection (as a reponse that is socially coded), and in this sense they may be viewed as merely reinforcing or confirming cultural taboos: blasphemy and obscenity – this interpretation arises from a focus on content and meaning rather than on the affective charge exerted by the works. In both cases, however, there is oscillation between disgust and pleasure; between experiencing abjection as a process that denies closure of meaning and therefore challenges binary logic and those processes of sublimation that give rise to the conceptual dimension of the image. The key to understanding the complex and ambiguous articulation of these works is not only the bringing together of the very high or sanctified and the low, but also the operation of colour and light as colour. In Serrano's Cibachrome photograph, light has been adjusted to produce a luminous surface of rich crimson against which the crucifix is suspended in urine and is illuminated with a brilliant yellow incandescence. The bubbles in the fluid appear as intense spots of light. The effect of this is to exert the double pleasure of voyeuristic gaze and that of social transgression. The work is evocative of colour as it is used in Baroque paintings such as those of Caravaggio, where colour as light denotes the divine and the glorious. It is this effect that permits an understanding of the claim that the obscene and the beautiful, the sacred and the profane are aligned. Though quite different in content, Sherman's image exerts a similar force. Here it is the chiaroscuro effect of light and dark that work modally to draw the viewer into and across the work; together with chromatic contrasts and harmonies it has the effect of obscuring representational elements. In Sherman's work, it is primarily the colour blue that carries the sensory charge. Kristeva tells us that because colour or chromatic experience exerts pressure on instinctual drive, it constitutes a 'menace to the self' (Kristeva, 1980: 220). This is particularly so with the colour blue: 'A possible hypothesis ... would be that the perception of blue entails not identifying the object; that blue is precisely, on the side of or beyond the object's fixed form' (225).

Kristeva makes it clear that abjection takes hold when there is a loss of self or a failure to separate from objects. If we bring together various dimensions of Kristeva's work related to the emergence of the subject, we may conclude that abjection does not rest solely on what disgusts and repels us, but is a continuation of a fundamental mechanism of separation originating as biological process. It is a process that continues throughout life as a precursor of language and the making and renewal of meaning as is evidenced in the works considered below.

Catherine Bell: beyond abjection

As discussed earlier, abjection gives rise to the *jouissance* of oblivion and the pleasure of transgressing the law. Thus the abject is related to perversion: a desire to look even when one is repelled or afraid. Abjection is related to the superego, an operation of the psyche that exerts control over the drives; in creative practice it can turn the drives aside, mislead, corrupt and misuse them in the striving for desirable cathexes or investment of the drives in what will emerge as the aesthetic image or internal structuring of the work. One of the effects of this can be found in humour and parody, which arises out of psychic processes that are directed towards defusing fear and trauma. Because it is a composite of conscious and unconscious elements, the superego constitutes ambiguous and fluid relations between the subject and the system of social laws and it is this dimension of abjection that is mediated in artistic practice. Hence, creative practice involves an ability to project oneself into the abject, to introject its logic and as a consequence, to pervert language through style and content. What distinguishes the making of art from schizophrenia (for example) is the capacity to mediate and sublimate the chaotic and ceaseless operation of drives. The work of Catherine Bell helps to illuminates the workings of abjection as fundamental to the creative process.

Catherine Bell: *The Gathering*

Though eclectic in form and content, Bell's works are linked by a sustained evocation of ambiguity, shock, pleasure and surprise that I suggest are indicators of abjection at work. The first is from the exhibition *The Gathering*, held at the Substation Centre for Art and Culture in Melbourne 2013. This exhibition was the result of a year-long artist residency at the St Vincent's Hospital's Caritas Christi Hospice in Kew and involved working with staff, patients and their families as well as volunteers. The making of this work is contextualised by the grief of terminal illness. Also during the residency one of the members involved in the group passed away. As I mentioned earlier, grief or grieving can be understood as a bridge between abjection and melancholia. This is so because melancholia is the result of an inability to separate from the lost object or unnameable other so that there is a constant attraction and movement toward it. Extreme melancholia, like trauma, results in an inability to symbolise or to 'speak' experience. The work of grieving therefore involves ways of articulating loss so that there is a partial recuperation through a renewal of language. Hal Foster has linked trauma as it relates to art to Freud's 'uncanny' and suggests that confrontation with the uncanny gives rise to the return of repressed material in ways that disrupt identity, social norms, and the social order (Steihaug, 1998: 28). However, this differs from trauma that is related to melancholia. The uncanny triggers negativity and expenditure that leads to a recuperation of the repressed object. Hence it is related to the ego or subject of language and to material that has been repressed in *relation to language* rather than to pre-Oedipal processes. Like depression, it is *exogenous* and relates to external events. Kristevan melancholia/trauma on the other hand is *endogenous* and relates to the pre-Oedipal infant and the trauma of separation of birth. It is this more profound trauma related to internal processes with which abjection articulates in creative practice – and that brings forth the new. The distinction is important because what is returned through processes of abjection is an alteration of language itself that permits emergence of a completely new object, one that has not hitherto been symbolised. Melancholia is a precondition for creative production because it instigates abjection as process. Intrinsic to grief is a kind of emotional menace and sense of abject danger. His fear of the unnameable thing that is articulated in Kristevan thinking as the body of the mother prior to separation of birth is also the fear of death – the unspeakable horror of what cannot be represented or seen. Moreover the threat that attends terminal illness and the loss of a loved one is the sense of becoming disenfranchised, disconnected and cast off by society. The dynamics of grief then, are like the dynamics of abjection: attraction and repulsion where movement towards the loved one is a movement towards death and movement away is separation and loss. This oscillation is instantiated in many of the works from *The Gathering*.

Heavy Petal (Figure 6) is a work made from petals from discarded bouquets at the hospice from which the artist has constructed what she call 'botanical collages'. The process of dehydrating the petals leads to a bleeding

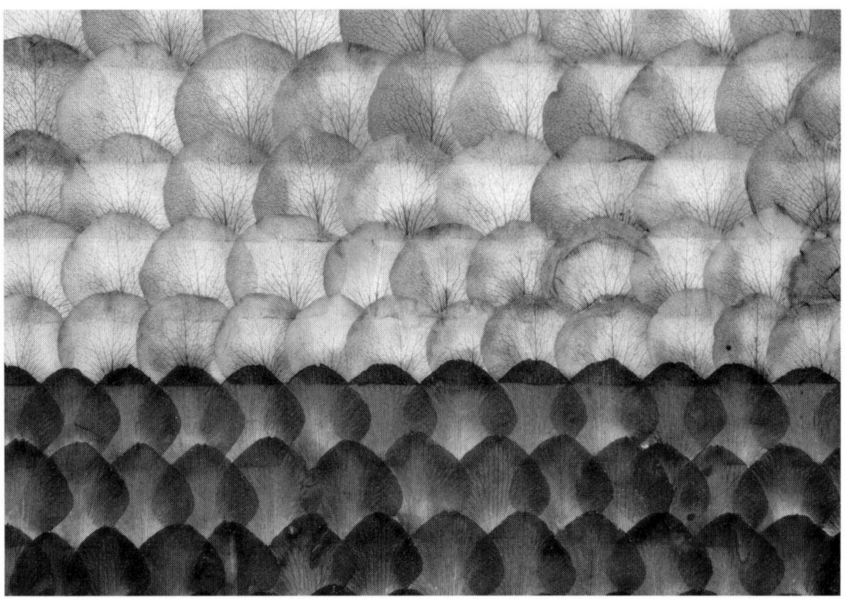

6 Catherine Bell, *Heavy Petal* (detail), 2012. Flower petals, conservation medium, wooden board, 25 × 30 cm. Courtesy the artist and Sutton Gallery, Melbourne. Photograph: Andrew Curtis.

out of colour, a kind of slow death of the flower as a living thing. The ritual recycling and making of the work becomes a counterpart of the collective trauma of death and loss (Bell, 2011). In this sense art making becomes a site of mourning. However, the completed work realises a new 'life form' and incandescent beauty. The image oscillates between sensory effects of colour, light and the almost abstract form of individual petals, and the whole image, which operates representationally to signify rows of headstones in a graveyard. The residual veins of the petals, skeletal, and like the veins under the papery skin of the aged and the sick – together with areas of sombre darkness and patches of blood red staining that has eluded the control of the artist in the making – operate in concert with the rhythms of repeated form and colour to exert forces of attraction and repulsion in the process of viewing. Moreover, what has occurred is a transformation, indeed a transubstantiation of the original bouquets into a new object, an object that is loaded with signification that gives voice, and therefore new meaning to the trauma of separation, of death and dying. The assuaging of grief is made possible through the 'language' of the artwork.

Because abjection is a demarcation between the pure and the impure, it also operates spatially to denote the proper place and order of things. It is this aspect of abjection that gives rise to both horror and humour. The Medusa's head writhing with snakes has long been regarded as one of the most horrific images in Western culture. It not only the repugnance of snakes that gives rise to this horror, but also the collapse of two different entities into one. Hence hybrid creatures and those with altered states, for example Robert Louis Stevenson's Jekyll and Hyde, exert both fear and fascination. Another body of work in this the exhibition articulates the workings of abjection in quite a different way. Bell not only uses discarded flowers from the patients' rooms, but also the blocks of green hydrated foam that provide supports for the floral bouquets. She uses her fingernails to sculpt vases or crematorium vessels out of the foam so that materially and visually there is a collapse of the demarcation between desirable object and waste matter, the sacred and the profane. Another sculpture fashioned from the foam, *Mountains of Mourne*, is a model of mountain ranges in Northern Ireland, the home of the nuns of the Sisters of Charity who tend the patients at the hospice. This work becomes both a de-negation of loss, but also an object of ambiguity, humour and whimsy. What lies beneath this effect is not only a displacement, re-orientation and transubstantiation of the foam that would normally have been discarded as garbage, but also the play of meanings engendered by the manipulation of scale and volume and the juxtaposition of content and form including the retention of the commercial labelling of the foam.

With reference to another of Bell's works from the exhibition, *Nanny Safari* (Figure 7), I would like to pursue the notion of abjection as a spatial concept that has a disorienting effect and a subsequent multiplying of meaning by disrupting established codes. This video installation demonstrates how abjection operates as social and political commentary without recourse to representation of violence, the obscene. In this image the *trompe l'oeil* effect collapses the inside/outside distinction as well as engaging with codes that perpetuate stereotypic perspectives regarding women and race. The image is part of a larger body of work that ostensibly depicts unequal relations between black and white women, casting black women in the position of servitude, as nannies of white babies. However, the composition of the works often disrupt this perspective by presenting the women in active stances and through a play of the way in which these women seem to have control and possession of the children. Indeed in one image not shown here a nanny is portrayed with a raised arm that ambiguously suggests an act of violence (perhaps towards her charge) or alternatively a position of repose. Such images are example of how artworks can be structured to invite a voyeuristic gaze and collusion in the implied criminality. The work shown here is a more nuanced evocation of subversive pleasure that operates through multiple visual inversions that work conceptually, to refuse binaries and remove notions of dominance. This is largely due to the spatial arrangement of the image whereby the white woman is located 'inside', a space of unpaid labour, traditionally considered

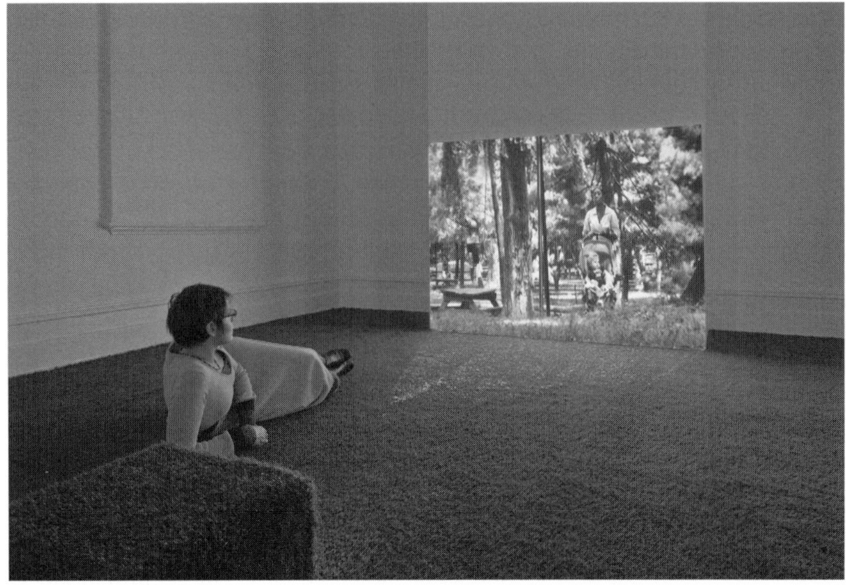

7 Catherine Bell, *Nanny Safari*, 2010 (Installation view). Dual audio visual projection, artificial grass. HD DVD 1,54 mins, HD DVD 2,35 mins. Courtesy of the artist and Sutton Gallery, Melbourne. Photograph: Christian Capurro.

the proper place for women, whereas the nanny is outside and is engaged (we assume) in paid work that bestows economic autonomy. Indeed both women are presented as equal in this regard despite their respective positioning. The intriguing power of this image is its capacity to evoke identification and pleasure as well as resistance to the positions made available through the ambiguity of image. Here, not only do we apprehend the forces of attraction and repulsion of abjection, but through the act of looking, experience implication of the superego within the embodied process.

To conclude, *Nanny Safari* and other works of Bell discussed eloquently demonstrate Kristeva's observation that that the subject of abjection asks not 'Who am I?' But rather 'Where am I?' (Kristeva, 1982: 8).

References

Barrett, E. 2011. *Kristeva Reframed: Interpreting Key Thinkers for the Arts*. London: I. B. Tauris.

Barrett, E. 2014. Beyond the Raw and the Cooked: Abjection as Art and Transgression. *Zetesis: The International Journal for Fine Art, Philosophy and the Wild Sciences* (Wet, Dry Thick Thin) 1(2), pp. 6–19. Birmingham: The Centre for Fine Art Research Birmingham University.

Bataille, G. 1973 [1957]. *Literature and Evil.* Trans. A. Hamilton. London: Calder and Boyars.

Bataille, G. 1988 [1954]. *Inner Experience.* Trans. L. A. Boldt, Albany: State University of New York Press.

Bell, C. 2011. Cooking up Crimes and Maternal Misdemeanours: From Food Ritual to Transgressive Performances. *Double Dialogues* 15, Winter. [Accessed 20 October 2013]. Available at: www.doubledialogues.com/issue_fifteen/bell.html.

Botting, F. and Wilson, S. 2001. *Bataille.* Basingstoke: Palgrave.

Hollier, D. 1989. *Against Architecture.* Trans. B. Wing, Cambridge, MA: MIT Press.

Krauss, R. 1996. 'Informe' Without Conclusion. *October* 78. Autumn, pp. 81–105. [Accessed 9 August 2008]. Available at www.jstor.org/stable/778907.

Kristeva, J. 1980. *Desire in Language: A Semiotic Approach to Literature and Art.* Ed. L. S. Roudiez, Trans. T. Gora, A. Jardine and L. S. Roudiez, New York: Columbia University Press.

Kristeva, J. 1982 [1980]. *Powers of Horror: An Assay in Abjection.* Trans. L. S. Roudiez, New York: Columbia University Press.

Kristeva, J. 1989. *Black Sun: Depression and Melancholia.* Trans. L. S. Roudiez, New York: Columbia University Press.

Poiana, P. 2013. Violence and Representation in the Works of Georges Bataille and Michel Leiris. *MLN* 128(4), September, pp. 1–8. [Accessed 20 September 2014]. Available at: http: //muse.jhu.edu.ezproxy-deakin.edu.au/journals/mln/v128.4poiana.html.

Steihaug, J-O. 1998. Discourse: 'Abject/Informe/Trauma: Discourses on the Body in American Art of the Nineties'. [Accessed 18 May 2014]: 1–41. Available at www.google.com.au/url?sa=t&.rct=j&q=&esrc=s&source=web&cd=1&ved=0CB8QFjAA&url=http%3A%2F%2Fwww.forart.

Stoeckl, A. 1985. Introduction. *Georges Bataille. Visions of Excess: Selected Writings 1927–1939.* Trans. A. Stoekl, C. R. Lovitt and D. M. Leslie Jr. Minneapolis: University of Minnesota Press: i–xxv.

Tyler I. 2014. The Wretched of the Earth. [Accessed 27 September 2014]. Available at: http://socialabjection.wordpress.com/2013/07/11/the-wretched-of-the-earth/.

9

Corpus delicti

Kerstin Mey

> Canova had a horse killed for 'Theseus and the Centaur' to study all states of mortal agony and to make use of it. (Canetti, 2014: 226)

Dying and death has intrigued artists for centuries. Antonio Canova's study of a creature's death struggle informed his conception of a life-size sculptural ensemble that captured his creative energy for fifteen years. *Theseus and the Centaur* (1804–09) represents a struggle between the two protagonists. In neo-classicist rendering, Canova shows Theseus kneeling on the chest of the centaur with his right arm raising a club in readiness to strike. In its expression of pathos the triangular marble composition resembles the *Antique Laocoön* group (AD 79). The inquisitiveness that drove Canova to study animal agony bears a close relation to the quest for knowledge in the human and animal anatomy that motivated artists like Leonardo da Vinci to dissect bodies, or at least to depict the process or results of such investigation as evident in work reaching from Hans Baldung Grien in the sixteenth century, to Rembrandt van Rijn a century later, or the anatomical drawings of George Stubbs in the late eighteenth century and early nineteenth century. Such explorations expanded the knowledge of the human body and its functioning, and developed effective ways of lifelike visual rendering. It could be argued that with the catastrophes of two World Wars, the Holocaust and countless other atrocities in the twentieth century, artistic concern moved to the human condition at large, to existential issues foregrounding charged and charging documentation of human suffering and loss (Kemp and Wallace, 2000).

However, over the past three decades, the re/presentation of demise and decease have become of growing interest to artists, stimulated by a range of different concerns. Nan Goldin's photographs of her circle of friends at the margins of society logged human suffering and expiry in the context of the first AIDS epidemic of the 1980s/early 1990s. It recorded the dignity of the dying, friendship, compassion and grief. Derek Jarman's film *Blue* (1993) or Sophie Calle's video *Couldn't Catch Death* (2007) give compelling insights into the relationship between life and impending death from very personal points of view. In a series of works, Finnish artist Terike Haapoja captures the cooling down of animal bodies after their annihilation with an infrared camera. In *Entropy* (2004), a life-size video projection of a horse, the corpse slowly vanishes from the screen as its body temperature gradually reduces to that of its environment. In the realm of 'object making' Damien Hirst's provocative displays of animal cadavers preserved in formaldehyde have both fascinated and repulsed audiences since the early 1990s.

This more recent preoccupation of artists with the transitory nature of life and the inevitability of death – of which Mark Quinn's *Self* (1991), a cast of the artist's head made of six pints of his own blood and kept in shape by constant refrigeration is another manifestation – echo wider public 'curiosity' and concerns. These are fuelled by the fact that for many in the West the immediate experience of the demise and death of others has been removed from everyday life. In the West death occurs predominantly by natural causes, and takes place in specialised institutions like hospitals, nursing homes and hospices. Their trained personnel deal with the period before and up to this event. Other institutions and social rituals meticulously regulate how we tackle the 'aftermath' in an orderly fashion and according to the requirements of specific cultural and religious conventions, of legal and ethical norms, and where possible, following the instruction of an individual with regard to how and where the mortal remains should be disposed of and how they wish to be commemorated (if at all). Advances in medicine, genetics and biotechnology have made the boundary between life and death more ambiguous and raised many related ethical concerns.

At the same time, and arguably more than ever – not least due to the exponential growth and saturation of our mediated culture with images – representations of dying and death inhabit our life worlds, and occupy increasingly our still and moving image screens. Fatalities are shown as spec/tac/ularised news of conflict and war from other parts of the world; they 'illustrate' reports on violence, homicides, tragic accidents and natural or manmade disasters.

Human expiry dominates many of the popular video games and films rendered in ever more perfectly simulated images. It could be said that the re/presentation of death lies at the heart of contemporary entertainment. It permeates all genres: sci-fi, historical epics, contemporary drama and comedy, and is particularly present in the moving images churned out by the Hollywood 'dream machine'.

Worryingly, the boundaries between flawless computer simulation and real atrocities committed in the name of ideology or religion, political and/

or economic interests appear increasingly blurred when, for instance, propaganda videos show executions and murder amplified through cinematic effects and HD technology. By drawing on filmic imageries as the main popular cultural reference framework, death is potently being used, as Michel Foucault argues, to disclose and enforce religious and political power, and to govern through fear (Foucault, 1998: 35).

It should also be noted that embedded reporting from acute conflict areas since the early 1990s, catalysed by continuous advances in the development of portable audio-visual recording equipment and mobile communication technologies, have contributed to the increased insertions of images of human malaise and death into daily life. And so too has the broadcasting of images taken by military satellites and aeroplane cameras that follow the trajectory of bombs and show how these hit (or miss) their targets, accepting any civilian casualty as unavoidable collateral damage in the supposed fight for democracy and freedom. The global proliferation of smart phone use and social media platforms has given rise to the activists and citizen-reporters capturing pictures of accidents and atrocities and disseminating those to audiences around the world.

At one level, it could be argued that reducing or removing intimate experiences of demise and loss of others from much of the personal and collective experiential horizons in the West, the absence of death in contemporary life, has at the same time elicited a 'toxic' mix of indifference towards human (and animal) suffering and annihilation, and intense curiosity and *Schaulust*[1] with regard to what dying means and what the expiry of life is like. This correlation of attitudes is both predicated and furthered by the focus on the individual (rather than a collective) that marks Western society. 'Disaster tourism' or traffic jams in the vicinity of serious road accidents, caused by drivers who slow down to catch a glimpse of the scene, are obvious indicators of a desire to directly stare into the face of death. In the absence of public or private occasions to directly encounter mortality (other than one's own), and of other moments that support an immediate experiencing and understanding of death, we turn to representations of dying and decease. These function as a substitute for the intractability and thus lack of experience and comprehension of our finitude.

Renderings of death by necessity transcend and transgress embodied experience and our systems of meaning (making). They rupture the symbolic order. Our fascination with death and the absence of an open and informed public discourse about the end of life has been both highlighted and exploited by Gunther von Hagens' *Anatomy Art*, a momentous public touring exhibition shown across the world including North America, Japan and Europe between 1995 and 2011. The evolving traveling exhibition consisted of a substantial (and over time much expanded) number of specimens of human and sometimes animal bodies: full corpses, body fragments, dissected organs and systems. Through exceedingly skilful preparation these specimens maintain their integrity and provide the highest possible detail. To achieve such extremely intricate and precise analytic visualisation of the complex human and animal anatomy, the Heidelberg-based pathologist and anatomist invented the process of Plastination in the 1970s to preserve tissue by replacing water in the cells with polymers such as silicone, epoxy or polyester resin. Plastination allows the conservation and stabilisation of large(r) bodily remnants. It was refined in the 1990s to deal with whole corpses, leaving surfaces and structures exposed, as required for demonstration purposes, and largely intact. In order to show specific body components and functions such as the nerve system, metabolism or muscle fibres, the cadaver has to be taken apart into its micro-structures and undergo a complete reconstruction. As the natural coloration of the body is lost in the complex process of Plastination, it has to be artificially reinstated, thus producing the hyperreal effect of many of these durable and odourless 'objects'.

The plastinated bodies could be easily mistaken for anatomical wax models from the eighteenth or nineteenth century, not least because the perfectly rendered models carry 'lively hues and fresh sheen' that make them 'truer to the colourful vitality that we expect to find within ourselves than the dull grey brown confusion that dominates the appearance of an actual dissection of a corpse' (Kemp and Wallace, 2000: 59). Therefore, the actual con/vergence between signifier and referent that marks the corpse appears obscured. Kristeva argues that

> [the] abject is not an ob-ject facing me, which I can name or imagine. Nor is it an ob-jest, an otherness ceaselessly fleeing in a systematic quest of desire. What is abject is not correlative, which, providing me with someone or something else as support, would allow me to be more or less detached and autonomous. The abject is only one quality of the object – that of being opposed to I. If the object, however, through its opposition settles me within the fragile texture of a desire for meaning … makes me ceaselessly and infinitely homologous to it, what is abject … the jettisoned object, is radically excluded and draws me to the place where meaning collapses. (Kristeva, 1982: 1–2).

The actual visual encounter of von Hagens' bodies works to initially mute such kind of reaction, as the special preservation of the cadavers heightens their object character and thus their supposed otherness that assures the subject. Only at second glance, and supported by the sensationalising publicity surrounding the public display of the dead, does the uncanny loom, the vaguely familiar and yet disturbingly strange and threatening of the cadaver, pointing to the 'border of my condition as a living being' (Kristeva, 1982: 4). It is at that moment that affective responses surface, which are associated with the abject and eventually trigger respective intellectual, ethical and legal considerations.

Compare von Hagens' corpses for instance to Kiki Smith's *Virgin Mary* (1992), a life-size replica of a female body exposing key aspects of its internal structure: bone, muscles and nerves. Made of wax, cheesecloth and wood, this figure is placed on a low steel plinth. It provokes a very emotional response to the partial un/veiling of corporeal realities that the artist has created by exploiting the 'organic' qualities of the malleable material and the juxtaposition between intact body zones like the breasts, the hands and the feet, and those seemingly 'skinned', subcutaneous, areas of the main body and its extremities. The affective dimension of the work is stressed by the figure's gesture that oscillates between opening up to the Other, seeking help, and supplication, thus suggesting a heightened degree of vulnerability both to external intervention and internal disintegration.

In contrast, von Hagens' early choice of body type, repertoire of postures and gestures reference well-known tropes from the canon of Western art history. The *Runner*, for instance, is one of numerous figures arranged in striking poses. It offers optimum sight of the body's voluntary muscles, i.e. those controlled by an individual's will. The figure's pose resembles Umberto Boccioni's *Unique Forms of Continuity in Space* (1913), a consciously sought similarity that is highlighted in the accompanying catalogue through the juxtaposition of photographs of both objects (von Hagens and Whalley, 2000: 73). Many of von Hagens' exhibits, like the *Chess Player*, *Swordsman* or *Horse and Rider, Soccer and Basket Ball Players* and *Skateboarder,* draw on and re-enact iconic images of the heroic male body. Towards the turn of the millennium von Hagens shifted his attention to employing tested artistic means of choreographing a figure – the harmonious *ponderation* and *contrapposto* or the *figura serpentinata,* which assist to visually connect the cadavers to the domain of fine art and its enduring symbolic authority – to postures and poses that have their origin in sensational sports images produced by stop motion photography or the promo shots for fashion and music. Nevertheless, all the well-proportioned and strangely timeless corpses exemplify the contemporary obsession with the perfected body: youthful, lean and fit. Von Hagens' spectacular choreography of death stays well away from the ugly and revolting corporeal realities that would immediately trigger revulsion. The staging of these cured and grotesquely vitalised bodies emulates visual symbols of power that are deeply anchored in the West, from Greek Antiquity via the Renaissance and Classicism to Modernism, and the various influences these have asserted on contemporary popular images of the human body through exposure and citation. He formally buys into the imageries of contemporary commodity culture as a means to mitigate against moral and ethical dissent. Recourse to such an established formal repertoire provides another means to successfully avoid any reference to the abject character of the corpse and related processes of abjection. It serves as an affirmative if ambivalent counter strategy to the principal transgression of the symbolic order, that is, death. 'It is not lack of cleanliness or health that causes abjection but what disturbs identity, system, order. What does not respect borders, positions, rules (Kristeva, 1982: 4).

Von Hagens' well-calculated provocation of staging dissected corpses copulating, premiered as part of the 'Cycle of Life' in the *Body Worlds* show in Berlin in 2009, brings together in a peculiar way 'Eros and Thanatos'. In this display, where the female sits on the reclining male facing away, the mechanics of sex and reproduction are demonstrated in deceased bodies, yet the focus on the biological aspects, married with the 'surreal' character of the dissected cadavers, suffocates any suggestions of wilful titillation, and stands in stark contrast to the surround of mirrored walls and opulent chandelier that hold strong connotations of a luxurious brothel rather than an 'Anatomy Cabinet'. In an age where pornography seems ubiquitous and has been one of the main catalysts in the development of the Internet, this morbid simulation of copulation still has the power to upset established norms of taste and morality that are bound up with accepted divisions between public and private. The same can be said about the controversial display of a *Reclining Pregnant Woman* shown in a provocative pose that deliberately references an erotic pose of the female body well tested in historical painting and 'soft' pornographic images. In this instantiation of the body, the gravid uterus is partially opened up to give sight to the eight-month-old embryo. It has frozen in time a symbiotic moment, where new life is developing inside the body: pre-symbolic and pre-subjective – not yet abject – but already abject in its condition of cadaver. It serves as a stark reminder of the proximity of life and death. This extreme scene that works so much against notions of the sanctity of life has the potential to particularly arrest and horrify the viewer, perhaps much more so then Damien Hirst's *Mother and Child (Divided)* (1993), a cow and her calf, each cut in half, and placed into two formaldehyde tanks situated in proximity to each other. Against the sanitised display of two different body halves, von Hagens' work intensifies the grotesque and the disturbing by showing the entwined bodies. Yet viewed in the context of the exhibition with its accumulated mass of dissected corpses – each more spectacular and bizarre than the next – there is such a degree of repetition at work of seeing stabilised carnal form that produces a degree of ennui and detachment similar to that occurring in pornography, where narrative details and the *mise-en-scène* are reduced to the bare minimum required for motivating and making plausible the situation in order to focus the viewer's attention on the sexual trans/action(s).

It could be argued that reinstating the 'parade and publicity' of death is fundamentally driven by a quest for (self-)know-ledge. Von Hagens' public anatomy lessons have been motivated by both enlightenment and public affront. It seems that an outright provocation of prevailing conventions of taste and an accompanying ethical controversy are necessary ingredients to elevate this public performance lecture from the general overload of images in order to capture public visibility and attention.

Von Hagens' performs his body art as perfectly staged spectacularisation, mixing in large doses of showmanship and 'self-stylisation' that converge the long tradition of the anatomist with that of the visual artist and the media-savvy entertainer. Sporting a black felt hat, it has been suggested that he seeks to evoke a visual connection of his public persona to the anatomist – as they are depicted for instance in seventeenth-century Dutch paintings. At the same time, he intentionally exploits a resemblance to the late Joseph Beuys with his trademark felt hat. The latter is underscored by von Hagens' cultivated mannerism when interacting with the public.

Von Hagens has taken the exploration of the human corpse out of the dissecting room and on to the public stage of the exhibition hall and the TV screen. Besides the public celebration of the human body, in its intricate design and wondrous functioning, he also directs public attention to disfigurement and physical signs of common diseases. The German title of the show, *Körperwelten*, translates into 'body worlds'. It does not only connote references to the natural sciences and medicine but also to the public spectacle of both freak shows and beauty contests. The title *Anatomy Art* chosen for the UK show in 2004 explicitly stakes a claim on the tradition of art history and the symbolic realm of high culture.

Von Hagens' intentional projection of his skills as anatomist on to the realm of art revitalises a historical and yet persistent understanding of this model of practice and its respective value hierarchy where creative talent converges with skill and learnedness. The intellectual and conceptual value of such anatomical art interventions receives additional emphasis through converging with science. While von Hagens stresses his intellectual abilities and educational intention in relation to his work, he rejects any responsibility for the reception of it within the context of art, insisting that

> Experience at exhibitions has shown that the aesthetic aspect of posed specimens make such an impression that visitors consider a number of these to be works of art. There is no dispelling of that conclusion either, because 'art is in the eye of the beholder'. No anatomical works of art have been created; they become works of art through the judgement of the visitor to the exhibitions. (von Hagens and Whalley, 2000: 34)

The selected 'milieus' for the display, (multi-purpose) exhibition halls or a museum of science, complicate such perception and respective validation mechanisms. The public acceptance of the work necessitates drawing on the privileged symbolic practice of art that constitutes an effective ground for a sublimating discourse on abjection. It is therefore perhaps not surprising that the event locations have been construed as sites for a dialogue between art and science, aesthetic appreciation and anatomical and medical education.

In this context it is also of interest to note that von Hagens' public dissection of a human corpse in front of a paying audience, randomly selected due to the large interest in the event, took place in a gallery in London's Brick Lane on 20 November 2002. This first public autopsy since the 1830s was intentionally situated within the immediate context of his *Anatomy Art* show in the vicinity at that time. An edited version of the event, intercutting scenes of the post-mortem analysis with audience reactions, was broadcast by Channel Four later that evening. The act of broadcasting played very much to the notion of a public '*Schauspiel*', literally a '*spectaculum*', a performance for the eyes, that had already emerged in connection to the live event and its deliberately scandalising promotion through the media. The corpse as a marker of the inevitable Other of life had to be comprehended by the majority of viewers from the distance of the camera/television screen. The broadcast documentation suppressed the noises and smells connected to the 'deconstructive' procedure, which could be experienced in the live event, and offered up the performance of the anatomist from a mediated distance. Therefore, the transmitting of audience responses served a dual purpose: it attested to the authenticity of the event, adding an affective dimension to draw in the television audience, and stimulated feelings of both awe and disgust.

The intense media promotion of that autopsy and the concurrent *Anatomy Art* show have raised suspicions that self-stylisation through spectacularisation, rather than an intellectual or moral obligation to publicly instruct and debate, has been the driving force behind von Hagens. Such impression is enforced by the 'maestro's' impressive showmanship.

Concerns regarding the legality of the procedure aside, both the exhibitions and anatomy lessons have raised considerable ethical and judicial issues pertaining to the dignity of human life (and death) and the supposed exploitation of human remains. Claims for exploitation were made on the grounds of allegations that corpses had been illegally acquired from Siberia and that bodies of executed prisoners from China were purchased. While such claims have not been substantiated, and while in the later part of the series of exhibitions, certifications of donation of the bodies were provided, the mere accusation contains significant implications for considerations of the abject and abjection by drawing attention to the objects of enquiry as corpses. From a social perspective these bodies were abject, not simply in the overt sense of them being cadavers, but because they were of unwanted, unknown lowly 'foreign' people, prisoners even. They were the detritus of everyday life; people who have been r/ejected from the 'body social'. Following others, Tina

Chanter argues that 'abjection is constitutive of the coherence and integrity of subjects and communities, such that a movement of rejection or expulsion is foundational to the identity of subjects and communities' (Chanter, 2008: 11). In other words, expulsion becomes constitutive of the other.

> In this sense, that which becomes other, that which is designated other, is constitutive of subjectivity precisely in its exclusion. The very possibility of being a subject, and of distinguishing other objects and subjects from oneself, owes itself to a preliminary and tentative positing of boundaries, a demarcation or discrimination of I from not-I that marks the moment of moving beyond primary narcissism. (Chanter, 2008: 11)

In the case of von Hagens' bodies, it is the theoretical knowledge of their supposed 'origins' that points to the socially abject, i.e. the insinuation that the former individuals committed crimes, were lawless and therefore imprisoned, or socially defunct and therefore expelled from the community and remained nameless. (The bodies as such do not bear resemblance to a particular individual, whether voluntary donor or not, due to the specific processes of their preparation, and therefore are difficult to place at least in terms of age, ethnicity and geography.) With the flow of capital underpinned by the increasingly ubiquitous digitisation and related transmission of information and communication globalising the world with potentially homogenising effects, from a Western perspective, there still appears a symbolic power hegemony at play – desperately kept potent by political rhetoric and the media – that casts the Chinese and Siberian bodies as outsiders. Stemming from beyond the boundaries of the crumbling political and economic imperium, even as remnant, these outcasts are constitutive of the West's increasingly weakening pan-national identity. In other words, beyond universal ethical concerns that the 'playing with the dead' may have raised, the exhibition of such bodies can be understood as a double attack on the necessary symbolic operations by which collective integrity is maintained.

Joel-Peter Witkin's and the Russian art group AES+F's grotesque 'play with corpses' present similar issues. Both artistic approaches have in common the use they make of the morgue and of anonymous dead for the staging of their photographic tableaux. Where Witkin's capture of bodies and body parts, skulls and skeletons revitalises the *vanitas* motif that featured prominently especially in seventeenth-century Dutch and Flemish painting, AES+F's work *Defile* (2000–7) converges traditions of photographing the dead with the contemporary fashion shoot.

AES+F's *Defile* consists of seven light boxes featuring one corpse per photographic image, each dressed up in an exuberant haute couture garment. The pictures of the bodies are taken from a bird's eye vantage point. Using the manipulative potential of the digital camera, all traces of their clinical surround are erased and the shrouded cadavers superimposed on to a white neutral background tilted to the vertical. In contrast to the lifeless bodies, their costumes are draped in an animate manner (in part invisibly propped up) that is disturbing. Positioned in front of a neutrally white background, with their toes pointed and their carnivalesque dresses swaying, they appear weightless and floating, like dancers. The exquisiteness of the extravagant clothes and their overly graceful arrangement support a beautiful and alluring, almost sublime appearance of the cadavers that is painfully ruptured by the cruel indicators of the actual toil of the individuals' former lives: their decimated physiques, their premature signs of ageing, the traces of disease and violence. It could be argued that the abject here is invoked in a double bind of the physical and biological on the one hand, and the social and ethical on the other. In terms of the former, the abject is connected to the material condition of existence, or more accurately, to the boundaries that demarcate respective physical integrity. Here the strong effects of the *Defile* series reside subcutaneously, that is, in the principally abject nature of death rather than at the level of its re/presentation per se. In relation to the body social, abjection is thematised in the 'public parade' of the corpses of anonymously dead: the remains of former subjects who have no one to bury their bodies, are not given a place to 'rest their souls' and have no one to commemorate their lives and safeguard their rights in death.

Considered superficially, these photographs may reference the tradition of posthumous portraiture, a practice that was established in the nineteenth century with the development of photography and survived in the West well into the first half of the twentieth century (Linkman, 2011: 69). Although there is no accessible survey history available, it is believed that the mourning portrait has survived in Eastern Europe, including Russia, to the present. Post-mortem photography is based on a strict protocol overseen by the funeral directors and is socially marked and associated with practices of embalming. It was first adopted by the more affluent elites, whose practice and respective values then spread during the later nineteenth and early twentieth century. Evidence shows that memorial photographs were taken of the 'dead in their bed or coffin, accompanied by the chief mourner(s), husbands, wives, parents and children (Linkman, 2011: 69). However, in AES+F's *Defile* project, the individuals are isolated from their surrounds and any human company, except of their own kind within the ensemble of the nameless deceased. And while these corpses have been carefully prepared, put in fancy dress and have been choreographed for their last memory picture, these interventions only contribute to emphasise that their physical appearance marks the abjection from the social 'organism' of Post-Communist Russia. The pronounced contrast between these physically and socially 'tarnished' cadavers on the one hand and their luxurious clothing, lightweight luminosity and radiant presence produced by the light boxes, on the other, lends this representation a deliberately provocative and problematic character. The grotesque simulation of beauty and grace has been modelled on and embodies contemporary values of consumption. It has come into being through a highly exploitative operation on the part of their privileged creators, the artists, who doubly objectify those vulnerable, 'forgotten' dead. It makes them into a powerful symbol for contemporary neo-liberal market capitalism, the 'abject' humus of exploitation and social oppression on which the obscene wealth of the few is being built, and which is deflected by the glamorous shine of the advertisement, the dream world of the silver screen and electronic display, the mirror facades of the temples of consumerism alongside the harmless and numbing décor of contemporary art. As Guy Debord (1983, unpaginated 34) noted more than half a century earlier: 'The spectacle is capital to such a degree of accumulation that it becomes image.'

Twenty-five years before AES+F's work captured public attention, Witkin's grotesque photographic spectacles of dead bodies provoked public controversy. *The Kiss* (1982), for instance, shows two halves of an elderly man's head arranged to embrace in a touching of the lips. His rather dishevelled exterior, the closed eyes and toothless sunken mouth suggest peacefulness until the gaze discovers the tumultuous array of arteries, sinews, flayed skin and muscles that surround the neck vertebrae. Witkin represents violent death employing two conflicting conventions – the classicist one of the suffering sublime body, and the anticlassicist, mannerist tradition of the grotesque, tortured, ruptured body and its creatural dimensions. However, it is not so much the latter that alludes to the process of abjection, it is the former. As Kristeva (1982: 3) states:

> The corpse (or cadaver: cadere, to fall), that which has irremediably come a cropper, is cesspool, and death; it upsets even more violently the one who confronts it as fragile and fallacious chance. A wound with blood and pus, or the sickly, acrid smell of sweat, of decay, does not signify death.

The irrational excess of violence, symbolised in the splitting of the severed head and the tortured neck, is counteracted with the stabilising centring of the arrangement, the symmetrical fusion of the skulls united in a kiss, and the dramatic black-and-white contrasting in this toned gelatin silver print. Interlocking the halves of the skull through the open mouth, he blocks off a liminal zone where entry to the body interior is given and where internal matter is ejected: saliva, mucus, vomit and blood. The kiss, a gesture of temporary convergence of I and Other, becomes a bizarre and destabilising encounter of the same.

Another black-and-white photograph from this series shows the post-mortem corpse of a young man. Roughly sawn up along the middle of his entire upper body, he is propped up on a chair, forced into position by metal straps or brackets. The staging of the cadaver offers a visual amplification of suffering of which the figure of *St Sebastian* has become the primary exemplification. In a later version of this motif, *Queer Saint* (1999), Witkin choreographs a fragile skeleton of a male, designated as such by the addition of a man's severed yet still physically intact head, complete with skin, hair and moustache, and penis and in front of a (surgical) cloth. Using attributes that have come to signify the Saint's martyrdom in Christian mythology, the artist partially moves the work into a more contemporary context by adding an eye mask, a recurring theme in his works, and a crown that verges between laurel and thorns, denoting both sanctity and suffering. Through attributes and title, the work is inserted into the long visual history of the depiction of sacrifice and excruciating agony by artists such as Matthias Grünewald, Hans Memling, Andrea Mantegna and El Greco. Yet it is also set in proximity to the homoerotic interpretation of the motif through which it served as an early gay icon and, as which, it has found explicit re/interpretation, for instance in the photography of Pierre et Gilles. However, the formal vocabulary employed by Witkin in the later version exploits the motif's iconic status yet returns to its gruelling foundations. It not only amplifies the freakish nature of the visual study but shifts its focus inescapably from Eros to Thanatos – nothing evades death: the great leveller, and no desire can hold annihilation.

Morbidity is placed centre stage in Witkin's series of still lifes, drawing on the Baroque and the tradition of the *vanitas*. *Still Life Marseille* (1992), for instance, consists of a partially opened up and emptied out head of a male. Eyes closed, the chubby skull rests on a table top, providing a container for roses and lilies in full bloom. It is surrounded by vegetables and fruits, some of them contained in a large tilted bowl. The opulent and sensual arrangement exudes an erotic charge that brings to the fore the dynamic nexus of human drives. In contrast, *Corpus medicus* (2000) showcases the lower body of a young(er) man laid out on a clothed table. Its staging gives full sight of the gaping wound where it was severed from its upper part – literally a *nature morte* – that juxtaposes the firmness of the corporeal exterior to the soft and squelchy mess of the violated interior.

Besides 'playing' with corpses and body fragments, Witkin has shown a lasting preference for picturing those who are physically and sexually different, deviating from the norm, including individuals who are maimed and disfigured. He uses his models and exaggerated theatricality to challenge dominant aesthetic paradigms and their principal motivation: to masque, battle, laugh off and conquer the absence of meaning created by death. Witkin effectively exploits a range of influential tropes and stylistic principles that have been associated with Western art from the Renaissance to Modernism. Inspired by the invention of photography and the Daguerreotype in particular, he employs traditional 'light writing' techniques, as well as excessive mark-making processes on the photographic surface to challenge the hegemonic aesthetic conventions and image-making operations as sublimating and controlling forces of signification. By distressing the shiny surface of the black-and-white image, the objects' semblance and beauty is ruptured, not dissimilar to the *punctum* that pierces the screen and offers a momentary glimpse of the real.

Witkin's formal repertoire and aesthetic registers do not conform to the contemporary *zeitgeist*, to prevailing creative practices. He articulates an Other that is situated in proximity to notions of obscenity and the prohibited; an Other that at the same time constitutes a necessary liminal part in the formation of current aesthetic sensibilities and 'norms'. This intentional positioning, both in art historical and creative terms, is well demonstrated in *Poussin in Hell* (1999), an epic picture foregrounding a masked female nude reclining on a mobile stretcher in a standard erotic pose. She is observed by a painter working at a canvas and endowed with the accessories of sadomasochistic practice. In the background towers a painting reminiscent of both El Greco's *St Francis Receiving the Stigmata* and Baroque renderings of religious ecstasy.

Giving visibility to those who, and to what exists at the margins of the 'acceptable' through forthright and transgressive expressions he demarcates and challenges the boundaries of established social and cultural practices. Yet it can be argued that their potential for critique is regarded as part of their fascinating (and terrifying) appeal within their place in contemporary art. Chanter (2008: 11) observes that through:

> the fluidity of imaginary, amorphous, invisible, excluded, unthought others, we can draw attention to the logic of abjection that grounds fetishistic discourses, a logic that such discourses utilize more or less consciously. There is an ambivalent inclusion of subjects, who are on the one hand situated outside of representation, in a mythical, indeterminate past that is mythologized as prior to civilized society, and on the other hand granted access to forms of representation that are nevertheless shaped and informed by their exclusion. Access is granted to these forms of representation only if those who are excluded acquiesce to their representation as subjects who conform to the imaginaries of dominant narratives.

Witkin's work goes some way towards articulating 'this logic of abjection [of] how discourses of racism, sexism, classism, heterosexism and nationalism are implicated in each other in ways that play off one another to produce their own internal others' (Chanter, 2008: 11).

Compared to AES+F's and Witkin's works, Andres Serrano's morgue series of 1992 has evolved from a different aesthetic approach. His large cibachrome prints zoom in on those details of human cadavers that aptly reveal the specific cause of death: drowning, asphyxiation, meningitis and pneumonia amongst others. A matter-of-fact caption supplied with each picture states the cause of death and aligns it to the physical signs of the fatality. An exception has been made for picturing a *Child Abuse*. The photograph gives sight only of the infant's closed eyes, surrounded by a pristine white cloth that is gently wrapped around the head. The image marks an eerie silence. An unthinkable offence committed in secrecy, unspeakable for its victims, inconceivable for the nearest and dearest. Widely invisible, this abhorrent crime continues to exist, not least through the absence of an open public discourse.

Serrano's approach in the *Morgue series* oscillates perpetually between the indexical and the symbolic, between revealing and concealing and between the forensic and the empathetic. He makes fruitful the uncanny to lay bare the revulsion that is part of sickness, physical violation, annihilation, while at the same time foregrounding through the exquisiteness of the arrangement, the frozen moment pregnant with meaning.

Although Serrano's corpses remain anonymous, their case histories and physical detail provide each corpse with elements of distinctiveness and significance as a victim of violent crime or fatal illness. Yet the pronounced close-up of the camera zooming in on a specific physical detail as *pars pro toto* unsettles identification and asserts a destabilising effect on the juxtaposition between object and subject, other and I.

The highly choreographed arrangement of the objects of study contradicts the factual statement of the cause of death. It moves the images from a document, from an 'arte faction' towards an 'arte fiction'. This is primarily achieved by the careful drapery of the shroud that frames the corporeal focal point, by the dramatising light and dark contrast, and the high resolution of the colour image. The intentional formal rigour of the composition lends these iconic pictures an expansive gravitas, solemn beauty and persuasive authority that overshadow their actual subject matter. The play with different economies of drives incites attraction and reflective delight, before dejection and disgust take hold.

Serrano's approach to the re/presentation of death contrasts vastly with Sue Fox's 'scopic regime' that governs her visual research, conducted in autopsies, mortuaries and crematoria in Manchester from the early 1990s onwards, through which she produced over 1500 images. A selection of this body of work that confronts death face on was published in *Post Mortem* (1997). Fox's image making documents the vulnerability, fragility and transience of the human body. Camera work and image edition underpin her positioning as inquisitive yet detached observer, who judiciously surveys, and registers, trying to control the visceral urge to grasp the irrational at the level of the phenomenon, to come to terms with the incomprehensible transience of life.

'Catching' a pathologist's hand at the moment when they pry open the rib cage to gut the male corpse, the materiality and messiness of the flesh fixates the gaze, as does the yawning cavity of a disembowelled cadaver or the peeling skin of a black male who has been dead for some time. The procedures applied by which the dead are prepared for their 'inhumation' – a most appropriate term – often seek to conceal what happens to the body when life expires: the excretions that occur at the point of total muscle relaxation, the awkwardness of handling a body in rigor mortis, the sensation of touching lifeless, cold flesh; the lingering stench of open wounds and putrefying flesh.

Some of Fox's photographs in the series deal with the deconstruction and decomposition of the cadaver, and its gradual disintegration and disappearance during incineration. She captures how the flames devour the skin first, then the soft tissue, muscles and organs until the skeletal structure lies bare and collapses into a pile of hot ashes. This pictorial journey, mapped through a series of carefully edited, poignant close-up images takes the viewer from the meaningful that builds on the recognisable presence of a carcass to the formless, where signification is invoked through 'situated' absence. Fox's work powerfully exemplifies how 'abjection returns to haunt the symbolic that it both founds, and from which it is rejected' (Kristeva, 1982: 13). Where Canova had focused his attention on creatural agony at the moment where death asserts its stranglehold, Fox, all matter of fact explores what remains. Without any pathos she stakes out the base from where all meaning making takes its beginnings.

Notes

1 *Schaulust* differs from curiosity and voyeurism in that the term signifies more generally the human desire across history and cultures to watch and take in situations that are rich of sensory stimuli. Voyeurism is marked by sexual denotations and often associated with the secretive behavior of observing other people in sexual contexts. Curiosity on the other hand denotes the active exploration of new sensory or factual situations for the purpose of information gathering and orientation. However, in current language use particularly in the media, the differences between *Schaulust* and voyeurism in particular are increasingly eroded.

References

Bataille, G. 1998. *Eroticism*. Trans. M. Dalwood, London and New York: Marion Boyars.

Bronfen, E. 1992. *Death, Femininity and the Aesthetic*. Manchester: Manchester University Press.

Canetti, E. 2014. *Das Buch gegen den Tod*. Munich: Carl Hanser Verlag.

Chanter, T. 2008. *The Picture of Abjection: Film, Fetish and the Nature of Difference*. Bloomington and Indianapolis: Indiana University Press.

Creed, B. 1993. *The Monstrous-Feminine: Film, Feminism, Psychoanalysis.* London and New York: Routledge.

Debord, G. 1983, *Society of Spectacle.* Detroit, MI: Black and Red.

Dekkers, M. 2000. *The Way of All Flesh. A Celebration of Decay.* Trans. S. Marx-MacDonald, London: The Harvill Press.

Foster, H. (ed.) 1998. *The Anti-Aesthetic. Essays in Postmodern Culture.* New York: The New Press.

Foucault, M. 1998. *The History of Sexuality: The Will to Knowledge,* Vol. 1. Trans. R. Hurley, London: Penguin.

Freud, S. 2005. *On Murder, Mourning and Melancholia.* Trans. S. Whiteside, London: Penguin.

Goodwin, S. Webster and Bronfen, E. (eds.) 1993. *Death and Representation.* Baltimore and London: Johns Hopkins University Press.

Kemp, M. and Wallace, M. 2000. *Spectacular Bodies.* Berkeley, Los Angeles, London: University of California Press.

Kristeva, J. 1982 [1980]. *Powers of Horror.* Trans. L. S. Roudiez, New York: Columbia University Press.

Linkman, A. 2011. *Photography and Death.* London: Reaktion Books.

Mey, K. 2007. *Art and Obscenity.* London and New York: I. B. Tauris.

Townsend, C. 1998. *Vile Bodies.* Munich, New York: Prestel.

Townsend, C. 2008. *Art and Death.* London and New York: I. B. Tauris.

von Hagens, G. and Whalley, A. 2000. *Anatomy Art – Fascination Beneath the Surface.* Heidelberg: Institute of Plastination.

Walsh, M. 2013. *Art and Psychoanalysis.* London and New York: I. B. Tauris, 2013.

Zimmermann, A. 2001. *Skandalöse Bilder – Skandalöse Körper. Abject Art vom Surrealismus bis zu den Culture Wars.* Berlin: Reimer Verlag.

10

Art is on the way: from the abject opening of *Underworld* to the shitty ending of *Oblivion*

Calvin Thomas

> At Monday's working lunch, Laurel Manderley's deceptively simple idea with respect to the package's contents had been to hurry back and place them out on Ellen Bactrian's desk before she returned from her dance class, so that they would be sitting there waiting for her, and not to say a word or try to prevail on Ellen in any way, but simply to let the pieces speak for themselves. This was, after all, what her own salary-man appeared to have done, giving Laurel no warning whatsoever that art was on the way. (Wallace, 2004: 280)

Segment 1: chiasmus

This writing will concern some 'theoretical' reading matters that I imagine informed the composition of two pieces of fiction, one by Don DeLillo, the other by David Foster Wallace, two pieces of literary art, each involving the other in the messy question of art and abjection, a miasmic chiasmus of art *become* abjection and abjection become art. In what follows, I intend both to *demonstrate* (to show, reveal, make the case) and, frankly, to *fabricate* (invent, devise, tell the lie) that the opening of DeLillo's massive 1997 novel *Underworld* – which depicts a historically real piece of art being passed through the defiles of a mechanically reproductive organ of mass culture to merge and mingle with a celebratory cascade of abjection – was influenced by DeLillo's reading of Dwight McDonald's 1957 essay 'A Theory of Mass Culture', *and* that the novella-length story that closes Wallace's 2004 collection *Oblivion*, an item called 'The Suffering Channel' – which envisions the miraculous rendering of real segments of abjection (specifically, human turds) as 'exquisite pieces of art' (Wallace, 2004: 239) – was inspired by Wallace's close inspection of my 1996 study *Male Matters: Masculinity, Anxiety, and the Male Body on the Line.*

With DeLillo, I intend to be demonstrative, relying on the standard scholarly protocols of interpretive argument based upon textual evidence. It is with Wallace, on the other hand, that I plan to be fabricative, by which disclosure I mean to say that, even though in the course of telling my story about Wallace's story, I will recur to a cluster of real, historical, biographical and autobiographical facts (about Wallace's writing and my own), I'll also be yanking a few items out of my ass. In other words, in aspiring to end up as an exquisite piece of art in its own right, this writing will press itself out in numbered segments of abjection.

Segment 2: parrhesia

I shit you not: I am being perfectly candid, honest, forthright, etc., when I declare that I fully intend to take artistic liberties – to fabricate, invent, imagine, even falsify (albeit *always* with a good conscience) – when surfing Wallace's 'The Suffering Channel'. I want these previews of coming averidicality to be taken seriously, and for two reasons.

One is that I still take *Nietzsche* seriously when he writes that the 'will to truth ... might be a concealed will to death' (2006: 364), when he interprets truth-driven ascetic idealism as being *suicidally* motivated by a rancorous hostility towards life, hatred of the human body, contempt for this-worldly existence, and, crucially, by 'the renunciation of any [and all] interpretation (of forcing, adjusting, shortening, omitting, filling out, inventing, falsifying, and everything else *essential* to interpretation)' (430). For Nietzsche, the 'will to truth' involves the desire for something *other* than interpretation, something *other* than the strong and noble *art* of forcing, inventing, falsifying, and so forth, something other than *art* as that vital and worldly realm 'in which *lying* sanctifies itself and the *will to deception* has good conscience on its side' (431–432). Desiring truth means denying ourselves the truly '*Nietzschean* affirmation ... the joyous affirmation of a world of signs ... without truth ... which is offered to an active interpretation' (Derrida, 1978: 292). *Our* affirmation of the *Nietzschean* affirmation of a world without truth thus involves us in a sort of personal and global *anti-suicide* pact, an agreement – *put in writing* – never to eliminate our own maps (of this world).

This specific language, figuring suicide as the elimination of one's own map, the erasure of one's own face, will of course be familiar to readers of Wallace's *Infinite Jest*, a terribly 'sad' novel amply saturated with discourse on suicide but also rich in a joyously Nietzschean affirmation of a world without truth: the world of play, the laughingly tragic, fate-loving affirmation of the world of *fiction*, of the world *as* fiction, the inescapably ironic affirmation of 'life as literature'.[1] And of course this language also reminds us, as if we needed reminding, that Wallace finally failed to live up to his end of our personal/global anti-suicide pact and in sad fact did end up ending his own life, eliminating his own map.

But this language also leads me to my other reason for stating up front that I intend to *lie* about Wallace and about the life and death of his writing. Toward the end of *Every Love Story is a Ghost Story: A Life of David Foster Wallace*, D. T. Max writes that 'over the past twenty-five years [Wallace's] mental life had run a huge circuit through the most astonishing complexities [only] to arrive at what many six-year-olds and nearly all churchgoers already understood' (2012: 286). Now, if what Herr Max here avers is in fact the case, if this noisome sentence accurately describes the 'truth' of Wallace's 'mental life' near the willed end of his physical life – if David Foster Wallace finally overcame his positive addiction to carnal irony to fully embrace a cretinous belief – then in all good conscience I must tell every damned lie about his fiction that I can devise. Honestly, I think I'd rather hang myself *myself* than accede to this ignoble, this *antibiographical* truth.

Segment 3: 'talk about stinko'

> Is cyberspace a thing within the world or is it the other way around? Which contains the other, and how can you tell for sure?
>
> ...
>
> Everything is connected in the end. (DeLillo, 1997: 826)

For the good anti-capitalist reader of Don DeLillo, the money-shot of his novel *Underworld* no doubt comes, appropriately enough, near the end, in the Epilogue, entitled '*Das Kapital*', which begins with discourse more than a little redolent of Max Horkheimer and Theodor Adorno's famous piece 'The Culture Industry: Enlightenment as Mass Delusion', albeit updated to address our fluidly cyber-sexual and woefully global postmodern times. The opening lines of *Underworld*'s Epilogue insist that the logic of late capitalism homogenises, flattens and devitalises the planet, finally and fatally making everything 'all part of the same thing' (DeLillo, 1997: 39) while pretending to spread only lively and happy heterogeneity everywhere. As our narrator, Nick Shay, explains:

> Capital burns off the nuance in a culture. Foreign investment, global markets, corporate acquisitions, the flow of information through transnational media, the attenuating influence of money that's electronic and sex that's cyberspaced, untouched money and computer-safe sex, the convergence of consumer desire – not that people want the same things, necessarily, but that they want the same range of choices ...
>
> This is what desire seems to demand. A method of production that will custom-cater to cultural and personal needs, not to cold war ideologies of massive uniformity. And the system pretends to go along, to become more supple and

> resourceful, less dependent on rigid categories. But even as desire tends to specialize, going silky and intimate, the force of converging markets produces an instantaneous capital that shoots across horizons at the speed of light, making for a certain furtive sameness, a planing away of particulars that affects everything from architecture to leisure time to the way people eat and sleep and dream. (DeLillo, 1997: 785–786)

But if there's something *un*-furtively Frankfurtian about this lecture, with more than enough 'mode of production' discourse to give even the least vulgar Marxist among us a critical boner, there's also something conspicuously and abjectly *Bataillean* about it as well. The language of the passage, involving silky and intimate flows of delusional satisfaction shooting off across our transnational horizons, invites us (or at least me) to imagine a sort of seminal overflow, discharge writ large, a vast deluge of ejacu-latté, a massive *load* of production in which wetly dreaming capital, doing its business as 'the spreading ooze of Mass Culture' (McDonald, 1998: 35), has 'succeeded in penetrating and dominating the very fantasy-kernel of our being' (Žižek, 1993: 10), saturating the collective-consumer unconscious with corporate jism, treating the whole global village to a facial. Here come the warm jets, all over our maps.

This globally warming cum-scene – this capitalist domination of/elimination on our once culturally distinct now glazed-over maps of the world – might best be worst described (in darkly dialectical terms, mixing Georges Bataille's excessive language with a few rank dollops of my own), as 'a magnificent but stinking ejaculation' (Bataille, 1985: 77), 'teeming with life and yet signifying death' (Thomas, 1996: 26). And this mashed-up description of the free market's malodorous money-shot seems apt enough when, a few more pages into '*Das Kapital*', we encounter this bit of transnational reportage – simultaneously (albeit artificially) seminal and shitty – coming to us from professional 'waste analyst' Nick Shay:

> They are trading garbage in the commodity pits in Chicago. They are making synthetic feces in Dallas. You can sell your testicles to a firm in Russia that will give you four thousand dollars and then remove the items surgically and mash them up and extract the vital substances and market the resulting syrupy stuff as rejuvenating beauty cream, for a profit that is awesome. (DeLillo, 1997: 804)

But our description, Bataille's and mine, seems even more fitting – especially if I alter the graphic appearance of my contribution to read 'teeming with *Life* and yet signifying death' – when we turn back to *Underworld*'s Prologue, which concerns, among many other cultural, historical and representational matters, a big soft glossy magazine called *Life* and a painting, like the Prologue itself, entitled 'The Triumph of Death'.

As I've already suggested, certain moments in *Underworld*'s opening –

called what it's called after the 1562 painting by Pieter Bruegel the Elder, but set at the 1951 Brooklyn Dodgers/New York Giants playoff game and organised in terms of the historical synchronicity between Bobby Thomson's pennant-clinching ninth-inning homerun (called 'The Shot Heard "Round the World"') and, on the other side of the world, the Soviet Union's reported test-detonations of atomic bombs in Kazakhstan – suggest DeLillo's familiarity with 'A Theory of Mass Culture', the 1957 essay in which 'Cold War' intellectual Dwight McDonald rails against the 'spreading ooze' of popular culture industrially produced and homogenised for 'the masses'. 'Like nineteenth-century capitalism', McDonald writes,

> Mass Culture is a dynamic, revolutionary force, breaking down the old barriers of class, tradition, taste, and dissolving all cultural distinctions. It mixes and scrambles everything together, producing what might be called homogenized culture, after another American achievement, the homogenization process that distributes the globules of cream evenly throughout the milk instead of allowing them to float separately on top. It thus destroys all values. (1998: 25)

McDonald is particularly repelled by *Life*, a high-circulation magazine that he thinks fatally erases the boundary between High Culture and popular kitsch by running features on esteemed philosophers and reproductions of long-seriously-regarded paintings nestled among schlocky stories about horses on skates, housewives at home plates, and Hollywood's latest feted celebs, as if these globular *quantities* of culture were all of the same globally significant *quality*. McDonald asks us to:

> Consider *Life*, a typical homogenized mass-circulation magazine ... Its contents are as thoroughly homogenized as its circulation. The same issue will contain a serious exposition of atomic theory alongside a disquisition on Rita Hayworth's love life; ... an editorial hailing Bertrand Russell on his eightieth birthday ... across from a full-page photo of a housewife arguing with an umpire at a baseball game ...; a cover announcing *in the same size type* 'A NEW FOREGIN POLICY, BY JOHN FOSTER DULLES' and 'KERMIA: HER MARATHON KISS IS A MOVIE SENSATION'; nine color pages of Renoirs ... followed by a full-page picture of a roller-skating horse. (1998: 25, italics added by me, for reasons to be discussed later)

DeLillo dramatises McDonald's argument – and especially his rancour against *Life* – in a conspicuously abject fashion at the opening to *Underworld*: near the climactic moment of Thomson's 'shot', Bruegel's 'Triumph of Death', as mechanically reproduced in the glossy pages of *Life*, is ecstatically torn out of that *poubellication*[2] by a nameless fan, thrown up into the air and made to let fall as celebratory confetti or 'happy garbage' (DeLillo, 1997: 45) on to certain historical personages depicted as attending the game: the criminally connected crooner/actor Frank Sinatra, the secretively cross-dressing lawman

J. Edgar Hoover – who 'likes to be around movie idols and celebrity athletes' and for whom 'fame and secrecy are the high and low ends of the same fascination, the static crackle of some libidinous thing in the world' (DeLillo, 1997: 17) – and, last but not least, the drunkenly libidinous and profusely vomiting fatso Jackie Gleason, who has consumed one too many ballpark franks. Mixing and scrambling shreds of falling paper (including the page of Bruegel that lands on Hoover's shoulder) with Jackie Gleason's chunky spew (which splatters Sinatra's pants and footwear), DeLillo's Prologue at its climax suggests not only his exposure to McDonald (and perhaps even Bataille) but also his own authorial/intestinal distress about the fate of language in the late days of late capitalism, his anxieties about art, sex, writing, history, commerce and culture as arenas of abjection in which fundamental distinctions between the representational and the real, the sacred and the profane – between high and low, life and death, law and crime, worth and waste (and, perhaps underlying all of *Underworld*'s anxieties, 'man' and 'woman') – all threaten to crumble.[3]

Now, since the anxiogenic issue here is indeed *language*, we should pay close attention to the author's own in those passages building up to the downward scattering of this 'thick issue' of *Life*, as described in the pages of the Prologue called 'The Triumph of Death', as well as those passages depicting the abject dissemination of the painting called 'The Triumph of Death' in and as one of those thrown-up pages of *Life*.

We are at Ebbets Field, in Brooklyn, early in the Prologue, early in the famous 'live-or-die' (DeLillo, 1997: 14) game:

> People stand in both decks in left, leaning out from the rows up front, and some of them are tossing paper over the edge, torn-up scorecards and bits of matchbook covers, there are crushed paper cups, little waxy napkins they got with their hot dogs, there are germ-bearing tissues many days old that were matted at the bottoms of deep pockets, all coming down around [Dodgers left-fielder Andy] Pafko. …
>
> People like to see the paper fall at Pafko's feet, maybe drift across his shoulder or cling to his cap. The wall is nearly seventeen feet high so he is well out of range of the longest leaning touch and they have to be content to bathe him in their paper. (DeLillo, 1997: 16–17)

Now even though Pafko plays *left* field, and not centre, DeLillo seems to want to situate this celebrity athlete in the same place where Oedipa Maas parks her Chevy Impala in Pynchon's *Crying of Lot 49*: to wit, 'at the center of an odd, religious instant' (1966: 24).[4] But in a sense that Dwight McDonald would no doubt endorse, the instant religion being brewed up at Ebbets is less miraculously 'odd' than all too odorously common. Speaking proleptically, we can say that the stench in question pre-emanates from those hot dogs getting their first adumbrating mention here, ordinary wieners fated to play their reeking part in the nauseous Gleason's discharge on to Sinatra's fancy pants-legs and shoes, the puke itself eventually prompting this exchange between the two celebrities, late in the pages of 'The Triumph of Death':

> [Gleason] rails at Frank: 'Nothing personal, pal, but I wonder if you realize you're smelling up the ballpark. Talk about stinko' …
>
> [Frank] says, 'It's not my stink. It's your stink, pal. Just happens I am the one that's wearing it.'
>
> Says Gleason, 'Hey. Don't think you're the first friend I ever puked on. I puked on better men than you. Consider yourself honored. This is a form of flattery I extend to nearest and dearest.' (DeLillo, 1997: 54–55)

Back in left field, early in the pages of Death's 'Triumph', we behold the more common 'people', the un-famous fans, eagerly attempting to extend themselves, in the form of torn-up germ-ridden waste-paper, to their nearest, dearest and better man, the otherwise untouchable Pafko. This devoted but stinko congregation, this increasingly indistinct mass of 'believers' – yes, the Prologue is awash with professions of belief, those bearing witness to the incredible game incanting such lines as 'I believe' and 'I'm still a believer. What about you?' (DeLillo, 1997: 42, 33) – they want to bathe themselves in Pafko's singular aura, even long to lean out and touch the hem of his uniform-garment but, arms too short, must content themselves with baptising the idolised sportsman in their mechanically reproduced tidbits of ballpark culture, their discarded articles of 'abject faith' (36).

But look, it's only the second *inning*, not the Second Coming, and DeLillo – the writer who John Leonard once tagged, not altogether baselessly, as a closet 'holy roller' who's 'afraid of the dark' (in Duvall, 2002: 73) – wastes little time highlighting the lowbrow lustre of this cracker-jack credo, this abject faith in redemption through consumption, this incontinent fall from the saving graces of Spirit and Holy Mass and True Religion into the spreading ooze of Sports and Mass Culture and Mob Fanaticism, by immediately having not St. Peter but 'hard-rock' Leo Durocher utter 'into his fist' the following sacred profanity: 'Holy fuggin shit almighty' (DeLillo, 1997: 17).

Sure as shit, a few more pages into 'The Triumph of Death' and we're visiting that phallo-fecal shrine, the ballpark crapper, where we behold

> men passing in and out of the toilets, men zipping their flies as they turn from the trough and other men approaching the long receptacle, thinking where they want to stand and next to whom and not next to whom, and the old ballpark's reek and mold are consolidated here, generational tides of beer and shit and cigarettes and peanut shells and disinfectants and pisses in the untold millions. (DeLillo, 1997: 21)

A few pages more and we get our first report that 'there's a man in the upper deck leafing through a copy of the current issue of Life [*sic*]' (DeLillo, 1997: 32). Meanwhile, on the opposite page 'in the [radio] booth [sportscaster] Russ

[Hodges] sees the crowd begin to lose its coherence, people sitting scattered on the hard steps, a priest with a passel of boys filing up the aisle, paper rolling and skittering in the wind' (33). The people sit; the holy man ascends; the waste-paper falls. 'Everything is changing shape, becoming something else' (33), while at the same time everything is becoming abjectly 'consolidated here' (21), everything simultaneously reified and liquefied to become all 'part of the same thing' (39), the same flow, the same generational (but anti-generative) tide of mass consumption and expulsion.

But turn to page 38.

> Look at the man in the upper deck. He is tearing pages out of his copy of Life [*sic*] and dropping them uncrumpled over the rail, letting them fall in a seesaw drift on the bawling fans below. He is moved to do this by the paper falling elsewhere, the contagion of paper – it is giddy and unformulated fun … It brings him into contact with the other paper throwers and with the fans in the lower deck who reach for his pages and catch them.

Letting fall his uncrumpled pages of *Life* also brings 'the man' into contact with the aforementioned 'auratic' personae seated below – Sinatra, Gleason, and Hoover – allowing the common anonymous fan to cover the famous names with his *Life*'s spreading ooze.

> Paper is coming down around the group, big slick pages from a magazine … Frank snatches a full-page ad for something called pasteurized process cheese food, a Borden's product, that's the company with the cow, and there's a color picture of yellowish pressed pulp melting horribly on a hot dog.
>
> Frank deadpans the page to Gleason.
>
> 'Here. This will help you digest.'
>
> Jackie sits there like an air traveler in a downdraft. The pages keep falling. Baby food, instant coffee, encyclopedias and cars, waffle irons and shampoos and blended whiskeys … And the resplendent products, how the dazzle of a Packard car is repeated in the feature story about the art treasures of the Prado. It is all part of the same thing. Rubens and Titian and Playtex and Motorola. And here's a picture of Sinatra himself with Ava Gardner and would you check that cleavage. Frank didn't know he was in this week's Life [*sic*] until the page fell out of the sky. (DeLillo, 1997: 39)

Following the metonymic line from Ava Gardner's cleavage back through the brand-name of the bra-maker Playtex to the very *tit* in the moniker of the art-maker *Titian*, we are indeed supposed to see that our mass cultural 'it' – *das Es* – has all become part of the same undifferentiated libidinous thing, the infantile (baby food) merging with the adult (blended whiskeys), mechanically reproduced pictures of 'Sinatra himself' sinking downward to darkness and extending on to the real star, 'Sinatra himself'. We're also supposed to see that these are of course not *real* things or *real* stars but merely representational matters that are falling, ecstatically and catastrophically, out of the sky, not actual encyclopedias and such but dazzling magazine adverts for these resplendent products, even if the real products represented as being advertised in *Life* become rather less resplendent and all the more abject the closer they come to Gleason's magnificent but stinking oral ejaculation, as witnessed by the Breugel-holding Hoover.

> Edgar stands with arms crossed and a level eye on Gleason folded over. Pages dropping all around them, it is a fairly thick issue – laxatives and antacids, sanitary napkins and corn plasters and dandruff removers. Jackie utters an aquatic bark, it is loud and crude, the hoarse call of some mammal in distress. Then the surge of flannel matter. He seems to be vomiting someone's taupe pajamas. The waste is liquidy smooth in the lingo of adland and it is splashing freely on Frank's stout oxford shoes and fine lisle hose and on the soft woven wool of his town-and-country trousers. …
>
> [T]he paper keeps falling … It is coming from all points, laundry tickets, envelopes swiped from the office, there are crushed cigarette packs and sticky wrap from ice-cream sandwiches, pages from memo pads and pocket calendars, they are throwing faded dollar bills, snapshots torn to pieces, ruffled paper swaddles for cupcakes, they are tearing up letters they've been carrying around for years pressed into their wallets, the residue of love affairs and college friendships, it is happy garbage now, the fans' intimate wish to be connected to the event, unendably, in the form of pocket litter, personal waste, a thing that carries a shadow identity – rolls of toilet tissue unbolting lyrically in streamers. (DeLillo, 1997: 44–45)

These last streaming jets of unbolted bum-wad pretty much say it all, encomp*ass*ing 'everything': the poetic merger of the ejaculatory with the meant-to-be-shit-stained (adumbrating the melding of seminal beauty cream and synthetic faeces in *Das Kapital*); the penumbral lyricism of 'personal waste' from wasted persons, coming on us from all points, the massive dispersal of a host of abject items simultaneously consumptive and expulsive, representational and real, from the menstrual to the monetary, from laxative ads to residual love letters, all the garbage happily but cadaverously falling in 'The Triumph of Death', including (the reproduction of) 'The Triumph of Death' itself. Eventually we see men themselves falling, male bodies deliriously dropping like liberated dingle-berries from the rims of outfield walls, all 'these men who drop from the high walls [but who] like to hang for a while before letting go' and who 'hit the ground and crumple' (DeLillo, 1997: 54) like paper, all these incredible 'cultural droppings' representing and vitally connecting the faithful and passionate fans, as per their most intimate wish, to the unendable 'event' of the shot heard 'round the world', but also, outside the conscious knowledge of everyone in Ebbets but Edgar, to reports of shots leading maybe to the end of the world, intimations of mutually assured destruction, of real rather than merely pictorial Death Triumphant, coming into Hoover's ear from Kazakhstan, all thanks to the secular miracles of technology and communication.[5]

> It seems the Soviet Union has conducted an atomic test at a secret location somewhere inside its own borders. They have exploded a bomb in plain unpretending language. (DeLillo, 1997: 23)

Now, what interests me about this last sentence is the way the (perhaps strategically) faulty punctuation (the omission of a comma, in plain unpretending language) makes it seem as if the ominous report from Kazakhstan were that the Soviets had 'exploded a bomb' not simply 'inside' their own national borders but 'in' the so-called 'plain unpretending language' itself, as if the *real explosion* were somehow *interior* to the merely representational words, as if there really were no difference between the intonated and the detonated. What interests me even more is the way this punctuationally undifferentiated manoeuvre gets replicated in a key sentence appearing later in the pages of 'The Triumph of Death' but already quoted in my text above: 'The waste is liquidy smooth in the lingo of adland' (DeLillo, 1997: 44). The 'waste' being referenced here is of course the taupe-colored vomit lyrically streaming out of Jackie Gleason's pie-hole, but, as in the earlier sentence, the withholding of the comma creates the impression that what is clearly now *exterior* to Gleason's body (to the point of splashing freely on to Sinatra's shoes) is still *interior* to language, as if the *real expulsion* were somehow 'in' the smooth advertising lingo itself, as if there were no difference between waste and word. And for yet another instance of authorial comma-withholding to excremental effect, consider this abject *ecce homo* showing up near the end of the Prologue, in which young Cotter Matthews is depicted as thinking: 'Shit man. I don't want to go to school tomorrow' (DeLillo, 1997: 58).

Shit man – at least there's a saving space of separation between the two words. But the absence of a prophylactic comma nonetheless begs the extimate question: 'Is [shit] a thing within the [man] or is it the other way around? Which contains the other, and how can you tell for sure?' (DeLillo, 1997: 826). Whatever we can or can't tell for sure, these linguistic consolidations (of transnational explosion with transpersonal expulsion, of shit with man and of man with shit) seem telling enough: they seem (to me, at least) to allow us to share DeLillo's view of the language of contemporary culture as being not a pristinely Heideggerian house of being but an exuberantly self-discarding stadium of abjection, a commercial dumping ground of personally explosive waste and fatally expulsive fallout, a debased cultural *qua* sphincteral arena in which all the talk coming out of all our holes is cadaverous chatter about stinko, in which all commodified *qua* commode-ified lingo misses any pro-creatively Living Word and expresses (or presses out) only the ultimate logic of late capitalism as massively anti-generative inside-out ass-fuck, the linguistically consolidated dropping of shit-man-turd-dick-f-bombs, the final, phallo-faecal, gravely rectal triumph of death: 'Holy fuggin shit almighty' (DeLillo, 1997: 17), it looks like 'Everything is connected in the [rear] end' (DeLillo, 1997: 826) of late capitalism.

Back, then, to McDonald's rancour against the spreading ooze of *Life*, back to the long quotation concerning that mag and to the words I strategically emphasised there, without then explaining the reason why: namely, '*in the same size type*' (1998: 25). As we've seen, what bugs McDonald in 'A Theory of Mass Culture' is that the significant actions of one JOHN FOSTER DULLES and the cinematic antics of whoever the hell KERMIA was get equal billing on the front-cover of *Life*, in the same size type. What we haven't seen, though DeLillo evidently has, is the front-page of the 4 October 1951 *New York Times*, which features, also 'in the same size type' and in symmetrically balanced opposition, two quantitatively similar headlines describing two qualitatively different events: in the top left corner, *GIANTS CAPTURE PENNANT, BEATING DODGERS 5–4 IN 9TH ON THOMSON'S 3–RUN HOMER*, and in the top right, *SOVIET'S SECOND ATOM BLAST IN 2 YEARS REVEALED BY U.S.; DETAILS ARE KEPT SECRET*. In other words, what I earlier in this segment of my writing inaccurately described as a real 'historical synchronicity' (between Thompson's and the Soviets' shots) was first historically described, or reported upon, in the *New York Times*, in the form of an abstract typographical equivalence. In yet other words – '*Nostra aetate*, as the popes like to say. In our time' (DeLillo, 1997: 805) – in *Life* as well as in our *Times* (the former no longer being published, the latter then and now capitalism's national newspaper of record), it is typographical writing, mechanically reproduced language itself, that pretends to keep high and low separate and distinct while actually making everything 'all part of the same thing' (DeLillo, 1997: 39), making everything in the world simultaneously crucial and trivial, bright and trite, libidinous and abject, teeming with life and yet signifying death, magnificent *qua* fucking stinko: 'The color is usually brown', like with the 'synthetic feces' 'they are making in Dallas' (DeLillo, 1997: 805), but it can also be taupe, the shade of the foul barf that Gleason lets fly in Brooklyn; it – our libidinous thing – can be lubricious and shiny, like the 'rejuvenating' seminal beauty cream manufactured in Russia and the 'resplendent' American products advertised in the glossy pages of *Life*, or, like the newspaper in the ancient riddle, it can just be black and white and read all over.

But is it *all* representational language that turns *everything* to synthetic shit in DeLillo's eyes? After all, it's really only so-called journalistic language, the writing of the *Life* of our *Times*, that pretends to be plain and unpretending (just the facts, all the news that's fit to print) and objectively prosaic (as opposed to subjectively poetic) while actually being completely reified and commercially debased (dispossessed of any intellectual or artistic integrity because always utterly dependent on corporate capital and the bounty of adland). But what about the serious novel? What about rigorously non-commercial art, firmly committed to negating reification?[6] Is there no longer any place in all of cyber-spatial postmodernism/late capitalism for writing that can effectively stage a real 'aesthetics of resistance' to the reifying lingo of adland, to the world *as* adland, straight-out serious and still pretty much modernist writing that possesses and displays that vital 'staying power' which McDonald calls 'the essential virtue of one who would hold his own against the spreading ooze of Mass Culture' (1998: 35)?

I can't 'tell for sure', but I'm fairly confident that DeLillo sees himself as the academic literary world sees him, as a very serious artist, an essentially virtuous novelist who never sells out but holds his own against capitalism's globally spreading, nuance-consuming, happily abject reifications, particularly in *Das Kapital* and 'The Triumph of Death'. But what might it mean for a man to 'hold his own'? What of one's own might one be holding if one holds one's own copy of 'The Triumph of Death' in one's hand? What's the actual fate of 'The Triumph of Death' in 'The Triumph of Death?' What 'really happens' to Bruegel's dead-serious art in DeLillo's dead-serious fiction?

Well of course nothing bad happens to the actual painting; the thing still hangs in the Prado, presumably safe from any ordinary or celebrity projectile vomiting. But it's interesting to note that for all my implied mixing and mingling of painting with puke in *this* writing, in DeLillo's writing the reproduction of 'The Triumph of Death' never really gets anything (of Gleason's) on it. For on the very same page of 'The Triumph of Death' where we behold the words 'Talk about stinko', DeLillo reveals that Hoover – for whom, let me remind you, 'fame and secrecy are the high and low ends of the same fascination, the static crackle of some libidinous thing in the world' (DeLillo, 1997: 17) – has taken the famous painting and secreted it away: 'He has the Bruegel folded neatly in his pocket and will take these pages home to study further' (54). And yet, in preceding pages, DeLillo pretty strongly intimates that Edgar's interest in 'these pages' is more perversely libidinous than aesthetically studious. 'He stands in the aisle and they're all around him cheering and he has the pages in his face' (50):

> He studies the tumbrel filled with skulls. He stands in the aisle and looks at the naked man pursued by dogs. He looks at the gaunt dog nibbling the baby in the dead woman's arms. … He finds a second dead woman in the middle ground, straddled by a skeleton. The positioning is sexual, unquestionably. But is Edgar sure it's a woman bestraddled or could it be a man? … Edgar loves this stuff. Edgar, Jedgar. Admit it – you love it. It causes a bristling of his body hair. Skeletons with wispy dicks. The dead beating kettledrums. The sackcloth dead slitting a pilgrim's throat. … The old dead fucking the new. (50–51)

Given all the icky sexual crackle of and on 'these pages', I think most attentive readers of 'The Triumph of Death' will 'get the picture' a few pages further on when confronted with DeLillo's description of Edgar's exit from Ebbets:

> They march toward the exit ramp with Edgar going fast. He turns toward the field on an impulse and sees another body dropping from the outfield wall, a streaky length of limbs and hair and flapping sleeves. There is something apparitional in the moment and it chills and excites him and sends his hand into his pocket to touch the bleak pages hidden there. (DeLillo, 1997: 55)

Yes, indeed, we get the picture – of J. Edgar Hoover *getting off* on the picture, 'making the scene with a magazine', as I once heard Tom Waits put it; we can easily imagine the cross-dressing Edgar holding his own and spreading his own when he takes these bleak pages home for further study, Edgar beating off to the rhythm of the dead beating kettledrums, Edgar in hiding with this body-hair bristling, holding his own wispy dick in one hand and 'The Triumph of Death' in the other, maybe even letting a load of his G-man jism splash freely and wastefully – counter-reproductively – on to Breugel's mechanically reproduced artwork with all its slit throats and dead babies and triumphantly fucking skeletons. Talk about stinko. Talk about 'no future'.[7]

Given this bleak scenario, we might conclude that Breugel's 'Triumph of Death' is not absolutely saved from an abject fate in DeLillo's vision of its (and our) mass-cultural reproduction. But is DeLillo's own 'Triumph of Death' itself any safer? Will DeLillo's *oeuvre* hold its own, and help us hold our own, against the fatally 'rich, chocolaty goodness' of mass culture's perversely global expansion?[8] I can imagine (because DeLillo prompts me to imagine) a smart perv like Hoover furtively jerking off to mechanically reproduced Breugel, but it's hard for me to believe that any man among us would want to do or spew similarly libidinous things on to *DeLillo's* bleak pages (though if any of the pages of *your* personal copy of *Underworld* happen to be stuck together, you are a far more serious reader than am I). As for DeLillo, closet holy-roller or no, at the end of the day, he is, I believe, 'still a believer' in the staying power of the novel, in the essential virtue of the art of fiction, a believer, I would say, if not in a modernist then at least in a resolutely *heteronormative and heteromasculinist* culture of redemption, a straight white High Culture in which True Life can never consort with 'daily seeping falsehearted death' (DeLillo, 1984: 22), in which real men cannot be (or want to dress as) women, in which potently seminal love letters cannot have gravely rectal destinations, in which real art cannot be faecal artifice, and in which truly aesthetically resistant writing can never present itself as actual outright shit.

Segment 4: speaking of 'speaking of speaking of shit' –

David Foster Wallace's 'The Suffering Channel' is a story about a story about a man 'who purportedly excreted pieces of fine art out of his bottom' (Wallace, 2004: 262), a fictional piece about a journalistic piece 'about somebody pooping little pieces of sculpture out of their butt' (246). Wallace's piece concerns one Virgil 'Skip' Atwater, a 'salary-man' writing for a magazine called not *Life* but *Style*, who, in July 2001 – yes, 2001, and yes, the editorial offices of *Style* are indeed located in one of the doomed towers of lower Manhattan's World Trade Center – takes it upon himself to investigate and report upon a Mr. Brint Molke (Mr. B. M.), abusively toilet-trained as a child, whose sole claim to mass-cultural fame as an adult involves his ability to produce signature pieces of sculpture out of his behind, not first defecating and then shaping these works by hand but rather 'miraculously' bringing 'fully-formed' heads of Anubis and Winged Victories of Samothrace and such directly, rectally, into the world.

Discussing 'allusions to Joyce' that 'are palpable' in Wallace's 'later work', Stephen Burn observes that 'one of the questions rehearsed by *Oblivion*'s 'The Suffering Channel' ... is effectively the question posed by Stephen Dedalus as he outlines his aesthetic theory near the end of *Portrait of the Artist*: '*Can excrement ... be a work of art? If not, why not?*' (2012: 25). Given all the 9/11 adumbration in *Oblivion*'s finale, though, one might also wonder if Wallace weren't conflating the Joyce allusion with a nod towards composer Karlheinz Stockhausen's amply vilified characterisation of the Al Qaeda attacks on America as 'the greatest work of art imaginable for the whole cosmos'.[9]

As previously announced, however, I like to imagine that Wallace wrote 'The Suffering Channel' at least partially under the influence of my *Male Matters*, a performative study of anxiously abjected masculinity organised around a fundamental Lacanian assertion about linguistic self-alienation out the wazoo, a statement according to which 'Th[e] subject, who thinks he can accede to himself by designating himself in a statement, is no more than [a lost, abject, or forsaken] object', and according to which 'the writer [asked] about the anxiety he experiences when he faces the blank sheet of paper ... will tell you who *is* the turd of his phantasy' (Lacan, 1977: 315). *Male Matters* is a book about what I call 'scatontological dysgraphia', about the bright writer's dark '*phantasy of being shit*' (Harari, 2001: 253), a book that I produced in the early 1990s while holding a post-doc at Syracuse University and while living near the campus in an apartment on Roosevelt Avenue that, as I much later discovered, was just around the corner from the Kensington Road dwelling where *Wallace* was at that very same time writing *Infinite Jest*, and a copy of which book (*Male Matters*, that is) I here claim to remember having sent to Wallace after a phone conversation I had with the writer a bit later in the decade – on Monday, 4 November, 1996, to be precise – when I was living in Iowa, and he was still in Illinois.[10]

It's mainly the fact (or what I'm here calling the fact) that 'I remember mailing *Male Matters* to Wallace' which leads me to imagine that his reading my book somehow helped him press out 'The Suffering Channel'. Of course, it's not as if David Foster Wallace had to take any cues from the likes of Calvin Thomas to know how to write about abjection; he had been eloquently 'speaking of speaking of shit' (Wallace, 1989: 256) and other matters for quite some time already. Nor would Wallace have needed my instruction in the finer (or coarser) points of cultural theory to envision the basic scenario of 'The Suffering Channel', for, according to the Max biography, Wallace studied with the brilliant queer theorist Andrew Parker even while an undergraduate at Amherst. Moreover, voracious reader that he was, it is not impossible that Wallace, prior to penning a fiction dedicated to the question of excremental art, had pored over all the various documents pertinent to my embodied arguments in *Male Matters* – all the stuff from Sigmund Freud, George Bataille, Julia Kristeva, Jacques Derrida, Jacques Lacan, Jane Gallop, not to mention James Joyce, that informs and infects my book – without ever having opened the gnarly volume itself.

But I just can't bring myself to imagine any other contemporary monograph in which all of this theoretically-pertinent-to-his-story stuff would have been so aptly consolidated, and thus so readily available for Wallace's inspection, than in my *Male Matters* (and I did, after all, I swear, send him a copy). Where else than in *Male Matters* would Wallace have been likely to witness, in such close proximity, all of the following abjection-related items, each, as I will spell out further below, receiving its own thematic or figural treatment at the end of *Oblivion*?

(1) Inquiry into the possible psychical consequences for the subject-in-process of the so-called 'cloaca theory' of childbirth that Freud imputes to all children: '"It is a universal theory among children," Freud writes, "that babies are born from the bowel like a piece of faeces: defaecation is the model of the act of birth" (*SE* 22: 100)' (Thomas, 1996: 85).

(2) Elaboration of Kristeva's quasi-cloacal idea in *Powers of Horror* that the fledgling subject-in-process must psychically abject the maternal body to avoid the sinking feeling of being entirely enmired in it/her himself: 'Abjection as a disruption of … archaic boundaries … poses a threat of "engulfment" to the subject, the threat "of being swamped by the dual relationship, thereby risking the loss not of a part (castration) but of the totality of his living being," the phantasmatic danger of "his very own identity sinking irretrievably into the mother" [Kristeva, 1982: 64]' (Thomas, 1996: 14).

(3) Consideration of Freud's Wolf-Man's childhood use of the term 'front-bottom' – a rather canny thing to call your country matters – to designate the vagina: 'In the case of Freud's speculation about the Wolf-Man's narrative, the disavowal of castration entails imagining the vagina as a "front bottom," that is, as a forward extension of the posterior region ... As Freud writes in 'Anxiety and Instinctual Life,' any "interest in the vagina, which awakens later, is also essentially of anal-erotic origin. This is not to be wondered at, for the vagina itself, to borrow an apt phrase from Lou-Andreas Salomé, is 'taken on lease' from the rectum" (*SE* 22: 101)' (Thomas, 1996: 76). And, finally:

(4) A pretty long exploration of Joycean 'inkenstink' and other matters emerging from Joyce's 'excrementitious intelligence', not excluding Stephen D's question about whether or not excrement can be art, but preceded by Lacan's suggestion that, when you get right down to it, real art can never avoid being excremental – 'The authenticity of what emerges in painting is diminished in us human beings by the fact that we have to get our colours where they're to be found, that is to say, in the shit ... The creator will never participate in anything other than the creation of a small dirty deposit, a succession of small dirty deposits juxtaposed' (Lacan, 1978: 176; Thomas, 1996: 114) – a suggestion that is itself preceded, at least in *Male Matters*, by that other Lacanian bit, already cited above, about the writer's anxiety when facing the blank sheet of paper, all of these suggestive bits and pieces prompting *this writer* to write that 'the knowledge that the creator cannot participate in his creation without placing his being in the shit, that insofar as he gives himself over to representation and to the other's gaze he pointedly stains himself and becomes caught up in a metonymic succession of small dirty deposits [juxtaposed] ... gives rise to [what I call] the anxiety of production, the creator's vertiginous, dysgraphic, scatontological anxiety when facing the blank white page, any surface in which he can see himself as something other' (Thomas, 1996: 114).

Now, to begin attaching these argumentative items from *Male Matters* to the fictional things that happen in 'The Suffering Channel', let's fold *MM* item #4 back on to *MM* item #1, let's say that if it's the good old cloaca theory that originally allows the subject both to account for his bodily origins *and* to 'see himself as something other', this 'theory' of one's being dropped into the world out of somebody's butthole will eventually and inevitably lead the subject to 'see himself' not as an orthopaedically 'ideal ego', as in the moment of the mirror stage, but rather as something far 'other' than anything he should ever want to look at, much less be. In other words, the cloaca theory can be sustained as a phantasmatic account of personal origins only for so long as the little theorist can manage to keep investing the stuff that comes out of his own body with some sort of oblative value (as Freud insists all children do do), but the theory must be dropped like a steaming hot potato as soon as the child learns to equate all turds everywhere with everything 'worthless, disgusting, abhorrent and abominable' (Freud *SE* 21: 100; Thomas, 1996: 84) in the world, as soon as he or she learns to assume 'the anal' as 'the symbol of everything that is to be repudiated and excluded from life' (Freud *SE* 7: 187; Thomas, 1996: 84).[11] But what this repression of the cloaca theory entails is that most normatively situated or 'socially refined' adults will be profoundly disturbed whenever the theory is partially unburied or reborn, whenever the rectal and the abominable get mixed up with the redemptive and the adorable: when, for example, worthless nuggets of human shit are presented as 'exquisite pieces of art' (Wallace, 2004: 238) worthy of aesthetic admiration, or, perhaps even more unsettling – because more deeply related to the disruption of 'archaic boundaries' before the erection of which it didn't cost the toddler any tokens of self-esteem to gleefully identify with its excrement – when turds get treated as human babies and/or babies get figured as turds.

The unsettling identification of 'baby' with faeces and vice-versa is crawling all over the Freud chapter of *Male Matters.* But this rather less than positive ID gets its most explicit thematic figuration in 'The Suffering Channel' during that story's lower Manhattan 'working lunch' sequence: 'Many of *Style*'s upper echelon interns convened for a working lunch at Chambers Street's Tutti Mangia restaurant twice a week, to discuss issues of concern and transact any editorial or other business that was pending, after which each returned to her respective mentor and relayed whatever was germane' (Wallace, 2004: 260). What's germane here is that these exquisitely coiffed and tailored upper echelon interns – the 'majority' of whom 'traditionally come from Seven Sisters colleges' (Wallace, 2004: 261), so you can just imagine – are sufficiently attracted to/repulsed by the talk of 'Skip Atwater's bizarre and quixotic pitch for a … piece on some sort of handyman who purportedly excreted pieces of fine art out of his bottom', or 'what came to be called the miraculous poo story' (Wallace, 2004: 262), that they cautiously begin to tell atrocious (but still basically adorable) poo-and-po-po-related stories of their own. The discussion starts with what later gets called 'the intracunnilingual flatus vignette' (involving some woman's haplessly farting in the face of the fellow going down on her), makes its way through a sophisticated comparative analysis of British, French and German toilets (one that will be quite familiar to anyone who's read Slavoj Žižek), but then abruptly comes to an end when one of the interns, named Laurel Rodde,

> who as a rule favored DKNY, and who wasn't exactly unpopular but no one felt like they knew her very well despite all the time they all spent with one another,

> and who usually barely said a word at the working lunches, suddenly said: 'You know, did anybody when they were little ever have this thing where you think of your shit as sort of like your baby and sometimes want to hold it and talk to it and almost cry or feel guilty about flushing it and dream sometimes of your shit in a little sort of little stroller with a bonnet and bottle and still sometimes in the bathroom look at it and give a little wave like, bye bye, as it goes down, and then feel void?' There was an uncomfortable silence. Some of the interns looked at one another out of the corner of their eye. They were at a stage where they were now too adult and socially refined to respond with a drawn out semicruel 'Oooo-kaaaay', but you could tell that a few of them were thinking it. (Wallace, 2004: 267).

OK, what I was thinking when I read this passage for the first time, in 2004, is that Wallace had at least glanced at the book I'm pretty sure I sent him as *un petit cadeau* back in 1996. But to relate what's more germane, I'll note the way Wallace's depiction of this intra-intern-al discussion at the restaurant called Tutti Mangia ('everybody eat') relates not only to *MM* item #1 (involving the speculative outcome of rectal parturition) but to *MM* item #2 (involving anxiety about engulfment in the muck of the maternal). For Wallace effectively sandwiches the Tutti Mangia segment into his extended narrational buildup to the major sex-scene *qua* engulfment scenario in 'The Suffering Channel', Skip Atwater's encounter with/immersion in *Mrs.* B. M., the gargantuan Amber Molke, in the front seat of the salary-man's 'enmired Cavalier' (Wallace, 2004: 306).

Skip's rented car is called a Cavalier because Wallace is following the standard convention of letting the brand-names of products or objects used or driven by fictional characters 'characterise' those characters.[12] The Cavalier is 'enmired' because it's sinking in the mud being produced by the wind-storming Midwestern downpour in which Atwater and Amber are caught. Wallace describes the Cavalier as being increasingly more deeply enmired on Amber's side, however, because the woman was herself 'less a person than a vista, a quarter ton of sheer Midwest pulchritude' (Wallace, 2004: 250), less a distinct human being than, as we'll see, an oceanic feeling surrounded by an 'immense sexual force field' (269), an erotic overflow of beautifully morbid obesity. At 6′1″, Amber is not quite as tall as Avril Incandenza, the self-centred and all-consuming maternal (death) figure in *Infinite Jest*, but she is much wider and heavier, outsizing and outweighing the adult but 'childlike' Atwater by far. Wallace provides ample details of the corporeal discrepancy between Amber and Skip, informing us that 'though technically fat, [Amber] presented more as simply huge, extrudent in all three dimensions. At least half a foot taller than the journalist, she managed to seem both towering and squat' (260). She 'had a head nearly twice the size of Atwater's own' (274), so that while 'her throat's girth was extraordinary – Atwater could not have gotten around it with both hands' (273), Amber's single hand 'could likely have gone all the way around Atwater's head and still been able to touch finger to thumb' (285).

Now, I can't read that last manual detail without thinking of (and taking far too literally) Lacan's infamous claim that 'if the mother's desire *is* for the phallus, the child wants to be the phallus in order to satisfy her desire' (2006: 582) – contrary, that is, to everything I'm supposed to know about the phallus's not being the penis and all that, I still see 'Atwater's head' here being figured as the tip or nozzle of the penis Amber Moltke would have if Amber had a great big dick instead of cavernous country matters between her legs, Atwater's whole body thus figured as the phallic endowment of this vista-sized maternal figure were *she* to be imagined 'holding her own' in one immensely sexy hand. As 'he continued to grip the Cavalier's steering wheel tightly with both hands and face directly ahead as though still driving' (Wallace, 2004: 269), however, Skip seems anxiously attracted less to Amber's hand than to her nearest leg, which for him 'was like something you could slide down into some kind of unimaginable chasm' (269). And sliding down 'something' into something unspeakably 'other' is pretty much what Atwater ends up doing, for the more the passenger side of the Cavalier sinks into the spreading Midwestern morass, the more Atwater is drawn into the multi-dimensionally extruding Amber, so that she in her vast totality becomes her own immensely engulfing front-bottom, an unimaginable chasm of devouring mud. And so eventually and inevitably

> they were kissing – or rather Atwater was kissing at the left corner of Amber Moltke's lip, while her mouth covered nearly the entire right side of the journalist's face all the way to the earlobe. The fluttering motions of his hands as they beat ineffectually at her left shoulder were no doubt similarly misperceived as passion. The movements of Amber's rapid disrobing then began to cause the rented sedan to heave this way and that, and drive it starboard side even more deeply into the overlook's mud, and a very muffled set of what could have been either screams or cries of excitement began to issue from the tilted vehicle; and anyone trying to look in either side's window would have been unable to see any part of Skip Atwater at all. (288)

Would-be spectators may not be able see any *part* of Skip, but it's fairly easy to see the pre-Oedipal *point* of the journalist's disappearance into the unbearably close horizon called Amber Moltke. Indeed, a few dozen pages later on, when Atwater is described as remembering the previous night's dream-like 'sensation of being somehow immersed in another human being, of having that person surround him like water', Wallace lets emerge the admission that 'it did not exactly take an advanced clinical degree to interpret' (312) these matters. But neither would Wallace have necessarily needed to read in *Male Matters* the lines from Kristeva's *Powers of Horror* about the subject's fear '"of being swamped by the dual relationship, thereby risking the loss not of a part

… but of the totality of his living being'" and so seeing "his very own identity [sink] irretrievably into the mother"' (Thomas, 1996: 14) to have produced the swampy scenario of Atwater's total immersion in Amber in the sinking Cavalier.

But I like to imagine that he did.

Moreover, to go forward and back to our old friend the 'front-bottom', I also like to imagine that language from *MM* item #3 played a part in informing Wallace's writing about two related 'unconscious signifiers' in 'The Suffering Channel', both of which seem to involve what I call a disturbingly 'forward extension of the posterior region' (Thomas, 1996: 76). The first signifier, extending from Brint Moltke himself, involves

> the arrangement of the artist's hands: their thumbs and forefingers formed a perfect lap level circle, which Moltke held or rather somehow directed before him like an aperture or target. He appeared to be unaware of this habit. It was a gesture both unsubtle and somewhat obscure in terms of what it signified. Combined with the [artist's] rigid smile, it was almost the stuff of nightmares. (Wallace, 2004: 248)

We are later told that 'no analogy for the digital waist level circle or aperture or orifice or void seemed quite right, but it struck Atwater as definitely the sort of tic or gesture that meant something' (Wallace, 2004: 253), the something meant of course pertaining to the artist's attractively 'repulsive talent' (253) for bringing visibly to the fore what's ordinarily left behind or blindly flushed into oblivion. Like but unlike the eye called window to the soul, Mr. B. M.'s 'unconscious ring' (253) or digital anus seems both to provide and to deny Atwater a glimpse into the sculptor's creatively transfiguring intestinal tract, 'the peculiar little unconscious signifier that Brint Moltke made when he sat, the strange abdominal circle or hole that he formed with his hands' (312) providing less a dreamy 'royal road to the unconscious' than a nightmarish Hershey Highway to same destination.

But speaking of dreams about butts that aren't butts, the other unconscious signifier of the front-bottom dispensation in 'The Suffering Channel' seems to me to emerge in *Style* intern Laurel Manderley's dream about a house, a rented duplex, with 'a front door that [wasn't] in front' (Wallace, 2004: 301). Laurel's dream

> had occurred the same night that the digital photos of Brint Moltke's work had appeared on the floor below the fax and she had felt the queer twin impulses both to bend and get them and run as fast she could from the cubicle complex …
>
> The dream involved a small house that she somehow knew was the one with the fractional address that belonged to the lady and her husband in Skip Atwater's miraculous poo story … The only specifically strange thing was that the house had two front doors, even though one of them wasn't in the front but

> it was still a front door. But this fact could not begin to account for the overwhelming dread Laurel Manderley felt, sitting there. There was a premonition of not just danger but evil. There was a creeping, ambient evil present, except even though present it was not in the room. Like the second front door, it was somehow there and not. (Wallace, 2004: 301–302)

The passage describing Lauren's dream and her feelings about it ends by insisting that 'there's no way to convey just why the two front door thing is so terrifying, since she herself can't even rationally explain it' (301–302), but one relatively rational explanation would involve these obvious and obscure overdeterminations: obviously, the dream is prompted by Lauren's ambivalent response to the faxed photos of Mr. B. M.'s ass-works, material from the man's backside brought to the front, but, more obscurely, it also follows her having heard Laurel Rodde's 'turd-baby' ruminations back at Tutti Mangia. In other words, since the dream involves Lauren's uncertainty about which one of the house's two openings she should run towards, the normal front door or the ambiently evil 'front door that isn't in front', her uncertainty may signify a return of the repressed cloaca theory, with corresponding doubts about from which of the two maternal apertures, front or back, she herself originally emerged. Moreover, as a possible future participant the maternal 'mode of production' herself, Lauren may have let Moltke's pieces and Rodde's ruminations prompt the unconscious terror of her own front-bottom someday popping out a massive dump rather than a little darling.

But the detail I find most compelling here is that Lauren's dream's locus is, again, a *rented* house – in other words, a house that is *taken on lease*. For the specific language from Freud about the 'front-bottom' that anyone reading *Male Matters* would surely have noticed stipulates that 'interest in the vagina, which awakens later, is also essentially of anal-erotic origin. This is not to be wondered at, for the vagina itself, to borrow an apt phrase from Lou-Andreas Salomé, is "taken on lease" from the rectum' (Thomas, 1996: 76). In other words, all artistic liberties taken, this correspondence releases me to assert as a fact proven beyond all reasonable doubt that *Lauren Manderley* read my *Male Matters*, even if the male who materialised her never actually did.

Segment 5: '*HELP ME*'

And so now to *MM* item #4, involving the scatontological implications of putting pen to paper, and to the many ways in which 'The Suffering Channel' connects the technology of producing script to the 'fantasy of being shit', 'the secular miracle of communication' to the breaking news of 'miraculous poo'. Note, for example, the frequent and ambiguous appearance of the word 'piece' itself –

'And then it will come out.'
'The piece, you mean' (Wallace, 2004: 276)

– used, as here, in such a way that it isn't always immediately clear which piece you mean: the piece of styled stool that will come out of Moltke's butt or the piece of commercial prose that will come out in Atwater's *Style.*[13] Note as well the way one mechanically reproductive piece of inter-office communicative technology (specifically, *Style*'s fax apparatus with its 'defunct ringer and missing tray') gets transfigured into a lugubrious shitting machine: 'The images [of Moltke's pieces that] Atwater was forwarding to Laurel Manderley began to emerge from the unit's feeder, coiled slightly, detached, and floated in a back and forth fashion to the antistatic carpet' (Wallace, 2004: 258–259) – though I have to say that while I hardly own the word 'coil' its appearance here puts me in mind of the 'dark, coiling figure' that I autobiographically 'let fall' on the second page of my *Male Matters.* And, speaking of white pages and of the shit that can figuratively sit upon them, note that when the editorial office of *Style* receives not faxed images but a real shipment of actual Moltkean artworks, the pieces get unpacked and arranged on the Executive Editor's desk as follows: 'Each sat on its own blank sheet of typing paper: it was the 20 pound rag bond used for executive letters and memos at *Style*' (Wallace, 2004: 293), these literally turd-laden pages of course not failing to remind yours untruly of what Lacan's writer will tell you when asked about the anxiety he experiences when facing any blank white sheet.

But regarding the strongest, most effluvial signs of scatontological dysgraphia in Wallace's piece of writing, let's say that the crux of the matter no doubt involves that moment in the narrative when Brint Molke moves his movements from the imaginary to the symbolic, when he goes from cloacal sculpture to assholey scripture. I refer to the scene in which Atwater emerges from the front door of his room at the Indiana Holiday Inn, ice-bucket in hand, and steps out on to the balcony:

> His shoe nearly came down in the message before he saw it and stopped, one foot suspended in air, aware at the same time that chlorine was not the only scent in the balcony's wind. The '*HELP ME*' was ornate and calligraphic, quotation marks sic. In overall design, it was not unlike the cursive … phrases of decorative icing on certain parties' cakes of his experience. But it was not made of icing. That much was immediately clear …
>
> [Skip] knew that great force of will would be required to try to imagine the various postures and contractions involved in producing the phrase, its detached and plumb straight underscoring, the tiny and perfectly formed quotation marks. Part of him was aware that it had not yet occurred to him to consider that the phrase might actually mean or imply in this context. (Wallace, 2004: 314–315)

Now, whatever the phrase might mean in Wallace's narrative context, in the scatontological context that I've been straining to lay out here, it's crucial that the deposited phrase contain some form of the first person pronoun, that the pressed-out phrase express '*ME*', that it work to 'set down my identity in scat' (Kinnell in Thomas, 2008: 49), materialise a signifier of self-recognition, 'physicalize' the 'consciousness' of self that is verily said to be 'nature's nightmare' (Wallace, 2004: 282).[14]

As for what Brint Moltke might have actually meant to imply by his 'brown cri de coeur' (Wallace, 2004: 315) on the balcony, we might note that the phrase 'help me' is after all a line from Kurt Neumann's 1958 horror film *The Fly*, the two words repeatedly squeaked at the end of the film by the tiny, fly-bodied but human-headed abomination helplessly caught in the arachnid's web and being steadily approached by the web's giant devouring producer. If we allow this cinematic allusion any purchase, then we are moved to ask who or what the film's immense spider might signify to the succour-seeking Moltke, and, given her graphically established 'devouring' obesity, Amber Moltke – less person than sinister vista, after all – would seem the most likely representational candidate. *Amber's* consuming passion, however, seems less gluttonously omni-sexual than massively monocultural, involving a trivially debased 'desire for recognition' unlike anything Hegel's masters or slaves would have found worth entertaining, a desire both to become one with and rise above the spreading ooze of mass culture, her erotically engulfing Atwater in the enmired Cavalier simply a part of her larger design to get the salary-man to publicise her husband's repulsive talent, to get Brint's creatively transfiguring *aufhebung*-hole out there into the mass-media spotlight, to project her husband and herself into the 'single great all devouring eye' (Wallace, 2004: 272) of American celebrity and fame.[15] As Amber explains to the as yet unengulfed Atwater in the sinking vehicle, the Moltkes' goal is

> to somehow stand out. To distinguish themselves from the great huge faceless mass of folks that watched the folks that did stand out. On the TV and in venues like *Style* … To be known, to matter, she said. To have church or Ye Olde Buffet or the new Bennigan's at the Whitcomb Outlet Mall get quiet when her and Brint came in, and to feel people's eyes, the weight of their gaze … To pick up a copy of *People* or *Style* at the beautician's and see herself and Brint looking back out at her. To be on TV. (283)

So does Moltke inscribe 'help me' with his asshole on the balcony because he wants Skip to assist him in getting 'to be on TV', or, hoping to spread his wings (rather than his cheeks) and fly away from Amber's all-American arachnid plan, is he pleading with Atwater to rescue him from precisely that fate? If the latter is the case, then Skip fails to fail to be an asshole in the end, for he indeed 'helps' get Moltke a (dark) spot on television.[16] Specifically, Atwater helps facilitate the planned broadcast appearance of the BM phenomena on a new venue called The Suffering Channel (a division, as we're told, of O Verily Productions); he helps orchestrate the artist's televised moment/movement of truth, his verily productive appearance on 'a clear Lucite commode unit atop a ten foot platform of tempered glass beneath which a video crew will record the real time emergence of either an iconically billowing and ecstatic Monroe or a five to seven inch *Winged Victory of Samothrace*, depending on dramatic last minute instructions' (Wallace 2004: 328). For the Executive Editorial decision has been made that *Style* will *not* publish the miraculous poo story as initially pitched by Skip but *will* cover TSC's broadcast of the proceedings by which the *truth* of Brint's self-purportedly hands-free faecal formalism will be *verified*. Verification of the artwork's authenticity is required, for the question is not simply why Moltke wrote 'help me': the question is if he really did inscribe these words 'direct(al)ly' with his ass, which would be pretty amazing, or if he just took his own quotidian crap and fashioned the calligraphy manually, which would be pretty disgusting. Similarly, as inquiring minds reading *Style* and viewing The Suffering Channel will surely want to know, does Moltke really bring fully formed stool stylings immediately out of his behind, or are he and ambitious Amber completely pulling out of their fundaments the story that he can perform this most secular of miracles? These are *questions* because no one has ever truly seen a single one of the pieces come out, not even the artist himself. And so, on the penultimate page of 'The Suffering Channel', there sit these words: 'Suspended from the studio's lighting grid to a position directly before the commode unit, a special monitor taking feed from below will give the artist visual access to his own production for the first time ever in his career. He believes what he sees will be public' (Wallace, 2004: 328).

This matter of publicly verifying the authenticity of fundamentally aesthetic production, establishing the truth behind the piece about the pieces established from behind, takes us back to the second segment of this (i.e., my) piece of writing, concerning the tension between *parrhesia* as truth-telling and *poesis* as yarn-spinning, the conflict between the production of truth as the will to death and the production of art as the will to *life* and to *style*. At the same time, this business about giving 'the artist visual access to his own production' resonates with what Slavoj Žižek calls 'fundamental fantasies' involving the subject's impossible desire to witness his own *birth* – his own mode of production, his own cloacal coming out of the original front-bottom – and/or his own *death*: given, that is, the common association of excrement with expiration, given that 'the corpse is the utmost in abjection' (Kristeva, 1982: 4), given that 'the horror we feel at the thought of a corpse is akin to the feeling we have at [the sight of] human excreta' (Bataille, 1986: 57), to *see* oneself shitting, even if shitting mere shit and not monumental art, could messily metaphorise the impossible act of seeing oneself coming to one's end, seeing oneself being wasted, becoming a cadaver.[17]

But as things seem to fall out, Brint Moltke *won't see shit*, and neither will we. Nothing, that is, gets verified in the end; there's no money-shot for any of us. Just as the reader at the inconclusion of *The Crying of Lot 49* is left, along with the novel's heroine Oedipa Maas, 'to wait for the crying of Lot 49' (Pynchon, 1966: 183), so the heroes and villains and readers and watchers of 'The Suffering Channel' are left suspended, constipatedly waiting for Moltke's next brown *cri de couer* to drop. For verily, a technical difficulty in the TSC studio would seem to deny both artist and audience visual access to *veritas*, the final production of truth, so that Wallace's last words in this long piece of fiction involve the fact that there's

> some eleventh hour complication involving the ground level camera and the problem of keeping the commode's special monitor out of its upward shot, since video capture of a camera's own monitor causes what is known in the industry as feedback glare – the artist in such a case would see, not his own emergent *Victory*, but a searing and amorphous light. (Wallace, 2004: 329)

This revelation of the *withholding* of revelation is consistent with Wallace's narrative strategies elsewhere. For example, in his introduction to Wallace's *The Pale King*, Michael Pietsch notes Wallace's notes for his final novelistic effort: 'One note says the novel is "a series of setups for things to happen but nothing happens" … Still another suggests that throughout the novel "something big *threatens* to happen but doesn't actually happen"' (Wallace, 2011: xii). Of course, what's different about 'The Suffering Channel' is that throughout the fiction something big *threatens* to happen that *did* actually happen. For this story is set at a historical juncture when certain of its characters, like *Style*'s Ellen Bactrian, 'had [but] ten weeks to live' (Wallace, 2004: 326), when a network of fundamentalists, without any 'warning whatsoever' (Wallace, 2004: 280), were planning to take a massive crap on a nation, to tear America a new asshole, a time when the greatest work of art imaginable for the whole cosmos was most definitely on its way.

Of course, we all know death is coming, that the absolute master's money-shot is perpetually aimed at each of our maps. Sometimes we can even see our own shitty ending's approach quite clearly. If we didn't possess that knowledge, that vision, that foresight, if we weren't at least dimly alert to that spoiler, if we were utterly oblivious to our utter oblivion, we wouldn't be 'fucking human beings', which means we wouldn't need or be able to lie, tell stories, craft fiction, make art.[18] And while we can of course always *read* the autobiographical stuff that we've written, *see* the self-expressive artworks that we've made, re-examine and even rearrange whatever succession of small dirty deposits we've managed to set down, we can never 'truly' see our own non-fictional endings. All of us body artists are constitutively denied real-time visual access to the shit that actually happens when we fully arrive at our will to truth's true destination. Just as Bruegel could behold his finished 'Triumph of Death' but couldn't witness his own life's finish, just as Brint Moltke could see only a spreading white glare but not his own *Winged Victory*, so, perhaps, at the moment of truth, at the instant of impact, on the morning of 9/11, when they gave cloacal birth to 'the tragedy by which *Style* would enter history' (Wallace, 2004: 245), the flying fundamentalists who penetrated our airspace and our offices couldn't see *their* winged victories, either, but only some shapeless and searing light.

As for Wallace's craft or sullen art in relation to my infinitely less significant own, I can say only that I'm grateful for the time during which Wallace seemed to believe that continuing to write fiction, to lie with a good conscience, to pit *poesis* against *parrhesia*, was the most productive way for him to help himself, to *help me*, and to help us, channel our abject suffering. I'd be lying if I said I didn't wish he still felt the same way.

Notes

1 The phrase 'life as literature' appears as the subtitle of an excellent book on Nietzsche by Nehamas (1987).

2 The word *poubellication* is a Lacanian pun mixing *publication* with *poubelle*, French for 'garbage can'.

3 Space limitations prevent my examining all the anxieties about differentiation-loss imputed to DeLillo in this essay, so here I will just say that his writing seems to me to participate in the heteronormative fear that psychically losing or representationally blurring or medico-technologically altering the distinction between 'man' and 'woman', between 'one sex' and 'the other', actually involves dissolving the boundary between bright shining 'life' and its dark shitty opposite, so that 'transsexuality' of any sort gets equated with abject ambulant death. For DeLillo, it seems, the internet's to blame for everything's now being turned into the same (witness the eponymous cyberspatial 'hyperlinking' of the deceased cross-dresser J. Edgar with the dead nun Sister Edgar as described on the penultimate page of *Underworld*). For a consideration of other (mainly theoretical) writers who seem to endorse this 'transsex=living death' ideology, see pp. 19–62 of Thomas (2008).

4 Pynchon's novel is a sort of ur-text for both DeLillo and Wallace, and so I will be alluding to it a few more times in what follows.

5 I allude here to Pynchon's reference in *CL49* to 'the secular miracle of communication' (1966: 180).

6 In *Dialectic of Enlightenment*, Horkheimer and Adorno write that 'Intellect's true concern is a negation of reification. It must perish when it is solidified into a cultural asset and handed out for consumption purposes. The flood of precise information and brand-new amusements make [*sic*] people smarter and more stupid at once' (2002: xvii).

7 As a sort of running counterthrust to DeLillo's heteronormativity, I have been letting drop phrases – carnal irony, cultural droppings, exuberant self-discard, culture of redemption, gravely rectal, and 'no future' – freely drawn from masterworks of queer theory by Leo Bersani and Lee Edelman. See the appropriate titles in the References.

8 Another allusion to Pynchon's *CL49*: Upon taking LSD, Oedipa Maas's radio DJ husband Mucho not only loses his distinct personal identity but discovers that 'Everybody who says the same words is the same person' (1966: 142). 'Rich, chocolaty goodness' is the advertising phrase that Mucho wants 'everybody' to say so as to become 'the same'.

9 For more on Stockhausen's remark, see http://nymag.com/news/9–11/10th-anniversary/karlheinz-stockhausen/.

10 I'm certain of the date of our talk because I remember that there appeared in that morning's *New York Times* a story about the controversy surrounding the fact that *Infinite Jest* had somehow not even been nominated for that year's National Book Award, and because Wallace was not aware that his name and picture were in the *Times* that day until I told him the news over the phone. How I came to be talking to Wallace in the first place is as follows: I was then teaching at the University of Northern Iowa; my department had that year received funds dedicated to bringing in a series of distinguished speakers/writers to the tune of 5000 dollars each, and I was calling Wallace to see if he were interested in coming over from Illinois to give a talk and to make some money. Wallace responded that for *that* kind of money I should find somebody more famous who really deserved it; he said he would be willing to drive to Cedar Falls IA from Normal IL and give a reading and maybe have dinner with some creative writing students if we paid his travel expenses, but that there was 'no way' he could accept 5000 dollars. 'It's a karma thing', he impressed me very much by saying. Now, my job at the time was to find people for whom there *was* a way to accept 5000 dollars without any karmic anxiety, and I indeed went on to find such people—without, as I now very much regret, ever going back to Wallace to see if he were really serious about driving over and giving a reading in Cedar Falls for chump-change.

11 Speaking of the transvaluation of the oblative value of a person's own personal shit, here is a bit from Freud that Wallace would have encountered in *Male Matters* if he in fact read *Male Matters*: 'After a person's own faeces, his excrement, has lost its value for him, this instinctual interested derived from the anal source passes over on to objects than can be presented as *gifts*. And this is rightly so, for faeces were the first gift that an infant could make, something he could part with out of love for whoever was looking after him. After this, corresponding exactly to analogous changes of meaning that occur in linguistic development, this ancient interest in faeces is transformed into the high valuation of *gold* and *money*' (*SE* 22: 100–101, Thomas, 1996: 79–80). This exchange between the fecal and the financial may help account for why Wallace in 'The Suffering Channel' repeatedly tags Skip Atwater, who 'could write a sweet commercial line' (Wallace, 2004: 270), as a 'salary-man.' Like the previously discussed 'Shit man' in *Underworld*'s opening, 'salary-man' – designating the man who writes only for

the 'salary' with and as which he is identified – is pretty much a scatontological signifier.

12 Here the word 'cavalier' describes not only 'what Skip himself believed was his chief flaw, an insufficient sense of the tragic' (Wallace, 2004: 245), and not only what Dwight McDonald considers the chief flaw of mass culture, this 'debased trivial culture that voids [all the] deep realities (sex, death, failure, tragedy)' (1998: 34), but also what Wallace himself believed to be the chief flaw of over-ironised and over-entertained but substance-starved American popular culture immediately prior to 9/11, which in 'The Suffering Channel' gets called 'the tragedy by which *Style* would enter history' (Wallace, 2004: 245). Such flaw-identification would seem to be one of the more obvious points of Wallace's story's indictment of American popular culture and the republic for which it stands: the story asks not 'can excrement be art?' but would we as a nation, in the summer of 2001, been so blithely consumed with and by trivially debased crap like *Style* and its countless cultural analogs had we any premonition, any 'warning whatsoever', that much more serious shit was coming, that 'art' in the form of Bin Laden's 'Triumph of Death' was imminently 'on its way'? But then again, when is death's triumph not on its way? And when do we not want to void that deep reality?

13 And just for good measure, there's a conspicuously cloacal clincher in which the journalistic 'piece' is described as being Skip Atwater's 'baby' (Wallace, 2004: 324).

14 As we are told: 'Registered motto of Chicago IL's O Verily Productions, which for complicated business reasons appeared on its colophon in Portuguese: CONSCIOUSNESS IS NATURE'S NIGHTMARE' (Wallace, 2004: 282).

15 Hegel, by the way, gets a mention in 'The Suffering Channel': one of Moltke's sculptures represents 'G. W. F. Hegel's image of Napoleon as the world spirit on horseback' (Wallace, 2004: 316). There is also a chapter on Hegel, called 'Piss Hegel', in *Male Matters*. I mean, I'm just saying …

16 Atwater is noted for his 'consistent failure to be an asshole' in the sort of professional world in which if you don't succeed in *being* an asshole you're likely to be treated as a turd and in which Atwater correspondingly 'was seen as having roughly the self-esteem of a prawn' (Wallace, 2004: 298).

17 Žižek writes that fundamental fantasies always involve the subject's preposterous ability to witness moments before or beyond its own temporal finitude, that is, moments of pre-origin or post-demise. Thus, in the fundamental fantasy, 'the subject is miraculously present as a pure gaze observing his own non-existence' (1996: 19).

18 Wallace to Larry McCaffery: 'Fiction's about what it is to be a fucking human being' (in Max, 2012: 178).

References

Bataille, G. 1985. The Jesuve. In Stoekl, A. ed. *Visions of Excess: Selected Writings, 1927–1939*. Trans. A. Stoekl with C. R. Lovitt and D. M. Leslie Jr. Minneapolis: University of Minnesota Press, pp. 73–78.

Bataille, G. 1986. *Erotism: Death and Sensuality*. Trans. M. Dalwood. San Francisco: City Lights Books.

Bersani, L. 1987. Is the Rectum a Grave? *October* 43, pp. 197–222.
Bersani, L. 1990. *The Culture of Redemption.* Cambridge, MA: Harvard University Press.
Burn, S. J. 2012. *David Foster Wallace's Infinite Jest: A Reader's Guide.* New York: Continuum.
DeLillo, D. 1984. *White Noise.* New York: Penguin.
DeLillo, D. 1997. *Underworld.* New York: Scribner.
Derrida, J. 1978. *Writing and Difference.* Trans. A. Bass. Chicago: University of Chicago Press.
Duvall, J. 2002. *Don DeLillo's Underworld: A Reader's Guide.* New York: Continuum.
Edelman, L. 2004. *No Future: Queer Theory and the Death Drive.* New York: Columbia University Press.
Freud, S. 1953–74. *The Standard Edition of the Complete Psychological Works.* London: Hogarth.
Harari, R. 2001. *Lacan's Seminar on 'Anxiety': An Introduction.* New York: The Other Press.
Horkheimer, M., and Adorno, T. 2002. *Dialectic of Enlightenment: Philosophical Fragments.* Trans. E. Jephcott. Stanford: Stanford University Press.
Kristeva, J. 1982 [1980]. *Powers of Horror: An Essay on Abjection.* Trans. L. S. Roudiez. New York: Columbia University Press.
Lacan, J. 1977. *Écrits: A Selection.* Trans. A. Sheridan. New York: Norton.
Lacan, J. 1978. *The Seminar of Jacques Lacan. Book XI, The Four Fundamental Concepts of Psychoanalysis, 1964.* Trans. A. Sheridan. New York: Norton.
Lacan, J. 2006. *Écrits: The First Complete Translation in English.* Trans. B. Fink. New York: Norton.
Max, D. 2012. *Every Love Story is a Ghost Story: A Life of David Foster Wallace.* New York: Viking.
McDonald, D. 1998. A Theory of Mass Culture. In J. Story, ed. *Cultural Theory and Popular Culture: A Reader.* Athens: University of Georgia Press, pp. 22–36.
Nehamas, R. 1987. *Nietzsche: Life as Literature.* Cambridge, MA: Harvard University Press.
Nietzsche, F. 2006. *The Nietzsche Reader.* Oxford: Blackwell.
Pynchon, T. 1966. *The Crying of Lot 49.* New York: Harper & Row.
Thomas, C. 1996. *Male Matters: Masculinity, Anxiety, and the Male Body on the Line.* Urbana: University of Illinois Press.
Thomas, C. 2008. *Masculinity, Psychoanalysis, Straight Queer Theory: Essays on Abjection in Literature, Mass Culture, and Film.* New York: Palgrave Macmillan.
Wallace, D. F. 1989. *Girl with Curious Hair.* New York: Norton.
Wallace, D. F. 1996. *Infinite Jest.* New York: Back Bay Books.
Wallace, D. F. 2004. *Oblivion.* New York: Back Bay Books.
Wallace, D. F. 2011. *The Pale King: An Unfinished Novel.* New York: Back Bay Books.
Žižek, S. 1993. *Tarrying with the Negative: Kant, Hegel, and the Critique of Ideology.* New York: Verso.
Žižek, S. 1996. *The Indivisible Remainder: An Essay on Schelling and Related Matters.* New York: Verso.

11

Base materials: performing the abject object

Daniel Watt

For he is not mad, he through whom the abject exists. (Kristeva, 1982: 6)

In his 1980 manifesto 'Reality of the Lowest Rank' the Polish director Tadeusz Kantor states, 'In the domain of the lowest reality, THE ESSENCE OF LIFE, bereft of STYLIZATION, GLITTER, false PATHOS, or ACADEMIC BEAUTY, is to be found' (Kantor, 1993: 124). The battle between the actor and the materials of their environment – the set, costumes and hybrid objects – in Kantor's theatre creates a stage space he terms the bio-object: neither human nor object, but an abject assault upon reality. It is in their artificiality that the audience encounters the Kantorian actor, as unalterably other, or as Kantor might term it 'death's emissary'. The actor in Kantor's theatre inhabits an in-between place, neither entity nor object.

In his 1968 text, *Towards a Poor Theatre*, Jerzy Grotowski quotes Artaud, 'Actors should be like martyrs burnt alive, still signalling to us from their stakes' (1991: 93). The level of psychophysical training required by the Grotowskian performer is often considered an attuned or peak condition, of an almost Olympic prowess. The attempt to locate performance within 'boundaries' and 'limits' inscribed within the actor, to rid them of external inhibitions, functions to elicit a form of sacrificial theatre at the limit of physical endurance and emotional containment.

Kantor and Grotowski were working during roughly the same period in a Poland overshadowed by the aftermath of Nazi, and then Soviet, occupation. Kantor had been a visual artist and experimented with theatre for many years before founding the Cricot 2 theatre with a group of artists, including Maria Jarema and Kazimierz Mikulski, in 1955. His early theatre work included performance happenings and versions of Witkacy plays in innovative and increasingly stylistic forms which would later be clearly 'Kantorian'. The period of his theatre works most widely known is often termed the 'Theatre of Death period' and includes his most famous performance, *The Dead Class* (1975), and also *Wielopole, Wielopole* (1980) and *Let the Artists Die* (1985). Kantor died in 1990 and Cricot 2 has continued to make work with a variety of members of the group.

Grotowski's theatre company, or laboratory, began in Opole in 1959; the phase of the group's work that is often explored includes their three most famous productions, *Akropolis* (1962), *The Constant Prince* (1965) and *Apocalypsis Cum Figuris* (1969). Grotowski's focus then turns to paratheatre, or 'closed work', in which there is not a performance end product but rather a participatory process that replaces the false divide between audience and actor. The training process in Grotowski's theatre laboratory was searching for an essence of acting that was based on first principles of movement that have been elaborated from 'organic impulses in an unblocked body going toward a fullness which is *not* of daily life' (Richards, 1995: 95). Grotowski died in 1999 but, as Kathleen Cioffi notes, 'the vision of the theatre that Grotowski and his actors introduced, was a belief that the theatre is a place where something sacred takes place' (Cioffi, 1999: 85), and that sense of the 'sacred' has influenced theatre practitioners for decades.

This essay examines the abject through the 'poor object' of Kantor's theatrical 'cricotages' and performance events and the intense 'sacrificial' total theatre of the Grotowskian performer. It argues that through the sacrificial abjection of the performing object in both Kantor and Grotowski's work a vision of base materiality, in a Bataillean sense, might lead us to reconsider the force of theatre as one that reveals the human, through a different type of communal event and the power of horror inherent in the sundering of selfhood in performance. Rather than embracing voguish avant-gardes, or posturing at alternative modes of representation, the task of performance becomes one of immersion in abjection and the generation of different forms of communal encounter that challenges identity.

So, what might an abject 'object' be? Julia Kristeva offers some reflection on the nature of the abject and how it differs from the object in *Powers of Horror*:

> The abject is not an ob-ject facing me, which I name or imagine. Nor is it an ob-jest, an otherness ceaselessly fleeing in a systematic quest of desire. What is abject is not my correlative, which, providing me with someone or something else as support, would allow me to be more or less detached and autonomous. The abject has only one quality of the object – that of being opposed to I. If the object, however, through its opposition, settles me within the fragile texture of a desire for meaning, which, as a matter of fact makes me ceaselessly and infinitely homologous to it, what is *abject*, on the contrary, the jettisoned object, is radically excluded and draws me toward the place where meaning collapses. (Kristeva, 1982: 1–2)

So the abject is not a 'thing', as such, something that would relate to a self that encounters it. So it resides alongside the object, in its alterity, but arises in a sense from a form of total exclusion from reabsorption into self. Encountering the abject is always destabilising, a sacrifice of self – a martyring, of sorts – into a base reality, where things and persons merge and disappear. It is not that identity disappears in the abject, but that it is altered; that certainty, and fixed place, of I, begins to vanish.

The process of production of a work of performance, and representation of character, relies upon a change of self, a sort of erasure in light of emergence. To play (although this is a difficult word in this context) someone else entails a working through and jettisoning of self in the first instance. Andrzej Wełmiński describes the dual process at work in Kantor's performances thus:

> The character created by an actor was identical with its performer; it was a form of self-presentation. Twin characters, doubles, replicas, split personalities, reflections, repetitions, copies, doppelgangers played a major part; a clear-unclear existence became their chief attribute. It was something more than an *alter ego*: it was an *ego alter*: a different me. (Wełmiński , 2014: 48)

There are echoes here of August Strindberg's note at the beginning of *A Dream Play*, where the 'characters, split, double, multiply, evaporate, condense, disperse, assemble' (Strindberg, 2000: 175). But where Strindberg's theatre may have begun a dissolution of character, it recouped all form into the 'consciousness … of the dreamer' (175), and, as bizarre as such might be, there is always a sense of another purpose to the performance – that that consciousness, as he says, 'rules over them all' (175). What Wełmiński points towards here, with the useful term 'clear-unclear' is a double movement between nothing and something, nobody and somebody, a something radically different to the all-knowing dreamer from whom 'there are no secrets, no illogicalities, no scruples, no laws' (175).

Antonin Artaud had already been experimenting with disrupting theatrical representation by a radical project of physical and psychical challenges; work that has deeply influenced many forms of theatre and performance practice through the last century. In her essay on Butoh, Bataille and Artaud, Catherine Curtin explains Artaud's attempts to pursue a theatre of bodily transformation:

> Artaud's theatrical ideas explored the body's infinite capacity for transmutation, as he wanted a multiplicity to be relentlessly created and affirmed, in intense moments of crisis, reflecting his own corporeality that was constantly in the process of being unravelled, disassembled and reborn. … He pared it down to the most basic elements, its marrow, sinew, flesh and flaying nerves, and proposed a new anatomical order forged from the material of abject fragmentation. Towards the end of his life he called for a 'revolution of the whole body', one

> that was metamorphosed and reconstituted to remain, as he had hoped early in his career, 'eternally incomplete'.
>
> In his first collection of poems, *Umbilical Limbo*, Artaud explores the body as if in a state prior to the symbolic, the imago in dissolution and 'images of threadlike, cotton wool limbs, images of limbs that are displaced and distanced'. (Curtin, 2010: 64)

This process of constant transformation echoes the encounter with the abject that Kristeva outlines, as even the body's form becomes dissolved into 'threadlike' limbs and a contorted struggling fleshy being, neither human nor object. But what remains from such a theatre, is there still 'someone' there, 'eternally incomplete' or not?

Who acts?

In a radio broadcast from October 1979, aimed at secondary school children, Grotowski offers two opposite definitions of the actor:

> the 'actor' can mean an individual who portrays or experiences some character, who acts somebody. That is one concept. Another possibility: the 'actor' means an individual in action, who aims not at acting, but at acting less than in daily life and who draws others to the simplest, the most human, the most direct actions – something so simple that it borders on the childish. Two polar possibilities. (Kumiega, 1987: 236)

Perhaps we need go no further with the question 'who acts?' for it seems that we may already have an answer. At a certain level an actor might simply be themself. But we all know it is not quite so simple as all that to *be* oneself, the *one* of *self* being the most complex of issues. And of course then we can ask, in what sense is acting a homogeneous practice, transferable directly using one specific method? Philip Zarrilli's text *Psychophysical Acting* cautions us to understand the work as a process, rather than system, stating, 'Enquiry is a process of exploration born out of intellectual and aesthetic curiosity. *Psychophysical Acting* [the book] is not and cannot be 'definitive' about either the questions around which the work is organised or the approach … taken to solving these questions at certain specific moments' (Zarrilli, 2009: 5).

Any approach to problem-solving must, as the actor's work might, be attentive to 'specific moments' – to the time of its question, as much as the question itself. In psychophysical acting we find an endless search for forms of selfhood, a figuring of action as thought and vice versa; a playing out of spirit and a drive not to represent but to *be*, in the sense of an eternal becoming. How might such deferred and mostly singular, interior, attempts to define being and identity enable an *act* at all? And how does the Kantorian actor attempt to explore this process of becoming? Wełmiński locates the issue between two polarities of identity, that of Kantor, his history and family, and that of the personal history of the individual actor:

> The crux was Kantor's reconstruction of his own life history. The artist himself referred to this as sleight of hand, a confidence trick of suspect legitimacy. Hired actors from a travelling theatre were to pretend to be the artist's 'Dear Absent Ones'. This was a trick, a circus act performed as part of a spiritual séance which Kantor himself had arranged. We were partly mediums, partly charlatans. On the one hand, we were enacting the roles of fathers, uncles, mother, aunt; on the other hand, we were ourselves. After a fashion, these stories of Kantor's were completed by each one of us. As we know, Tadeusz had a weakness for falsifying his own history, and such a method suited him very well and often pleased him exceedingly. Thus, each actor is, in their own singular way, a co-creator of his individual story. (Wełmiński , 2014: 49)

There is much play here around the figures of the charlatan, medium, cheap sideshow magic tricks and the air of the mistrusted travelling player. A quality of the criminal and abject is evoked that hints at trickery and subversion, as though performance itself were a 'sleight of hand' that substitutes one identity for another. The tradition of psychophysical practices, which, in a Grotowskian manifestation, require intense physical training, and differ in many basic ways from the practices of Kantor's Cricot2 company, are as much about an elaboration of an environment of training as a moment of performance, and in many ways the Cricot2 company were also engaged in endless rehearsals (training) for an event (a performance) that only marked a particular moment in the exploration of that process.

The question 'who acts?' might also be asking something of all those hidden relations between practitioners, teachers, students of the psychophysical and the Kantorian 'Cricotage', and all the further complex lineages and genealogies of the work through other cultural practices and manifold theatre forms, martial arts, ritual practices, circus and cabotin etc., and the environments of such work – the university, the theatre 'school', the workshop – all entailing careful elaboration of 'the political', 'the spiritual', and the very act of witnessing, training, appropriating and even misappropriating, that this would suggest. But the ultimate boundary is drawn by the individual performer, at work upon themselves, and striving to show something to an audience. Their encounter with themselves is one, to recall Andrzej Wełmiński's words, that *alters* their *ego*; that challenges limits and forces the actor to encounter a state of abjection where the body is returned to heterogeneous possibility rather than homogeneous self-assertion and production.

It is worth pausing here a moment to consider Georges Bataille's notion of Base Materialism, as it demonstrates the foundation of human projects in the most abject of elements. Rather than locating human endeavour in will, power, intellect or skill, Bataille sees a more basic, and somewhat degrading origin to human achievement, one quite amusingly elaborated in his essay, 'The Big Toe', where 'men obstinately imagine a tide that will permanently elevate them, never to return, into pure space. Human life entails, in fact, the rage of seeing oneself as a back and forth movement from refuse to the ideal, and from the ideal to refuse – a rage that is easily directed against an organ as *base* as the foot' (Bataille, 1985: 20–21).

The rage experienced by this frustrating beginning in the abject, and the revulsion against all that evokes it, goes some way to describing the difficult position of the actor in relation to other identities, for, as we have seen, its ego-altering activities bring us to the verge of this movement between 'refuse and the ideal' – both being and its founding alterity, at once. What remains difficult, even for Bataille, is to maintain the destabilising and disorienting force of such a thinking of the abject, without it collapsing back into something applied, as Benjamin Noys points out in his essay 'Bataille's Base Materialism':

> Bataille's achievement is to create an unstable discourse that communicates this possibility of matter as difference, and to provide a culture medium to carry this contagion of base matter … Bataille produces a very *different* thought of matter. The weakness of his thought at this point is that it also tries to translate the instability of base matter into political terms. (Noys, 1998: 503)

So, even Bataille's Base Materialism – an entirely *different* thinking of matter – is in danger of reaffirming a project for the abject, putting that which evades and destabilises work, *to* work. For the power of the base and abject is that it destroys boundaries, from the bottom up. The actor is always in danger of becoming useful again.

But it is in that sense (of boundaries) therefore that another preoccupation, the issue of community, occurs. For how indeed can we come together as actors, or those who act, without prejudice, without goal and intent and allow the work of bodies and minds to do their heterogeneous unfolding? Is there not always some point of idealism, or a pragmatic agenda that dissolves the sense both of subject and community – a dissolution at the very heart of 'who' that destroys the opportunity to 'act'; a kind of recouping of an abject dissolution into another object of accumulation?

The 'who' of 'who acts?' seems to return a resounding 'me', against the 'you' of the audience. But again this must be viewed in terms of the manifold approaches that might be taken to the elaboration of this skill – achieved through practices within the hermetic confines of the workshop. It is in this context that it is worth returning momentarily to Zarrilli, to underline the absolute specificity of each performer, practice and process. He writes:

> The 'problem of the body' is like a virus – it constantly mutates and surprises us. Since our individual bodyminds do not stand still and can be multiple, and since no two bodies, no two selves, no two ensembles, and no two dramaturgies are

> the same, the tactics I use in the studio and rehearsal room must constantly shift to the ever-changing ways in which the problem of the body is manifest in this actor's bodymind, this ensemble's collective body, the demands of this dramaturgy on the actor's bodyminds at this particular moment. (Zarilli, 2009: 5)

Each work might be said to exist in a given 'particular moment', rendered real through the experience of the actors in their process. This does not culminate in a straightforward presentation of the work, or even event of the work, but rather a specific situation of the work; a specific situation that we might provisionally term 'the community'. I would like to attempt to maintain the question of 'who' as a dual one – not simply the opposition between passivity and action, but rather as an ethical demand, arising from abjection's initiation of the Kristevan 'collapse of meaning' (Kristeva, 1982: 2), which uncovers the nature of community as one which points towards an experience of death, or the dissolution of communality, by using the work of Maurice Blanchot, Giorgio Agamben and Jean-Luc Nancy as means by which to reveal acting, in the form of a striving for a different self, as a work that reveals another form of reality through its engagement with what is base and abject.

Who watches?

The question of 'acting' falls continually between the work of the actor falling away from themself, and the act of the agent attempting, through a decision, to assume subjectivity, however briefly such an interval may last. Recalling Grotowski again, such a reaching for subjectivity might be said to be 'acting less than in daily life' (Kumiega, 1987: 236).

We might start with an extreme example, to offer some purchase on what this 'acting less' might deliver in terms of community. In the psychophysical actor the focus on extreme presence actually seems to come full circle, into total absence of selfhood and ideally some form of communion based on their 'self-sacrifice'. It seems to bear much similarity to the absence at the heart of the Acéphale community of Georges Bataille and others, and this is why I have chosen to trace, briefly, a theoretical path through Blanchot and Nancy (who elaborate their thought on community through Bataille) and finally to the issue of ethics against morality in Agamben, to trace the implications of such a transformation into the abject object beyond the implications for the individual.

In his short book *The Unavowable Community*, talking of the Acéphale group, and Bataille, Maurice Blanchot writes:

> That is the sacrifice that founds the community by undoing it, by handing it over to time the dispenser, time that does not allow the community nor those who give themselves to it, any form of presence, thereby sending them back to

> a solitude which, far from protecting them, disperses them or dissipates itself without their finding themselves again or together. The gift or the abandonment is such that, ultimately, there is nothing to give or to give up and that time itself is only one of the ways in which this nothing to give offers and withdraws itself like the whim of the absolute which goes out of itself by giving rise to something other than itself, in the shape of an absence. An absence which, in a limited way, applies to the community whose only clearly graspable secret it would be. The absence of community is not the failure of community: absence belongs to community as its extreme moment or as the ordeal that exposes it to its necessary disappearance. (Blanchot, 1988: 15)

Blanchot's lengthy consideration of the paradoxical structures of community and the evolution of a return to myth through the failure of art and politics is a complex one that engages with Jean-Luc Nancy's text *The Inoperative Community*. There is not space here other than to trace some of the issues and sketch a rough trajectory of the thinking. Suffice to say that Blanchot's concept of the absence of community supplies us here with a sense of the endless momentum of that which oscillates between the solitude of the individual and the work of the collective. This is not simply the replacing of the one with a unity of ones, or indeed the founding of a new singularity through such sacrifice. It is the process of this sacrifice that is community itself, in much the same way that the abject, and the object, as *not I*, initiates a crisis in the subject. Nancy states it clearly:

> Community therefore occupies a singular place: it assumes the impossibility of its own immanence, the impossibility of a communitarian being in the form of a subject. In a certain sense community acknowledges and inscribes – this is its peculiar gesture – the impossibility of community. A community is not a project of fusion, or in some way a productive or operative project – nor is it a *project* at all. (Nancy, 1991: 15)

This strikes me as offering a way to think about the coming together of acting practices. If they form some kind of coherence, some community of practices, it is only through the impossibility of that drawing together that it functions. And if it is a form of practice that comes together without fusion, and project, in mind, it suggests its form of being as an attempt to return to mythic dimensions of the subject in which dispersal is the key. Recall Zarrilli's statement about the problem of the 'body being a virus'; its 'mutation', and 'surprise', the fact of its multiple identities manifest in one specific site at one specific time. This 'event' must be understood in the sense of the death at the founding moment of the collective, be they ensemble or Acéphale group. As soon as it occurs there is no being remaining through which it can take place, least of all those that survive to witness it. The struggle of coming to *act* is one founded on the point at which one assumes agency as subject. Work aimed to inaugurate any form of community dissolves the event by which a decision can be made, through the subject, and returns us to impossibility, governed, perhaps, by the overwhelming desire to repeat such an impossible project.

There is a similar process at work in Kantor's Cricot2 company, where those works that we think of as 'Kantor's' are the product of intense collaborative processes that have resulted in the view of Kantor as something of a tyrannical director (perhaps his creative heterogeneity challenging the established homogeneous culture of stagnant acting forms). But the work was far from the edict of a singular creative mind; it emerged from a form of practice that both effaced the individual performer but also guaranteed their individuality, as Wełmiński explains, citing Porębski:

> It isn't possible to talk about the Cricot 2 Theatre performances without mentioning the creative function of the group as a whole. There are still many mythical misconceptions out there about the director 'shaping' the 'human matter' or 'using actors as paint' (now that really is a fatuous idea!) about actors-as-dummies, devoid of individual traits, just milling about on stage like spinning tops, and other such descriptions.
>
> The reality is that the creation of a performance is a very complex process, reliant on the joint effort of many people. It is a collaborative work – a team endeavour, and the creative process never stops. As Mieczysiaw Porębski noted: 'The leading idea was not working *on* the actor, *on* the role – but collaboration with the actor, as independent as the author of the performance and being not so much a performer as a subject in their own right, with their own unique personality, their own path, history and the potential yet to discover. (Wełmiński, 2014: 50–51)

It is important to underline that no formulation, no regime, no system can recover the essential quality of dissolution, of absence, we might even chance to say *failure* so necessary in the encounter that generates community (here the actor and the audience). In Levinasian terms, that is the foundation of ethics – the pure openness to the other, without condition. To inaugurate other agendas, as function and project, would stand in danger of jeopardising the opportunity to resist programmed structures of performing being enabled by the actor's encounter with 'alter ego' or a descent into abject alterity; to re-emerge in a new form of being whose subject begins the process again.

By way of closing this excursus into the issue of the community, and moving us towards a short case study, I would like to briefly introduce Agamben, as a coda to Nancy and Blanchot, with a passage from his curiously fragmentary text, *The Coming Community* that offers a useful drawing together of ethics and disappearance as a process of being as possibility, as opposed to the redundant closure of morality and efficacy, which again resembles that movement into an abject object that the actor attempts.

> This is why ethics has no room for repentance; this is why the only ethical experience (which, as such, cannot be a task or a subjective decision) is the experience of being (one's own) potentiality, of being (one's own) possibility – exposing, that is, in every form one's own amorphousness and in every act one's own inactuality.
>
> The only evil consists instead in the decision to remain in a deficit of existence, to appropriate the power to not-be as a substance and a foundation beyond existence; or rather (and this is the destiny of morality), to regard potentiality itself, which is the most proper mode of human existence, as a fault that must always be repressed. (Agamben, 1993: 43)

In a world increasingly bound by ways of being governed by modes of appearance the issue of absence seems increasingly to be, well, *absent*. Of vital importance here is the fact that potentiality remains genuinely open, and not bound by a strict definition of what it might become (thence arises the issue of morality, repentance and the baggage of the predetermined). All forms of acting may have to embrace a further abandonment of selfhood, rather than a concentration within the body of the performer, to offer what its real gift might be – 'the experience of being potentiality'.

'A weight of meaninglessness, about which there is nothing insignificant': a brief case study

In April 2008 a colleague at Loughborough University and I took a group of ten undergraduate students to Poland to explore the work of Tadeusz Kantor and Jerzy Grotowski, through workshops and lectures. It was a wonderful trip, the students experienced work they had previously only encountered at a distance and were immersed in ways of working that offered fresh perspectives on their usual acting processes. As a pedagogical experience it was a great achievement. As an encounter with forms of acting approaching the abject it was very revealing.

For the second phase of the trip we were accommodated, and worked, in the Grotowski Center work site at Brzezinka. Amidst the usual days of training and lectures we were treated to some examples of work in progress. Of particular interest was the piece *Poppy Seed Lady*, presented by Agnieszka Pietkiewicz. Our group assembled in a small wood-floored room above the main kitchen area to see this work-in-progress at close hand. It was April, and still quite chilly deep in the forest work centre, but not chilly enough to merit the baking hot stove that pumped its heat through the room lending a certain soporific edge to our engagement. Agnieska's work, with Grzegosz Ziolkowski, was certainly accomplished. The students were clearly impressed. I was torn however by a feeling that what we were witnessing was of an entirely different order to either a work-in-progress or even a short piece of theatre. Agnieszka somewhat disappeared to be replaced by movements and gestures springing from some unfathomable well of otherly experience. I reiterate: it was a stunningly accomplished piece of work. As witnesses we watched in awe, helped by the incredible heat and increasing humidity of the cramped room. I felt deeply privileged to be shown the intimacy of this actor vanishing before our eyes. And that was it. *Vanishing*. It seemed to me, having thought much on the experience since, a work of death, at the deepest level. This is certainly not a criticism.

It was a revelation of death, not in a Kantorian tradition, but in terms of the actor's *being* itself. She was not an articulated emissary of another world, but *becoming* death – that constantly collapsing interval between I and we. And this was achieved through a total presence to herself as a performer, certainly through a personal journey, and one without, no doubt, a 'definitive' route that led to it. And in that total presence she became absent, or to offer it in relation to Agamben, 'exposing ... in every form one's own amorphousness and in every act one's own inactuality' (Agamben, 1993: 43). This describes very well for me the ethical encounter with abjection; the necessity continually to put oneself in question, one's own being rendered uncertain.

Kristeva describes the sense of dissolution at the heart of the abject, a few lines on from the passage cited at the beginning of this essay. She writes:

> A massive and sudden emergence of uncanniness, which, familiar as it might have been in an opaque and forgotten life, now harries me as radically separate, loathsome. Not me. Not that. But not nothing, either. A 'something' that I do not recognize as a thing. A weight of meaninglessness, about which there is nothing insignificant, and which crushes me. On the edge of non-existence and hallucination, of a reality that, if I acknowledge it, annihilates me. There, abject and abjection are my safeguards. (Kristeva, 1982: 2)

This could serve very well as a description of many Kantorian performances, as the 'reality of the lowest rank' assails the spectator and the actors transform themselves from persons to things, from memories to repetitive movements. In the Grotowskian performance contexts it is the body passing beyond simple signification, and form, and collapsing into the meaninglessness (and consequent freedom) of total awareness.

It might be described in other terms, one of which might be ecstasy – as this usefully returns us further to the private space of the actor. Blanchot describes it thus:

> One can write the word (ecstasy) only by putting it carefully between quotation marks, because nobody can know what it is about, and, above all, whether it even took place: going beyond knowledge, implying un-knowledge, it refuses to be stated other than through random words that cannot guarantee it. Its decisive aspect is that the one who experiences it, is thus no longer there to experience it. (Blanchot, 1988: 19)

On the one hand the very process of the work might deliver it into a position where hermetic ritual practice and obsessive regimen obscure the work and transform it into an accomplished circus trick clouded in the mystery of mastery, and on the other giving it over to a quasi-religious avowal of collective radicalisation that finds in its own community only the affirmation of the other initiates. But beyond such dangers there is always the desire to produce a form of performance that challenges the actor and provides a means through which to question the self and reveal other means of encounter with the world. Of course, the lineage of Kantor's and Grotowski's works are complicated, but it is worth returning to Artaud to draw together the power of an acting process not predicated on simplistic reiteration and representation. Curtin puts it rather poetically:

> Artaud intended that every myriad aspect of the actor's body would be included and perpetually in process, just as he employed every part of the anatomy to interrogate the suffering at the core of his own being. Through a highly trained physicality the actor would become totally immersed in his actions, which involved a studied concentration brought to every movement, gesture and facial expression. This would be supported by an understanding of the musculature and pressure points, so that the actor could connect with specific sites of the spectator's body, '[t]o reforge the links, the [magical] chain'. Most important were the rhythms of the breath, so that the performer would connect with hidden layers of emotion and sensation. These internal dynamics were stressed, which required the actor's complete mastery over his impulses. It was this consciousness and rigour that were at the heart of Artaud's *Theatre of Cruelty*, connecting the chaos of his proposed performance with the order and discipline necessary for radical deconstruction and transcendence. This would involve a sense of physical urgency with the actors pushed to the limits of self-experience in radical and ceremonial stagings where their bodies are laid bare, aflame, coiled and in crisis. (Curtin, 2010: 65)

Whether we determine this form of radical performance 'a sacrifice', or the encounter with the abyssal in the abject object an incommunicable experience to those who witness it, these practices are in a privileged space to reveal a power inherent in all acting; becoming other through oneself, open to the dissolution of the abject. A moment ago I called it a work of *death*, we could call it *ecstasy*, or, for Emmanuel Levinas, and for Giorgio Agamben, it might be an ethics of becoming. They strike me as enabling the same moment of questioning though: 'who acts?'; and in that question continues the exigency of the task of performance, which is a struggle to guarantee freedom, and that is also a freedom *not* to be, to become absent, to explore the abject and encounter the base unforming of the self; to guarantee the impossibility of community through the ecstatic task of the body in performance. It is the isolated experience shared by all. The struggle is not *how* to communicate it, or indeed *what* is being communicated, but the coming to know *who* is communicating, and finding there an unknown thing, somewhere between oneself and an object, something frighteningly familiar, base and abject.

References

Agamben, G. 1993. *The Coming Community*. Trans. M. Hardt. Minneapolis: University of Minnesota Press.

Bataille, G. 1985. *Visions of Excess: Selected Writings, 1927–1939*. Ed. A. Stoekl. Trans. A. Stoekl with C. R. Lovitt and D. M. Leslie Jr. Minneapolis: University of Minnesota.

Blanchot, M. 1988. *The Unavowable Community*. Trans. P. Joris. Barrytown: Station Hill.

Cioffi, K. 1999. *Alternative Theatre in Poland, 1954–1989*. Amsterdam: Harwood.

Curtin, C. 2010. Recovering the Body and Expanding the Boundaries of Self in Japanese Butoh: Hijikata Tatsumi, Georges Bataille and Antonin Artaud. *Contemporary Theatre Review* 20(1), pp. 56–67.

Grotowski, J. 1991 [1968]. *Towards a Poor Theatre*. London: Methuen.

Kantor, T. 1993. *A Journey Through Other Spaces: Essays and Manifestos, 1944–1990*. Ed. M. Kobialka. Minneapolis: University of Minnesota Press.

Kobialka, M. 2009. *Further On, Nothing: Tadeusz Kantor's Theatre*. Minneapolis: University of Minnesota Press.

Kristeva, J. 1982 [1980]. *Powers of Horror: An Essay on Abjection*. Trans. L. S. Roudiez. New York: Columbia University Press.

Kumiega, J. 1987. *The Theatre of Grotowski*. London: Methuen.

Nancy, J-L. 1991. *The Inoperative Community*. Minneapolis: University of Minnesota Press.

Noys, B. 1998. Bataille's Base Materialism. *Cultural Values* 2(4), pp. 499–517.

Richards, T. 1995. *At Work with Grotowski on Physical Actions*. London and New York: Routledge.

Strindberg, A. 2000. A Dream Play. In *Plays: Two*. Trans. Michael Meyer. London: Methuen.

Wełmiński, A. 2014. Function and Significance of the Theatre Company in the Development of Cricot 2 Productions. In Fazan, K., Burzyńska A. R., Bryś, M. Trans. A. MacBride. *Tadeusz Kantor Today: Metamorphoses of Death, Memory and Presence*. Berlin: Peter Lang, pp. 43–60.

Zarrilli, P. 2009. *Psychophysical Acting: An Intercultural approach After Stanislavski*. Abingdon: Routledge.

Index

abject art 3–6, 11, 12 n.4, 17, 27 n.5, 30–3, 35, 44, 91, 100, 119, 121, 133, 135
Abject Art (Whitney Museum exhibition) 1–7, 9–10, 14, 30–3, 35–6, 42, 47
absorption 56, 129, 191
Abstract Expressionism 24, 72
abstraction 56, 60–1, 67, 68 n.17, 74, 76, 78, 79–81, 83–6, 87 n.3, 88 n.8, 114, 140, 170
Acéphale group 196
acting 10, 22, 165, 197–200
actor *see* acting
Ades, Dawn 113
Adorno, Theodor 162, 185 n.6
AES+F 9, 152–4, 156
aesthetic 2, 4, 7, 8–9, 17, 22, 30, 32, 33, 35, 44, 63, 71, 110, 114–15, 119, 130, 132, 134–6, 138, 150–1, 155–6, 173, 183
aesthetics of resistance 171–2
Agamben, Giorgio 16, 195, 197–9, 200
ageing 116 n.2, 153
agency 37–41, 47, 196
aggression 51, 53, 58–9, 63–4, 123–4
AIDS 36, 41, 144–5,
Aliens (film) 7
Allport, Gordon 109
Altamira 67
ambiguity 15, 25–6, 34–5, 52, 97–8, 132, 135, 138, 141, 142
ambivalence 8–9, 15, 25, 34, 111, 120, 128, 149, 156, 180
American art 2–3, 12 n.4, 30, 56, 84
anamorphosis 72, 76
Andre, Carl 5, 10
animal 3, 7–8, 18, 58, 90–102, 110, 113, 116, 116–17 n.7, 137, 144–7
animalism 7, 91, 108,
animality 7, 92, 108, 133, 137
anthropocentrism 7, 96
anthropology 2, 15
anthropomorphism 101
Antipodean 6, 82, 100
anus 72–3, 74, 96, 114, 179
Anzieu, Didier 123–4
art history 62, 86, 87 n.6, 148, 150
Artaud, Antonin 10, 35, 113–14, 189, 191–2, 200
assemblage 109, 111, 114
attraction 7, 8, 34, 97–8, 130, 132, 135, 139, 140, 142, 157
Australia 6, 8, 20, 72, 73, 74, 77, 82–6, 99, 100, 130
autobiography 83, 102, 161, 181, 184–5
autopsy 9, 151
avant-garde 2, 9, 57, 190

Bacon, Francis 8, 105, 109, 110, 112–16, 116–17 n.7, 119–29, 129 n.2
Bakhtin, Mikhail 8, 125, 126
Barbay, Vanessa 91, 99
Baroque 137, 155, 156
Barthes, Roland 8, 125, 126–7, 129 n.3
Bataille, Georges 4, 8, 11, 12 n.5, 15, 18, 31, 51, 55, 62, 66, 68 n.17, 112, 131, 135, 137, 163, 165, 174, 183, 191, 195

abjection 1–2, 16, 32–3, 97, 131, 133–6, 163
base materialism 3, 54, 61, 67, 110, 113, 190, 193–4
heterology 16, 133
informe (formless) 18, 32, 68 n.5, 90, 93, 100–2, 133
sacred 133, 136
sacrifice 52, 55–6
Beardsworth, Sara 34
beautiful (Burke) 110
beautiful (Kant) 5, 20
beauty 20, 30, 98, 99, 110, 133, 150, 154, 156, 157
Becker, Ernest 107
Bell, Catherine 8–9, 130–1, 132, 138–42
Bellmer, Hans 8, 105, 109, 110–12, 113, 114–16, 116 n.6
Benjamin, Walter 15
Benveniste, Émile 57
Beugnet, Martine 18, 21, 27 n.4
Beuys, Joseph 150
bio-object 10, 189
Blanchot, Maurice 55, 195–6, 197, 199
blurring 15, 22, 63–4, 66, 77
bodily fluids 34, 65, 108–9
blood 11, 67, 93, 94, 95, 109, 120, 145, 154, 155
mucus 2, 108, 154
saliva 2, 101, 109, 136, 154
semen *see* sperm
sperm 6, 65–6, 74, 76, 107, 108, 163, 172
spit *see* saliva
urine 2, 6, 120, 137
vomit 31, 68 n.6, 154, 165, 166, 168, 169, 171
see also menstruation
Bois, Yve-Alain 100
Bolívar, Simón 73–4
border 2, 14, 15, 31, 34, 47, 51, 52, 91, 94, 97, 98, 99, 102, 106, 107, 121, 123, 124–5, 132, 147, 149, 169
borderline 18, 62, 66, 91
boundary 3, 8, 35, 66, 91, 94, 105–6, 108, 109–10, 113, 120, 123–4, 145, 164, 185 n.3, 193
Bourdieu, Pierre 28 n.14, 53–4, 67 n.1
bourgeois 52, 53, 60, 125, 134
Bourgeois, Louise 91, 102
Brenez, Nicole 18, 21
Breton, André 32, 51, 56–9, 61, 65, 67, 137
Bruegel, Pieter (the Elder) 164–5, 171, 185
Butler, Judith 5, 7, 40, 46, 47, 48
abjection 3–4, 31, 37–8, 39, 121
Bodies that Matter 37, 39, 40
Excitable Speech 40–1
Gender Trouble 36–7, 39, 40
performativity 37, 39–41

cadaver *see* corpse
Callen, Anthea 59
Canada 5, 6, 30, 36, 38, 42, 43, 44, 48
Canova, Antonio 144, 158
capitalism 125, 134, 154, 162, 164, 165, 170–1
Caravaggio 137
catharsis 10, 35, 95
Céline, Louis-Ferdinand 2, 10, 35, 54, 68 n.7
Chanter, Tina 152, 156
chiaroscuro 5, 137
Chicago, Judy 3, 46
Chile 74
cinema 12 n.4, 18–26, 27 n.4, 27–8 n.11, 146, 170, 182
Clark, Timothy James 52, 62, 63, 67, 68 n.13, 72, 77, 78
colour 24, 59, 67, 83, 86, 113, 116, 123, 134, 135, 137–8, 139–40, 147, 157, 175
communication 15, 57, 123–4, 146, 152, 169
community 16, 42, 48, 152, 194, 195–7, 200
conceptual art 21
contamination 38, 106, 137
contemporary art 5, 7, 8, 30, 47, 71, 90, 99, 101, 121, 154, 156
contour 52, 60, 119
corpse 9, 15, 55, 98–9, 107, 108, 145, 147–55, 156–8, 183, 184
Courbet, Gustave 54, 77–8, 81, 82, 87 n.5
Creed, Barbara 7
Cricot 2 theatre company 11, 189–90, 193, 197
crime 15–16, 19, 67, 152, 157, 165
criminality 15, 130–1, 141
Cubism 86, 109

Dada 84
Dalí, Salvador 56, 65
Danto, Arthur 17, 21, 26
David, Jacques Louis 72, 76, 77, 78, 81, 87 n.4, 88 n.8
Davila, Juan 6–7, 72–86, 87 n.5, 88 n.8, 88 n.9, 88 n.10

death 9, 15, 52, 73, 76, 85, 99–100, 107, 108, 110, 112, 132, 139–40, 144–6, 148–9, 151, 153–8, 161, 162, 163, 165, 170, 172, 177, 183, 184, 185 n.3, 187 n.12, 189, 190, 195, 196, 199–200
death drive 18, 21, 71, 132
Debord, Guy 24, 154
Deleuze, Gilles 106, 113–14, 135
  figural 114, 117 n.8
DeLillo, Don 10, 185 n.4, 186 n.7
  Underworld 160–72, 185 n.3
Dempsey, Shawna 5, 30–1, 32, 36, 37, 41–3, 47–8
Derrida, Jacques 174
desire 2, 18, 22, 26, 63, 67, 76, 95, 98, 109, 112, 130, 138, 155, 158 n.1, 178, 182, 183, 197
  heteronormative 64
  lesbian 42
  sexual 64, 94, 108, 111
  see also Kristeva, Julia
deviance 6, 36, 41–2, 43, 47
dialectical materialism 51
Didi-Huberman, Georges 66
Dionysian 106, 133, 136
disfigurement 56, 62, 128, 150, 155
disgust 17, 21, 33, 94, 107, 108–9, 115, 116 n.3, 122, 133, 136, 137, 138, 151, 157, 176
Dobell, William 72–3, 83
dolls 110–12, 114–16, 116 n.5, 116 n.6
Douglas, Mary 15, 106, 107, 116 n.1
doxa 126–7
Drew, Marian 91, 99–100
drives (psychoanalysis) 18, 21, 24, 33–4, 57, 62, 63, 64, 71, 105, 132, 134, 138
Duchamp, Marcel 5, 17, 21, 26, 65
Dutch painting 150, 152
dying *see* death

ecstasy 132, 133, 156, 199, 200
ego 14, 19, 26, 27 n.3, 112, 124, 132, 139, 175, 191, 193, 194, 197
El Greco 155, 156
empowerment 94–5
epistemology 16, 19
equine 96, 98
eroticism 2, 15, 47, 149, 155, 156, 175, 177, 180, 182
ethics 19, 96, 145, 148, 150, 151–3, 195, 197–8, 199, 200
excess 41, 44, 46, 59, 61, 62, 133, 136, 154
exclusion 2, 4, 16, 32–3, 35, 37, 38, 121, 124, 136, 152, 156, 191
excrement 2, 3, 10, 33, 59, 74, 75, 76, 108, 134, 135, 136, 137, 168, 169, 173, 174, 175, 176, 183–4, 186–7 n.11, 187 n.12
experiential 9, 130, 146
extremism 10

faeces *see* excrement
fascism 112
fat activism 44, 46–7
Favell, Rosalie 5, 30–1, 32, 36, 37, 38–41
Fédida, Pierre 61
female animal 93–5
femininity 41, 42, 44, 65, 95
feminism 5, 30, 31, 36, 39, 42, 43, 44, 46–7, 48, 68 n.17, 93–4
figuration 6, 10, 51, 59, 60–1, 66–7, 73, 74, 75, 114, 128, 134, 161, 176, 178
film 4, 5, 7, 9, 12 n.4, 18, 20–6, 27 n.6, 27–8 n.11, 41, 43, 71, 85, 145, 146, 182
First Nations 6, 38
forbidden 21, 58, 93, 130
formalism 6, 53, 55, 135, 183
Foster, Hal 4, 8, 17–18, 20, 25, 27 n.5, 32, 33, 105, 111, 121, 131, 139
Foucault, Michel 15, 52, 53, 146
Fox, Sue 157–8
fragmentation 8, 105, 106, 109–10, 112–15, 124–5, 128–9, 191–2
Freud, Sigmund 15, 21, 24, 28 n.12, 34, 62, 63, 64, 72, 78, 82, 92, 139, 174, 175, 176, 180, 186–7 n.11
Fried, Michael 66, 71, 72, 88 n.8
Fuente del Salín 67

Gardner, Ava 167
gaze 59, 71, 76, 77–8, 81, 95, 121, 128, 130, 137, 141, 154, 158, 175, 187 n.17
gender 3, 7, 20, 33, 37, 39–40, 40–1, 73, 95, 121
Gérôme, Jean-Léon 57
Gestalt 119–20, 122
Gleason, Jackie 165–71
goddess 30, 44, 94
Goldin, Nan 144–5
Grandrieux, Philippe 5, 18, 27 n.3, 27–8 n.11, 28 n.12
  La Vie nouvelle 18
  Sombre 5, 18, 21–6, 27 n.6
Greenberg, Clement 7, 55–6, 66–7
grief 131, 139, 140, 145

Grosz, Elizabeth 109
grotesque 31, 34, 35, 47, 110, 111, 112, 121, 148, 149, 152, 154
Grotowski, Jerzy 10–11, 189–93, 195, 198, 199, 200

Hagens, Gunther von 9, 146–52
Hainge, Greg 27 n.10, 27–8 n.11
Hawke, Bob 73
Heffernan, Julie 91, 98
Hegel, Georg Wilhelm Friedrich 71, 78, 82, 182, 187 n.15
Heidelberg School 79
heteronormativity 46, 172, 185 n.3, 186 n.7
heterosexuality 3–4, 37, 39, 40, 41, 43, 74
  heterosexism 44, 156
high culture 150, 164, 172
Hirst, Damien 87 n.1, 145, 149
Hogan, Paul 73
Hollier, Denis 21, 27 n.7
homosexuality 10, 36, 37, 39, 41, 42, 43, 47–8, 65, 72, 73, 74
Hoover, J. Edgar 165, 167, 168, 169, 171, 172
Horkheimer, Max 162, 185 n.6
horror 10, 11, 27 n.6, 31, 33, 56, 76, 108, 122, 139, 140–1, 183, 190
  horror film 7, 22, 25, 182
Houser, Craig 3, 32
human–animal 8
humour 41, 42, 43, 48, 138, 140, 141
hybridity 96

identification 14, 20, 22, 26, 37, 41, 42, 47, 52, 82, 121, 122, 135, 142, 157, 176
identity 4, 5, 8, 10, 15, 16, 18, 22, 31, 34, 36–7, 38, 46, 57, 58, 59, 90, 91, 92, 93, 101, 106, 109, 110, 111, 115, 120, 122, 125, 139, 149, 152, 168, 174, 179, 182, 186 n.8, 190, 191, 192–3
  lesbian 39, 41
  national 12 n.4, 86, 152
  sexual 6, 63, 64–5
ideology 68 n.16, 75, 86, 112, 146, 185 n.3
illness 108, 116 n.2, 139, 157
immanence 5, 18, 19, 23, 26, 27 n.9, 196
immediacy 14, 19, 20, 116, 145, 146
impurity 7, 54, 60, 93, 99, 116 n.6, 140
interpretation 6, 16, 19, 40, 75, 131, 133, 137, 155, 161
irony 6, 44, 46, 72, 95, 107, 108, 125, 161–2, 186 n.7, 187 n.12

Jones, Leslie 3, 32
Jouhandeau, Marcel 4, 7, 10, 12 n.12
jouissance 11, 34, 66, 132, 136, 138
Joyce, James 26 n.1, 62, 173, 174, 175

Kant, Immanuel 5, 17, 20, 78
Kantor, Tadeusz 10–11, 189–93, 197, 198, 199–201
Kazakhstan 164, 169
Keating, Paul 73
Kelly, Ned 73, 82
Kelley, Mike 121, 135–6
Kline, Franz 61
Krauss, Rosalind 4, 27 n.8, 32, 55, 56, 62–3, 63–4, 68 n.5, 68 n.8, 100, 101, 131, 133, 135
Kristeva, Julia 5, 6, 7, 57–8, 61, 66, 68 n.11, 139, 174
  abjection 1–2, 4, 7, 8, 9–10, 11, 12 n.1, 12 n.5, 14–5, 16, 18, 19, 22, 25, 26, 27 n.8, 31, 32, 33–5, 36, 41, 48, 54, 61–2, 68 n.7, 81–2, 87, 90–9, 100, 101, 102, 105–8, 115, 116, 116 n.3, 120, 124, 125, 130–6, 138, 139, 142, 147–8, 149, 174, 178–9, 190–1, 192, 195, 199
  chora 35, 95
  desire 14, 34, 108, 132, 147, 190
  love 24–5
  Pollock, Jackson 61, 66
  Powers of Horror 1, 2, 7, 11, 12 n.5, 26 n.1, 31, 33, 82, 87, 90, 105, 120, 174, 178, 190
  Revolution in Poetic Language 1
  semiotic 19, 22, 95, 115, 134–5

Lacan, Jacques 2, 14, 17, 18, 33–4, 57, 71, 74, 78, 82, 88 n.7, 92, 173, 174, 175, 178, 181, 185 n.2
  mirror stage 2, 14, 33–4, 175
  Real 17–18, 75–6, 121
  Symbolic order 34, 35, 37, 41, 57, 92, 94, 115, 120, 146, 149
Laurence, Janet 91, 100
Lascaux 52
late capitalism 162, 165, 170, 171
Lautréamont, Comte de (Isidore Ducasse) 35, 56–9, 60, 62
law 15–16, 28 n.12, 34, 37–8, 92, 106, 121, 132, 138, 165, 191
lawless 15, 152
Leiris, Michel 68 n.15, 112–13, 136–7

Leonardo da Vinci 63, 144, 163
lesbian 3–4, 5, 30–1, 36, 38–9, 41–8
Levinas, Emmanuel 19, 26, 27 n.3, 200
  Other 19, 23, 28 n.15, 197
  Same 19, 23
Leviticus 93, 99
libidinal 64, 73, 165, 167, 170, 171, 172
libidinous *see* libidinal
liminality 91, 154, 156
literature 2, 4, 9, 10, 11, 25, 26 n.1, 35, 91, 132, 161, 185 n.1
logos 16
Lomas, David 56, 65

Madí 83–6
Malevich, Kasimir 76, 81, 88 n.8
Mallarmé, Stéphane 57
Manet, Édouard 6, 51–6, 59–67, 67 n.1, 68 n.4, 68 n.6, 77, 87 n.6
Mapplethorpe, Robert 5, 73
masculinity 6, 10, 95, 173
mass culture 160, 163, 164, 166, 170, 171, 172, 182, 187 n.12
materiality 5, 22–4, 27 n.9, 27 n.10, 27–8 n.11, 55, 75, 106, 107, 112, 119, 120, 123, 134, 158, 190
maternal 2, 35, 37, 65, 91–3, 95, 112, 177, 178, 180
  maternal body 34, 37, 115, 121, 174
matter 7, 8, 34, 53, 61, 62, 63, 66, 98, 112, 113, 120, 123, 124, 132, 133, 141, 154, 194, 197
McDonald, Dwight 160, 164–5, 170, 171, 187 n.12
McGinn, Colin 106–7, 115
meaninglessness 14, 62, 199
melancholia 131, 139
menstruation 3, 15, 93, 107, 108, 116 n.3, 168
Métis 6, 38
Michelangelo 73, 74
Millan, Lorri 5, 30–1, 32, 36, 37, 41–3, 47–8
mind–body dualism 3, 33, 110
mirror stage *see* Lacan, Jacques
Mitchell, Allyson 5, 30–1, 32, 36, 37, 43–8
modern art 10, 17, 30, 55
modernist 5, 10, 26, 52, 55, 56, 62, 72, 76–7, 81, 82, 87 n.2, 171, 172
monstrous feminine 7, 42
morality 149, 195, 197–8
mortification 126–7, 128
Mother (psychic figure) 2, 24, 25, 33–4, 92, 93, 95, 116 n.3, 120, 132, 134, 139, 174, 178, 179
music 11, 22, 71, 148

Nancy, Jean-Luc 195, 196, 197
nationalism 5, 12 n.4, 86, 152, 156
naturalism 57, 60, 77
Nazism 10, 32, 112, 189
negation 7, 58, 82, 107, 133, 141, 185 n.6
Neyrat, Roger 85
Nietzsche, Friedrich 161, 185 n.1
nihilism 22, 133
Nochlin, Linda 57, 64
Noys, Benjamin 194

objectification 5, 7, 16, 19, 126–7
obscenity 31, 75, 121, 131, 133, 134, 135, 137, 141, 156
Oliver, Kelly 33, 92

pain 39, 41, 113, 126
parrhesia 183, 185
patriarchy 68 n.16, 92, 95, 96, 102
Penwarden, Charles 9
Péret, Benjamin 65
perversion 34, 63, 64, 90, 94, 97, 112, 115, 130, 131, 138, 171
phenomenology 23, 123
photography 32, 56, 100, 111, 115, 148, 153, 155
Picasso, Pablo 109, 113
Piccinini, Patricia 91, 96
Pietkiewicz, Agnieszka 198–9
Plastination 9, 147
pleasure 27 n.7, 30, 62, 64, 66, 131, 137, 138, 141–2
poetics 22, 23, 64
political 37–8, 39, 41, 47, 48, 72, 74–5, 100, 135, 136, 141, 145–6, 152, 193
politics 33, 39, 46, 47, 84, 135, 196
  extreme 10
  feminist 5, 43, 44, 46
  gender 37
  lesbian 5, 31
  queer 46
  sexual 4
Pollock, Griselda 55, 68 n.17, 93–4
Pollock, Jackson 6, 12 n.8, 51, 56, 60–1, 63, 66–7, 88 n.8
pollution 107–9

polymorphous perversity 63, 64, 112
Pop art 6, 74
postcolonialism 86
postfeminism 43, 47
postmodernism 6, 36, 63, 71–2, 75, 76, 81, 86, 162, 171
  postmodern art 63, 71, 75–6
power 10, 11, 20, 40, 93, 112, 146, 148, 152, 193
Power, John Joseph Wardell 86
pregnancy 93–4, 95, 149
prehistory 52, 66
prohibition 15, 20, 34–5, 47, 97, 130, 132, 133, 134, 136, 156
production 163, 180, 183
  capitalist 134
  creative 131–2, 135, 136, 139
psychoanalysis 1, 2, 3, 11, 14, 15, 18, 32, 33, 61, 68 n.17, 73, 75, 123–4, 136
psychophysical 189, 192, 193, 195
psychosis 58, 61, 115
Puig, Manuel 74
purgation 9, 10, 57
purification 7, 9, 11, 15, 35, 95–6, 108, 116
purity 7, 15, 33, 36, 54, 60, 137

queer theory 30, 46, 174, 186 n.7
Quin, Carmelo Arden 84–5

realism 27 n.9, 54, 110, 115
reception 9, 46, 150
religion 2, 15, 35, 75, 90, 92, 93, 95, 116, 116 n.3, 145, 146, 156, 165, 166, 200
representation 8, 14, 19–21, 51, 66, 76, 87 n.3, 109, 120, 123, 127, 135, 165, 170
  narrative 114
  theatrical 191
repulsion 8, 17, 22, 31, 33–4, 35, 52, 53, 119, 121, 122, 130, 135, 139, 140, 142, 145, 176
resignification 5, 37–8, 40, 43, 47
rhetoric 54, 67 n.1, 152
Richard, Nelly 75
Rifkin, Adrian 11, 12 n.12, 68 n.4
Rites of Passage (Tate exhibition) 9
ritual 2, 9, 15, 67, 90, 106, 107, 108, 140, 145, 193, 200
Rose, Jacqueline 10, 63
Rothfuss, Rhod 84
Rrap, Julie 91, 96, 98
Russia 152, 153, 163, 170

sacred 2, 15, 26, 27 n.3, 133, 136, 137, 141, 165, 190
sacrifice 10–11, 52, 55–6, 63, 67, 155, 189, 190–1, 195–6, 200
sadism 6, 51, 56, 61, 62, 64, 66, 67, 68 n.8, 68 n.9, 68 n.15, 68 n.17, 135
Sartre, Jean-Paul 23, 129 n.3
Saville, Jenny 91, 94
sculpture 10, 32, 43, 74, 85, 94, 96, 100, 102, 111, 113, 141, 144, 173, 179, 181, 187 n.15
self 2–3, 8, 11, 18, 19, 31, 34, 66, 90, 97, 98, 105, 106, 108, 115, 120, 121, 122, 124–9, 129 n.3, 132, 133, 138, 173, 182, 191, 198, 200–1,
selfhood *see* self
Serrano, Andres 5, 9, 31, 121, 128, 137, 156–7
Seuphor, Michel 84–5
sexuality 3, 4, 15, 33, 43, 51, 63–4, 110
Sherman, Cindy 7, 31, 121, 137–8
shock 18, 113, 136, 138
sickness *see* illness
signification 5, 7, 22, 24, 40, 57, 62, 90, 101, 132, 133, 140, 147, 158, 179–80, 182, 199
Silverman, Kaja 122
Sinatra, Frank 164–5, 167, 169
skin 31, 76, 96, 120, 123–4, 140, 148, 154, 155, 158
Smith, Joshua 72–3, 83
Smith, Kiki 3, 7, 31, 91, 94, 121, 148
sociology 32, 33
sovereignty 16, 40
spider 101–2, 136, 182
Steihaug, Jon-Ove 133, 137
Stoekl, Alan 137
Strindberg, August 191
style 19, 54, 55, 68 n.13, 74, 79, 82, 127, 132, 134, 138
subjectivity 4, 14, 19–20, 33–4, 35, 39, 57, 58, 60, 63, 101, 105, 112, 122, 126, 132, 195
sublime 78, 87, 87 n.2, 99, 133, 153, 154
sublimation 2, 35, 42, 47, 76, 77, 78, 81–2, 87 n.5, 137, 138, 151, 156
superego 138, 142
surface (of a painting) 7, 53, 55, 60, 62, 63, 75, 81, 120, 123

Surrealism 6, 32, 51, 54, 56, 58–9, 60, 61, 62, 63–6, 67, 68 n.9, 84, 86, 109, 112, 137
Sylvester, David 116, 127

Taylor, Simon 3, 4, 7, 32
Taylor, Sue 111, 117 n.9
technology 23, 169, 181
  biotechnology 145
The Fly (film) 182
theatre 4, 10–11, 39, 189–93, 197, 199, 200
Thomas, Calvin 174
  Male Matters 160, 173–5, 176, 178, 180, 181, 186–7 n.11, 187 n.15
Torres Garcia, Joaquín 84–5
Tovey, Donald 11
transgender 46
transgression 4, 8, 30, 47, 53, 74, 76, 94, 105, 106, 110, 131, 135, 136, 137, 138, 146, 149, 156
transsexuality 73, 185 n.3
trauma 17–18, 34, 39, 121, 138, 139–40
truth 76, 79, 87 n.2, 133, 161–2, 183–4, 185
Tyler, Imogen 135, 136

uncanny 72, 98, 99, 128, 139, 147, 157
unconscious 21–2, 24, 27 n.3, 27 n.5, 37, 39, 61, 75, 82, 116, 138, 163, 179–80

video art 3, 8, 30, 41, 42, 43, 75, 141, 145
video games 9, 145
viewing 4, 8–9, 66, 77–8, 115, 130, 132, 133, 135, 136, 140
Vigneault, Louise 66
violence 15, 21, 24, 40, 55, 58, 60, 61, 64, 115–16, 141, 154
voyeurism 137, 141, 158 n.1

Wagner, Richard 11, 71
Wallace, David Foster 10, 160–2, 173–85, 185 n.4, 186 n.10, 186–7 n.11, 187 n.12, 187 n.18
  Infinite Jest 161, 173, 177, 186 n.10
  The Pale King 184
  'The Suffering Channel' 10, 160–1, 173–85
Warhol, Andy 5–6, 17, 77
Wełmiński, Andrzej 191, 193
White Cube (gallery format) 7
Whitney Museum (of American Art) 1, 2, 3, 4, 5–7, 9, 14, 30–3, 35–6, 42, 47
Witkin, Joel-Peter 9, 152, 154–6

Zarrilli, Philip 192, 194, 196
Žižek, Slavoj 6, 71–2, 75–6, 78, 81–2, 87 n.1, 176, 183, 187 n.17,
Zurek, Amy 31–3